36910053

Best Practicable Environmental Option Assessments for Integrated Pollution Control

Volume I: PRINCIPLES AND METHODOLOGY

London: The Stationery Office

Commissioning Organisation:
Environment Agency
Government Buildings
Burghill Road
Westbury-on-Trym
Bristol
BS10 6EZ

Recycled Paper
Printed on recycled paper. Envirocote 115 gsm.
85% minimum recycled waste. Mixed de-inked and
unprinted waste, oxygen bleached.

STANDING ORDER SERVICE

Are you making full use of The Stationery Office's Standing Order Service?

The Standing Order Service is a free monitoring of the publications of your
choice from over 4,000 classifications in 30 major subject areas. We send you
your books as they are published along with an invoice.

With a standing order for class 22.07.020 you can be supplied automatically
with [all supplements to/new editions of this title/further titles in this series]*
as they are published.

The benefits to you are:

● automatic supply of your choice of classification on publication

● no need for time consuming and costly research, telephone calls and
  scanning of daily publication lists

● saving on the need and the costs of placing individual orders

We can supply a wide range of publications on standing order, from individual
annual publications to all publications on a selected subject. If you do not
already use this free service, or think you are not using it to its full capability,
why not contact us and discuss your requirements?

You can contact us at:

The Stationery Office
Standing Order Department
PO Box 276
London SW8 5DT

Tel 0171 873 8466; fax 0171 873 8222

Contents

1 Introduction

On 1st April 1996, Her Majesty's Inspectorate of Pollution (HMIP) together with the National Rivers Authority and the Waste Regulation Authorities formed the Environment Agency with responsibility for England and Wales.

1.1 When Integrated Pollution Control (IPC) was first introduced in April 1991 only general guidance on how environmental assessments for IPC could be conducted was available. Several fundamental questions were posed by the legislation and accompanying regulations:

- how could an operator demonstrate that the choice of process represented the Best Available Techniques Not Entailing Excessive Cost (BATNEEC) having regard to the Best Practicable Environmental Option (BPEO) for those IPC processes where this is required by section 7(7) of the Environmental Protection Act 1990 (the Act);

- what kind of environmental information could an operator provide to demonstrate that no harmful releases to the environment occur; and

- how could HMIP use this information in determining an IPC application?

1.2 Over the next five years, HMIP conducted research and carried out case studies with the aim of developing practical approaches to these aspects of IPC. The Royal Commission on Environmental Pollution made recommendations in its twelfth report[1] on how to assess the BPEO (see box 1). HMIP considered the recommendations made by the Royal Commission and at the same time considered how environmental and economic assessments could be carried out. The first draft document was discussed within HMIP in April 1992, and then within the Department of the Environment a few months later. After an encouraging response, further detailed case studies were carried out as well as research to establish the necessary data.

1.3 In July 1993, a draft methodology was presented at a seminar organised by HMIP to give a preliminary airing of the proposals to outside bodies. The seminar provoked widespread response from participants, and several follow up meetings were held between HMIP and other organisations to explore specific issues. These comments were taken into account in preparing a formal consultation document[2] which was issued in April 1994.

1.4 A total of 91 organisations responded to the consultation exercise, making a total of

---

THE SEVEN STAGES OF BPEO
ASSESSMENT

Define the Objective
Generate Options
Evaluate the Options
Summarise and Present the
 Evaluation   maintain
Select the BPEO   audit
Review the BPEO   trail
Implement and monitor*

The seventh stage is ongoing and follows the choice of BPEO. It is not covered in this guidance.

Box 1

---

almost 1500 separate comments. Almost all of those who responded recognised the need for guidance in this area and welcomed the document. Several, generally constructive, criticisms were also made. HMIP considered the comments made and at the same time it established a programme of case studies, involving operators of specific sites, the site inspector and HMIP policy units, to test the draft guidance. In 1995 the final drafts of the technical guidance were produced and presented to an advisory group involving industry trade associations, NGOs, independent experts, regulatory bodies and Government Departments. Further comments were received from members of the advisory group and a series of bilateral meetings was held with the Confederation of British Industry and the Chemical Industries Association.

1.5 This work has culminated in the publication by the Environment Agency (the Agency) of this guidance which sets out a methodology for assessing harm and comparing options for specific industrial processes to determine BATNEEC having regard to BPEO, as well as outlining the kind of economic information required to gauge the practicality of process options. It is one of a series of considerations which should be taken into account by operators and the Agency alike and should not be used without recognising other legal requirements, in particular section 7(2) of the Act. The net result should be the selection of the process and abatement option which represents BPEO in accordance with section 7(7) of the Act.

1.6 This guidance has been drawn up by the Agency as an example of how the appraisal of BPEO required of some processes under IPC can be carried out. Experience with IPC applications to date has demonstrated that operators would benefit from such guidance.

1.7 In the view of the Agency this guidance is suitable for the broad range of processes covered by

1

RELATIONSHIP BETWEEN ANALYSIS AND ASSESSMENT

	Activity	Short name
Administrative legal and other detail	Description of the process or processes and associated management systems	Process description
	Estimation of the quantity of substances released and their dispersion in the receiving environment	Analysis[4]
	Effects on releases on the environment and the generation of costs	*Assessment*

Box 2

IPC, and strikes an appropriate balance between the need to justify any choice of process option, and the need to keep administrative and financial burdens on operators to a minimum. The Agency therefore anticipates that the methodology described in the guidance will be widely used, and is encouraged by indications that a number of applicants for authorisations under IPC have already based their submissions on it.

1.8 Nevertheless, the use of this particular methodology is not compulsory. It is an example of how a BPEO appraisal could be carried out. Neither is the methodology a prescriptive approach to be applied rigidly in all cases. It is intended to be a framework which can be applied flexibly and imaginatively as appropriate to particular circumstances.

1.9 The methodology is not meant to replace expert judgement but is an aid to the process of determining BPEO. It should not be used in a mechanistic way. The selection process for the final option should have weighed the relevant factors based on expert judgement. If used in a commonsense fashion, the methodology will provide the means for doing this in a clear, and fully auditable way.

1.10 BPEO must be assessed in all relevant cases. Individual operators may find that a modified form of the methodology or a different approach best suits the circumstances of their own particular process. Operators should be able to justify the methodology they have adopted. It is recognised that some parts of the assessment may be commercially confidential. The methodology provides an indication of the degree of detail and rigour with which the Agency expects that this should be done. Operators who wish to use alternative methodologies should bear this in mind.

1.11 The guidance is published in a combined format:

● Volume I: Principles and Methodology

● Volume II: Technical Data (for consultation)

1.12 Volume I includes all the guidance on the methodology and its application. Volume II contains data that the Agency has put together to support the methodology. However there are differences of opinion amongst experts about the methods by which Environmental Assessment Levels (EALs), in particular, should be derived. For this reason a working group of experts from industry and academia is being set up by the Agency to comment on the methods used for determining EALs etc and to recommend alternatives if appropriate. Thus Volume II is a consultative draft and feedback from users of the methodology is encouraged. The values therein are temporary and should be viewed with caution. There is a possibility that, as a result of the deliberations of the working group, some values could be increased as well as others being decreased.

1.13 There are three other main areas of activity to complement this guidance note.

● First, a consortium of operators, regulators and environmental groups has produced guidance on environmental analysis[3]. Their guidance provides information on tools for conducting analyses, such as predictive mathematical models and supporting data bases. The relationship between the material covered in that guidance and this is shown in box 2.

● Second, is the provision of economic information on industry sectors and cost information on process and abatement options. This will be included in the revisions of the IPC Guidance Notes[4], starting with the revised notes for waste disposal and recycling and the minerals industry.

● Third, the Agency is currently working with industry to produce "good practice" guides on how to undertake BPEO assessments for different sectors of IPC. The first such guide is for batch processing within the chemical industry[5].

1.14 The BPEO methodology represents a first step in an evolving approach to environmental assessment of IPC processes. Further refinements will be made in the light of experience with using the methodology in practice, and as more research information becomes available. The Agency will work with industry and others to analyse the lessons learned from applying the guidance note and refine the approach as required.

1.15 The application of the methodology should ensure that sufficient information is provided by an operator to enable the environmental effects of releases to be properly assessed. It should ensure that the process or abatement option chosen represents the "BATNEEC to minimise pollution to the environment as a whole having regard to the BPEO". In this regard, application of the guidance will assist the Agency in fulfilling its vision to "protect and improve the environment as a whole by effective regulation, by our own actions and by working with and influencing others".

2 Purpose and scope of the guidance

2.1 The guidance sets out principles and a methodology which can be used for BPEO assessments of IPC processes in a consistent way. Such assessments should be practical, transparent and compatible with the requirements of part I of the Act and relevant Statutory Instruments. The technical data to be used with the methodology is contained in Volume II of this guidance.

2.2 By following the guidance, operators will be able to provide an audit trail to support the justification of their proposals which will assist the Agency in determining a new application or reviewing an existing authorisation.

2.3 The methodology is designed to be used for BPEO assessments of industrial processes which are controlled by the Agency under the integrated pollution control regime (ie those processes which are prescribed for central control under section 2 of the Act and referred to as Part A processes in the Regulations[6]), but normally excluding those processes which are likely to involve the release of substances into only one environmental medium.

2.4 BPEO assessments will normally be carried out by current or prospective operators of such processes, or by consultants acting on their behalf. The Agency is likely to refer to the methodology during their evaluation of an operator's submission and any subsequent determination of authorisation conditions.

2.5 The applicant must, in the following circumstances, present to the Agency matters[7] on which he relies to establish that he will achieve the objective of ensuring BATNEEC having regard to BPEO will be used:

- as part of applications for Authorisation submitted to the Agency for new processes;

- as part of applications submitted to the Agency for variations to existing processes;

- as a requirement of a condition in an Authorisation.

2.6 At the present time this guidance note only addresses the environmental effects of releases from a process (for example solid waste, discharges to river, and emissions from chimneys). It does not deal with some indirect environmental effects consequent upon the operation of the process, for example, the environmental effects of:

- transport and disposal of waste

- transport and fate of products;

- extraction and transport of raw materials; or

- disturbance of natural habitats by the physical presence of the plant itself.

2.7 The methodology may also be used by developers submitting Environmental Impact Statements to a Planning Authority under the Town and Country Planning (Assessment of Environmental Effects) Regulations 1988 (SI 1199). However, the Agency only recommends the use of the methodology with respect to developments which will subsequently require an authorisation from the Agency and its use is only appropriate to that part of the Environmental Statement which addresses the releases from the process as described above. Nothing in the guidance obviates the need for developers to meet other requirements of Environmental Statements under the above regulations.

3 Principles

3.1 Legislative background

3.1.1 Part I of the Environmental Protection Act 1990 introduced a new system of Integrated Pollution Control (IPC) and provided the framework for controlling releases from certain prescribed industrial processes and ensuring compliance with relevant EC Directives on pollution control. The Agency is responsible for regulating prescribed processes in accordance with IPC.

3.1.2 Section 4(2) of the Act states that the functions of the Agency under Part I of the Act are to be exercisable for the purpose of preventing or minimising pollution of the environment due to the release of substances into any environmental medium. The Environment Act 1995 also contains a range of new powers and duties for the Agency.

3.1.3 Under section 6 of the 1990 Act no process prescribed for central control may be operated without an authorisation from the Agency. In determining an authorisation, section 7 of the Act requires the Agency to include conditions for achieving the objectives set out in section 7(2). These objectives are to ensure that in carrying out a prescribed process the Best Available Techniques Not Entailing Excessive Cost (BATNEEC) will be used:

- for preventing the release of substances prescribed for any environmental medium into that medium, or where that is not practicable by such means, for reducing the releases of such substances to a minimum and for rendering harmless any substances which are so released; and

- for rendering harmless any other substances which might cause harm if released into any environmental medium.

3.1.4 Furthermore, where the process is designated for control by the Agency and is likely to involve the release of substances into more than one environmental medium, section 7(7) of the Act requires that BATNEEC will be used:

"for minimising the pollution which may be caused to the environment taken as a whole by the releases having regard to the Best Practicable Environmental Option (BPEO) available as respects the substances which may be released".

3.1.5 In addition, section 7(2) requires that conditions should be placed within an authorisation to ensure the objectives of compliance with:

- any direction given by the Secretary of State to implement European Community or international obligations relating to environmental protection;

- any statutory environmental quality standards or objectives or other statutory limits or requirements (see section 3.3.4 below);

- any plan made by the Secretary of State under section 3(5) of the Act (eg the National Plan for Reducing Emissions of SO_2 and NO_x[8]).

3.1.6 Some guidance on the operation of IPC under Part I of the Act is given in "Integrated Pollution Control: A Practical Guide" issued by the Department of the Environment and the Welsh Office[9]. The document explains the Act and the Regulations made under it as they apply to IPC in England and Wales. It also considers the interpretation of the requirements of the legislation, and deals in some detail with the meaning of BATNEEC. The description of BATNEEC provided below summarises the relevant considerations.

3.2 Best Available Techniques Not Entailing Excessive Cost (BATNEEC)

3.2.1 The term "BATNEEC" is not defined in the Act, although section 7(10) provides that:

"References to the best available techniques not entailing excessive costs, in relation to a process, include (in addition to references to any technical means and technology), references to the number, qualifications, training and supervision of persons employed in the process and the design, construction, lay-out and maintenance of the buildings in which it is carried on."

3.2.2 Further interpretation has been provided[9] by considering the words "best available techniques" separately and together.

3.2.3 *"Best" means most effective in preventing, minimising or rendering harmless polluting releases. There may be more than one set of techniques that achieves comparable effectiveness - that is there may be more than one set of "best" techniques.*

3.2.4 *"Available" should be taken to mean procurable by the operator of the process in question. It does not imply that the technique has to be in general use, but it does require general accessibility. It includes a technique which has been developed (or proven) at pilot scale, provided this allows its implementation in the relevant industrial context with the necessary business confidence. It does not imply that sources outside the UK are 'unavailable'. Nor does it imply a competitive supply market. If there is a monopoly supplier the* technique counts as being available provided that the operator can procure it.

3.2.5 *"Techniques"* *is defined in section 7(10) of the Act. The term embraces both the plant in which the process is carried on and how the process is operated. It should be taken to mean the components of which it is made up and the manner in which they are connected together to make the whole. It also includes matters such as numbers and qualifications of staff, working methods, training and supervision and also the design, construction, lay-out and maintenance of buildings, and will affect the concept and design of the process.*

3.2.6 **"Not entailing excessive cost"**, in the context of techniques, applies if the benefits of employing the techniques outweigh the costs. The benefits in this context relate primarily to the prevention of environmental damage, and the costs relate primarily to the costs of applying BAT. The act of balancing the benefits against the costs will involve judgement. In general, the greater the environmental damage, the greater the costs of BAT that can be required before costs are considered excessive.

3.2.7 The consideration of BATNEEC requires an approach which is as objective as possible. The concern is with what costs in *general* are excessive; the lack of profitability of a particular business should not affect the determination. The fact that a firm may be unable to afford to reduce releases to the required level should be disregarded in assessing BATNEEC.

3.2.8 The considerations above apply equally to the determination of what is "not entailing excessive cost" for existing plant as for new plant. However, in the case of existing plant an additional factor to take into account in the assessment is the configuration of the existing plant, which may make it excessively costly (in relation to the harm which would be avoided) to fit particular types of abatement technology.

3.2.9 The Agency must decide what is BATNEEC in relation to each application, and translate that decision into conditions to be included in the authorisation. However, it is desirable that there is broad consistency in these decisions, especially between processes of the same kind. To assist in achieving consistency, IPC Guidance Notes are published by the Agency for all processes coming within IPC, and provide information on the best available techniques for new plant and their application to existing plant. The Notes also set out the release levels which the Agency believes can be achieved by their use.

3.3 Assessment of harm

3.3.1 The Act requires BATNEEC to be used to prevent or minimise releases of prescribed substances and to render harmless any substances which are released and which might cause harm. Within the context of the Act, "harm" means:

> "harm to the health of living organisms or other interference with the ecological systems of which they form a part and, in the case of man, includes offence to any of his senses or harm to his property; and harmless has a corresponding meaning".

However, the Act does not define the nature of the effects which may be considered harmful or the level in the environment at which they may occur. Therefore, the Agency has developed a practical approach to the assessment of harm, and this is described below.

3.3.2 The environmental consequences of a particular process will depend on a number of factors. These include the magnitude of the releases, ambient pollutant concentrations, as well as the composition, structure, response and function of the receiving environment.

3.3.3 Complete knowledge of this type is rarely available. However, there is a considerable amount of laboratory and field based data on the sensitivity of individual receptors to particular pollutants.

3.3.4 This information has formed the basis for the development of environmental quality objectives and standards such as those used in water quality control. Environmental criteria of this type provide a "benchmark" against which the relative harm/harmlessness of releases from prescribed processes can be assessed. Indeed, the Agency must specify in an authorisation conditions that it considers appropriate for achieving compliance with Environmental Quality Standards (EQSs) prescribed by the Secretary of State under certain enactments. Where an EQS is, or is likely to be, breached the Agency has to come to a view as to the most appropriate manner in which environmental concentrations can be reduced.

3.3.5 The Agency proposes to use EQSs to define the upper bound of the concentration of a substance in the environment which can be considered tolerable. A release of a substance which contributes to a predicted environmental concentration above the EQS may be considered intolerable.

3.3.6 At present, statutory EQSs exist for only a limited number of substances. In the context of this guidance it is therefore proposed that environmental harm can be judged by considering the environmental concentration of a substance in comparison to a reference level for that substance. The reference level expresses the relative potential for harm of that substance. The Agency has called these reference levels "Environmental Assessment Levels" (EALs). The guidance proposes their use at several stages of a BPEO assessment.

3.3.7 Provisional EALs for each environmental medium have been derived from a variety of published United Kingdom and international sources. The provisional EALs and a detailed description of their derivation are presented in Volume II of this guidance note. In many cases both long-term and short-term EALs are given. It is very important, particularly with short-term EALs, that they are only used in exactly the same way that they have been formulated (eg averaging periods and percentile exceedances). The values recommended for use will be kept under review as further information about the effects of substances on the environment becomes available.

3.3.8 In the specific cases where there is an EQS for a substance in an environmental medium, the EAL has been set equal to the EQS. Account will be taken of new EQSs as they are established.

3.4 Significance and priority of releases

3.4.1 A judgement needs to be made about the extent to which releases need to be prevented, minimised and rendered harmless to meet the requirements of BATNEEC and BPEO. This judgement will involve balancing the effects of the releases on the environment against the costs of measures to prevent, minimise and render harmless. The greater the effects on the environment, the less likely any given costs will be considered excessive.

3.4.2 To help further focus operator and regulatory effort, a mechanism has been developed to determine whether each substance released should be a "priority for control". The search for techniques to further minimise pollution to the environment as a whole should be focused on the releases identified as priority for control. Other releases can be considered of lower priority, although the effects of these releases may need to be included in the assessment of the identified control options.

3.4.3 Another mechanism has been developed to define a lower boundary, below which releases can be considered to be less significant for the purposes of detailed assessment. For releases below this level, the environmental harm would be small and the chances of improvement remote. A detailed evaluation of environmental effects would generally

not then be necessary, and further environmental protection measures would generally not be required unless the costs involved are very low.

3.4.4 For the purposes of applying the above approach, a method is needed by which the concentrations of substances in the environment resulting from releases from the process can be compared. This can be undertaken by comparing releases based on an EAL. The Agency proposes the following rules of thumb for identifying into which of the above categories releases could be allocated. Firstly, releases could be considered priority for control if the predicted environmental concentration (PEC) resulting from the release (which includes the process contribution (PC) to this concentration and the ambient concentration) is high compared to the EAL. Alternatively, releases could also be considered priority for control where the process contribution alone is more than a small fraction of the EAL. In this context, high compared to the EAL is taken to be around 80%, and a small fraction of the EAL is taken to be around 2%.

3.4.5 Releases can be considered insignificant if the process contribution alone is less than a very small fraction of the EAL. In this context, a very small fraction is taken to be 0.2%. This value has been chosen to provide a factor of ten between a release which can be considered insignificant and a release which could be considered a priority for control.

3.4.6 It is emphasised that these percentages have been put forward purely as rules of thumb for the purposes of efficient allocation of resources of both the operator and the Agency, and that they represent a pragmatic choice based on experience with applying the concepts set out here in the case studies and elsewhere. As further experience is gained with using the methodology set out in this guidance, these rules of thumb may be subject to refinement.

3.4.7 To summarise, releases could be considered as priority for control if:

$$PEC \geqslant 0.8 \ EAL;$$
$$\text{or } PC \geqslant 0.02 \ EAL.$$

Releases could be considered insignificant if:

$$PC \leqslant 0.002 \ EAL.$$

3.4.8 To be useful in practice, it should be possible to identify insignificant releases without needing to undertake complex environmental modelling to determine the process contribution to the environmental concentration of each substance released. For this purpose, simple, generalised methods can be used to make a conservative estimate of the process contribution from the amount of a substance released. Further guidance on these methods and suitable assumptions are given in Volume II of the guidance note.

3.4.9 Although the methodology pays great attention to concentration as the principle measure of the environmental presence of a pollutant, it is foreseeable that other measures may be appropriate and operators may wish to use other measures of environmental effects where they believe these are relevant.

3.5 Best Practicable Environmental Option

3.5.1 Where a process may involve the release of substances to more than one environmental medium, the Agency will need to determine whether the proposed operation represents BATNEEC having regard to the BPEO for the pollutants concerned. As the Act does not define the BPEO, the Agency has adapted the definition given by the Royal Commission on Environmental Pollution (RCEP) in their Twelfth Report[1] to the requirements of IPC. The (IPC) BPEO can be considered as:

> **"the option which in the context of releases from a prescribed process, provides the most benefit or least damage to the environment as a whole, at acceptable cost, in the long term as well as the short term."**

3.5.2 Note that, because section 7(7) of the Act refers specifically to "the substances which may be released", this definition of the IPC BPEO is restricted to the releases from the prescribed process, and therefore excludes other environmental effects, such as those arising from the production and delivery of raw materials for the process. In addition, although an IPC authorisation covers all releases from the process, including, in particular, solid and liquid waste streams, it cannot regulate the method of disposal of the waste streams. It cannot therefore control the ultimate releases from waste to air or water. The IPC BPEO therefore also excludes the environmental effects arising from the disposal of these waste arisings. Having said that, the operator should be aware of the final disposal options. Further discussion on the assessment of waste arisings is given in paragraph 3.5.16 and section 7.7 below.

3.5.3 It has been argued that this definition represents too limited an interpretation of the BPEO concept as originally put forward by the RCEP. However, the Agency is constrained by the terms of the legislation in this regard.

3.5.4 The RCEP described a BPEO as "the outcome of a systematic consultative and decision-making procedure which emphasised the protection and conservation of the environment across land, air and water". It also described how to select a BPEO and the steps involved were summarised under the following headings:

- define the objective;

- generate options;

- evaluate options;

- summarise and present the evaluation;

- select the BPEO;

- review the BPEO;

- implement and monitor.

3.5.5 Throughout all the above steps an audit trail should be kept. Indeed RCEP stated that "The presentation of information, opinions and conclusions reached at different stages of the BPEO study is clearly important. The decision maker, and other persons, should be able to see separately the data or scores relating to each aspect of the decision for each option".

3.5.6 The RCEP's recommendations have been adapted in developing the framework described in this technical guidance note for generating IPC process options, for evaluating these options, and for determining the site-specific BPEO.

3.5.7 A key element in the assessment of the BPEO is the evaluation of the impact of releases on the environment as a whole. The integrated assessment of the impact of releases on the environment as a whole is extremely complex. The effect of a release on the environment will be dependent on many factors, including:

- the amount of each substance released;

- the rate of release of each substance;

- other release characteristics, such as release location, release velocity, concentration of substances in the released material, temperature of released material;

- the physical properties of the released substances (such as its physical form, or particle size);

- the chemical properties of the released substances;

- the nature of the receiving medium, particularly its dispersive and transfer characteristics and how these vary with time;

- ambient concentrations of released substances already in the environment;

- the location of receptors in the environment sensitive to the released substances; and

- the degree of sensitivity of these receptors to enhanced concentrations of released substances.

3.5.8 If there were complete knowledge about all of these factors, it would, in principle, be possible, by the use of modelling or monitoring or a combination of the two, to predict or measure the effects of all the released substances on all sensitive receptors in the environment. However, in practice, knowledge about these factors is limited. In addition, although progress is being made in this area, comprehensive assessments of impacts can be time-consuming and costly. On the one hand, there is the need to make a sufficiently accurate assessment of environmental impacts to provide confidence that resources allocated to environmental improvements result in at least commensurate benefits and that they are not being mis-allocated. On the other hand, there is the possibility of expending greater resources on the assessment itself than could be justified by any environmental improvement. Clearly the level of detail in the assessment should be influenced by the significance of the impacts.

3.5.9 This is not a problem unique to the UK. However, experience elsewhere offers no simple solution. In many countries a simpler, technology-based approach is taken to the control of polluting releases. Where the approach contains a consideration of risks to the environment (for example in European Union legislation relating to the control of new and existing chemical substances[10,11,12,13], or in the risk assessment approach developed in the Netherlands to regulate the risks from chemical substances[14] and the risks of accidental spills from industrial sites[15]) a simplified approach based mainly on the concentration of the polluting substance in the environment in comparison to a reference concentration, such as the no effect concentration, is used.

3.5.10 In the light of this, a similar, simplified approach is proposed for the assessment of the direct environmental effects of releases from prescribed processes for the purposes of evaluating and determining the BPEO. The direct environmental effect of a substance released to a particular environmental medium is assessed as the ratio of the process contribution to the EAL for that substance in that medium. This quantity is denoted the environment quotient (EQ) for that substance in that medium.

3.5.11 Where there are several substances released to more than one environmental medium, a broad indication of the overall direct effects on the

environment of all of these releases can then be obtained by summing the environment quotients. The sum over all releases to a single medium is denoted the environment quotient for that medium. Mathematically:

$$EQ_{(Substance)} = \frac{\text{Process contribution}}{\text{EAL}} \, ...(1)$$

$$EQ_{(Medium)} = EQ_{(a)} + EQ_{(b)} \cdots + EQ_{(i)} ...(2)$$

Where:
EQ is Environmental Quotient, and
a...i are substances released to a particular medium.

It might sometimes be appropriate to demonstrate the overall effects in water, air and land by summing the three environmental quotients. The index so produced is called the "Integrated Environmental Index" (IEI).

$$IEI = EQ_{(Air)} + EQ_{(Water)} + EQ_{(Land)} ...(3)$$

3.5.12 Clearly these indicators do not provide a scientifically accurate assessment of the effects of the releases on the environment. They are based, for example, on assumptions that effects are linearly proportional to the concentration of a substance in the environmental medium into which it is released; that the EALs correspond to identical levels of effect for all substances and all media; and that there are no synergistic or antagonistic effects between substances. However, for the purposes of *comparing* control options at a particular location, where the nature of the receiving environment will be effectively the same for all options, the EQs provide simple, robust indicators of *relative* impacts which are sufficient for the majority of applications.

3.5.13 Because this methodology is concerned with authorising releases to the environment which may be maintained on a continuous basis, its primary focus is on the long-term effects on the environment. However, there will also need to be consideration of the possible short-term effects of peak, short-term releases. In this case, a similar approach can be used, involving the comparison of short-term concentrations in the environment with short-term EALs. However, care should be taken in assessing short-term effects in as much that short-term concentrations should be expressed on the same basis as short-term EALs (eg averaging periods and percentile exceedances).

3.5.14 The main focus of this part of the methodology is releases to air and to water. Subsequently, the major transfer in the environment will be from air to land by deposition. The methodology outlined above should therefore be applied primarily to:

- the concentration in air from releases to air;

- the concentration in water from releases to water; and

- the concentration on land from releases to air and deposition on land.

3.5.15 As well as the direct effects for which EQs and the IEI provide indicators, released substances can have indirect effects on the environment. Indirect effects include changes in the environmental conditions brought about by the released substance which then affect sensitive receptors, for example changes in climate brought about by releases of greenhouse gases. Two indirect effects of particular concern are global warming and photochemical ozone creation at ground level. The possible effects of a rise in the average temperature of the earth's surface are very wide-ranging and include a rise in sea-level and shifts in climatic zones. Ozone is a highly reactive pollutant which, at ground-level, may exert a number of damaging effects on human health, vegetation and materials. It is therefore important that releases of gases which contribute to these effects are minimised wherever possible. Methods for assessing the relative contributions of different substances to these effects have been developed in international fora[16,17], and are increasingly being applied to assess environmental effects, for example, in the context of life cycle assessment[18]. The EA proposes that these methods be used in the context of BPEO assessment to provide indicators of the two indirect effects of global warming and photochemical ozone creation. Further details of the methods are given in sections 7.5 and 7.6 below.

3.5.16 Finally, an indicator is proposed for waste arisings. Many processes will generate quantities of solid or liquid waste, ie material not released to air or water, and the treatment and disposal of this waste may have some effect on the environment. The method proposed to compare waste arisings for the purposes of BPEO assessment is based on that developed by the UK Government Industry Working Group on Priority Setting and Risk Assessment[19]. The resulting indicator depends on the quantity of waste arising and its hazardous nature. It does not depend on the method used to dispose of the waste. It is again a relative indicator suitable for the comparison of options for a particular process operated at a specific site. In such circumstances, it is not unreasonable to assume that the same waste treatment and disposal methods will be used for similar types of wastes and therefore that differences between the effects of different waste treatment and disposal methods can be disregarded. The indicator should include all waste arisings taken off-site for disposal, but should not include material which is reused or recycled. The calculation of this indicator is described in more detail in section 7.7 below.

3.5.17 In summary, the EA proposes to base its assessments of the environmental effects of releases from prescribed processes on the following indicators of environmental impact:

- indicators based on the long term environmental concentrations of the released substances;

- indicators based on the short term environmental concentrations of the released substances;

- indicators based on the contribution made by releases of substances to global effects of concern (in particular, global warming and the generation of ground level ozone); and

- an indicator based on the hazardous nature of any waste produced.

The EA will generally expect the relative environmental effects of the control options being considered in the BPEO assessment to be presented in terms of these indicators. However, an operator is free to use alternative indicators if they are fully justified and provide at least an equivalent degree of transparency and as good an audit trail.

3.5.18 The above list is neither exhaustive nor exclusive, and other, additional indicators could be used if appropriate. For example, the effects of the following releases may also need to be considered for specific processes:

- odours,

- visible plumes,

- exceedance of critical loads,

- foreseeable but unplanned releases.

It is for the operator to decide which additional indicators may be necessary to provide the most complete description of the relative effects of the control options being considered.

3.6 Assessment of costs

3.6.1 The general methods of economic option appraisal are broadly common across both the public sector in the UK and the private sector. The justification of, and procedures for, public sector appraisal are given in the HM Treasury publication, *Economic Appraisal in Central Government: A Technical Guide for Government Departments*[20]. This spells out how social cost benefit analysis should be used for public sector project and policy appraisal. The particular application of this approach to cases with environmental effects is further detailed in the Department of the Environment publication, *Policy Appraisal and the Environment*[21]. Social cost benefit analysis aims to consider all the impacts from a project or policy intervention by using money values as a common denominator for those 'external' effects which do not normally carry a price.

3.6.2 Commercial or financial appraisals have common ground with social cost benefit analysis in terms of the comparison of options and the handling of streams of payments over time. Where commercial appraisals differ, however, is that they normally address only the private costs of the operator or company concerned: they do not cover impacts which are external to the operator.

3.6.3 The methodology in this guidance is an intermediate form, which goes beyond the scope of financial appraisal but not to the full extent of social cost benefit analysis. External effects are considered in terms of the specified environmental impacts of each option, but comparisons are made directly rather than through the medium of money valuation of such impacts. The method is based on a comparison of the relative costs and relative environmental effects of a number of alternative options in order to identify the best option for which costs are not excessive.

3.6.4 Further details about the assessment of costs are presented in section 7.9 below.

3.7 Determination of the BPEO

3.7.1 The final justification of the BPEO should weigh all relevant factors based on expert judgement: first on the part of the operator in compiling an application; and second by the Agency in determining an application. It should be emphasised that the methodology set out in the guidance should not be used in a mechanistic way. If used in a commonsense, non-mechanistic fashion, the methodology provides the means for demonstrating compliance with the requirements of the Act in a clear and fully auditable way.

3.8 Sensitivity analysis

3.8.1 Throughout the assessment, uncertainties about many of the assumptions made could influence the results of the assessment. This does not necessarily invalidate the methodology used to undertake the assessment, but highlights the importance of sensitivity analysis as a technique to explore the importance of any uncertainties.

3.9 Presentation

3.9.1 It is important that any BPEO assessment is presented in a clear and logical fashion with a good audit trail. The adoption of the methodology herein will contribute to the achievement of this objective. However, the inclusion of mass balances, process flow diagrams, decision flow diagrams and reasons for no further consideration of a technique etc. are likely to make the assessment easier to scrutinise.

4 A methodology for BPEO assessments

4.1 Introduction

4.1.1 The remaining parts of this volume explain a methodology for BPEO assessments which the Agency has developed for use by operators and inspectors of IPC processes. The methodology can be separated into six stages as shown in box 3. Sections 5 to 10 below describe each of the six stages of the methodology.

BPEO ASSESSMENT METHODOLOGY FOR IPC PROCESSES

1) DEFINE THE OBJECTIVE
e.g. produce a product or provide a serivce and meet the objectives of IPC

2) GENERATE OPTIONS FOR ACHIEVING THE OBJECTIVE
Generate available techniques
Screen the techniques
Select a small number of options to achieve the objective

3) ASSESS THE OPTIONS
Environmental assessment
Economic assessment

4) SUMMARISE AND PRESENT THE ASSESSMENT
Set out all factors used in evaluation

5) IDENTIFY THE BPEO
Justify Choice

6) REVIEW THE BPEO
Sensitivity testing
Ensure there is an audit trail

Box 3

4.2 Requirement to carry out a BPEO assessment

4.2.1 Before undertaking a BPEO assessment, operators are advised to consider, for each process that they operate, whether the BPEO requirement of section 7(7) of the Act is relevant to the process in question ie if both of the following criteria are met:

- the process is one for central control (ie the process is listed as a "Part A" process in the Regulations[7]); and

- the process is likely to involve the release of substances into more than one environmental medium.

4.2.2 If the first criterion is not met then the operator should consult with the local authority regarding authorisation of the process if it is prescribed as a "Part B process" in the Regulations[7].

4.2.3 If the process is <u>not</u> likely to involve the release of substances into more than one environmental medium, then although section 7(7) of the Act does not apply, much of this methodology would still be relevant and could be used.

4.3 Sensitivity analysis

4.3.1 In using this methodology, there may often be considerable uncertainty about many of the figures employed. To understand the effects of this uncertainty, sensitivity analyses can be conducted to obtain an idea of how likely the worst case assumptions are and what influence that would have on the choice of a site-specific BPEO.

4.3.2 The operator is expected to judge where sensitivity analysis might be appropriate. For example, it might be carried out at each stage of the assessment wherever the degree of uncertainty over any particular figures might affect the final choice of BPEO. Examples are given below.

- Assumptions about the **mass release** of any one substance from an option would have a significant effect on the EQ for that substance, if the PC turned out to be high compared to the EAL. If that substance is not released (or released in much less quantities) from other options then the ranking of options may be influenced solely by that one substance. If the assumptions have a high margin of error (because, say, they were based upon only one or two samples) then the operator could improve the accuracy of the figure (say by taking more samples).

- When identifying and comparing **the cost** of each option, the cost-effectiveness result may be sensitive to the context in which an individual abatement technique is applied. For example, plant is designed for a specified range of operating conditions, and to operate beyond that range or under different conditions may entail additional operating and/or capital costs.

- Assumptions about the **ambient concentration** of any one substance might have a significant effect on the PEC for that substance, and therefore influence the generation of options. If the resulting PEC is greater than 80% of the EAL and the assumption of ambient concentration for that particular substance has a high margin of error (because, say, there is little or no background monitoring data available) then the operator could improve the accuracy of the figure (say by undertaking appropriate environmental monitoring).

4.3.3 As well as the ongoing sensitivity analysis described above, operators could, after completing the comparison of options, examine whether the differences in scores of each option are significant, what factors had the largest influence on the scores, and what effect would changes to those factors have on the final decision. The operator could then either improve the accuracy of his data, or justify why not, as appropriate and, if necessary, repeat the relevant environmental or economic assessments.

4.4 Reduction in the scope of environmental effects to include in the assessment

4.4.1 The work involved in undertaking each one of the environmental assessment techniques described below for many options releasing many substances to all media may be not inconsiderable. However, it is not the intention that considerable resources need to be committed to processes with only limited impact in terms of one or more of the environmental effects, described in Section 7 below. In such cases the scope of the assessment can be restricted to specific environmental effects which require further consideration appropriate to the

particular process concerned and the workload could therefore be lessened. For example:

- where test of insignificance demonstrates that many substances are released in only insignificant amounts (in which case the PC, background concentrations and PECs will only need calculating for a few substances);

- where there are no releases, (or only insignificant releases) to one of the three media (in which case modelling for that medium will not be necessary and that $EQ_{(medium)}$ will not need calculating);

- where, there are no solid wastes for disposal in amounts greater than 1 kg/year; and / or

- where releases affecting ozone creation and/or global warming are insignificant.

4.4.2 If all the environmental effects are insignificant, then detailed environmental assessment of several options is not necessary. The BPEO can be justified by reference to the identification, screening and selection of techniques undertaken in developing the preferred option.

5   STAGE 1: Define the objective

The starting point for a BPEO assessment is to define the objective of the particular IPC process on which the assessment is to be performed. For example, for a new IPC process the objective might be, *"to produce a product or provide a service and operate the process in accordance with the aims of Integrated Pollution Control"* (see box 4).

THE AIMS OF IPC INCLUDE:

- to prevent or minimise the release of prescribed substances and to render harmless all substances which are released;

- to develop an approach to pollution control that considers releases from industrial processes to all media in the environment as a whole;

- to improve the effectiveness and efficiency of pollution controls on industry;

- to provide the appropriate framework to encourage cleaner technologies and the minimisation of waste;

- to maintain public confidence in the regulatory system through a clear and transparent system that is accessible and easy to understand and is clear and simple in operation

Source: Integrated Pollution Control: A Practical Guide Department of the Environment 1995

Box 4

6 STAGE 2: Generate options to meet the objective

6.1 Introduction

6.1.1 BPEO cannot be looked at in isolation from the other aims of IPC (see box 4) and options considered must therefore meet all the other aims of IPC. In effect this means carrying out a fundamental examination of the whole process. The operator should examine which techniques are feasible for each step of the process. The process might be broken down, for example into the following aspects:

● the chemical synthesis route;

● the process technology; and

● abatement plant.

6.2 Identifying a preferred option

6.2.1 At this stage techniques should be evaluated in terms of their potential to prevent, minimise and render harmless releases. The "cleanest" feasible techniques for each step of the process, should be identified. A configuration of techniques can then be chosen as the preferred option for achieving the objective developed in stage 1.

6.2.2 Establishing a preferred option at this early stage can reduce the workload for operators. Ideally all practicable options should be assessed in detail. However, the benefits of doing this may be outweighed by the costs incurred by the applicant in carrying out detailed environmental assessments of several options.

6.2.3 For example, the preferred option for a new process should include the latest, cleanest techniques which minimise releases. An analysis of environmental effects of the preferred option could then be made to check if the releases have an insignificant effect on the environment. In such a case detailed environmental assessments of several other options might not be required.

6.2.4 For existing processes the preferred option might be the existing techniques unless there are already plans to upgrade the plant (for example as a requirement of an improvement programme). This might be especially true in cases where the options being considered only relate to installing new pollution abatement equipment on existing processes. The principles in the following paragraphs apply to both new and existing processes.

6.3 Identification and quantification of substances released from the preferred option

6.3.1 All substances which may be released from the preferred option should be identified whether prescribed or not. Guidance on which substances may be released can be found in the relevant IPC Guidance Notes. Sufficient information should be provided by the operator to enable the extent of the releases to be quantified. For example:

● the concentration of substance in the release;

● proposed release rate (quantity per unit time); and

● an estimate of the total annual load released.

6.3.2 The above information should be provided for the following:

● peak releases, which may be as a result of periodic fluctuations in the plant throughput or a consequence of start-up or shut-down operations;

● proposed normal operating conditions; and

● fugitive releases.

Mean concentrations of routine releases should be expressed as flow weighted averages.

6.3.3 In the case of releases of trade effluents to sewer, the above information should be supplied, together with an estimate of the final load released to the receiving water. Information on typical removal rates of the pollutant during sewage treatment can normally be obtained from the local water company. The removal rates assumed should be clearly stated in the data supplied.

6.4 Test of Insignificance

6.4.1 In principle, all substances which may be released from the preferred option should be identified, but then their impact should be assessed to avoid taking insignificant releases through the rest of the assessment.

6.4.2 The word insignificant in this context means that the environmental effects are insignificant. One way of judging insignificance is by estimating the concentration in the environment that would result from a release, (the process contribution or PC) and comparing that to the EAL. To provide a quick way of checking whether environmental effects will be insignificant, the Agency has developed a method to calculate threshold release rates for each substance to the relevant medium for different stack heights or aquatic dispersions. This method has been developed from the relative potential for harm of each substance in each environmental medium (expressed as the EAL) and dispersion from certain typical stack heights or into typical aquatic conditions

6.4.3 Operators can simply compare the release rate of each substance with the thresholds to determine if a release is insignificant. Volume II includes tables thresholds of insignificance.

6.4.4 The operator should also determine if there are any other significant environmental effects.

- Short Term Effects

- Global Warming

- Ozone Creation

- Waste Arisings

- Other Environmental Effects (see section 7.8)

6.4.5 The concept of insignificance discussed here cannot be unambiguously defined as a fixed percentage of the EAL. However, the Agency proposes that, as a rule of thumb, insignificant substances are those where:

- the long term PC in air is less than 0.2% of the long term EAL for air;

- the long term PC in water is less than 0.2% of the long term EAL for water;

- the deposition rate on land is less then 0.2% of the MDR for land;

- the short term PC in air is less than 0.2% of the short term EAL for air; or

- the short term PC on waste is less than 0.2% of the short term EAL for water.

6.4.6 It should be noted that a substance can be insignificant for one medium but not for another. Similarly a substance can be released in insignificant quantities with respect to long term effects but not short term and vice versa. Furthermore, the cost of preventing or minimising an "insignificant" substance may be so small that it is still justified to make improvements to the preferred option.

6.4.7 If all substances released in insignificant amounts from the preferred option and no other significant environmental effects are identified, then detailed environmental assessment of several options is not necessary. The BPEO can be justified by reference to the identification, screening and selection of techniques undertaken in developing the preferred option.

6.5 Prioritising the substances released in terms of environmental effects

6.5.1 In order to minimise pollution to the environment as a whole having regard to BPEO, attention must focus during option generation on priorities so far as environmental effects are concerned. Before generating further options it is helpful therefore to prioritise substances released from the preferred option in terms of their environmental effects. The ways that this can be done include those described below.

Comparison with IPC Guidance Notes

6.5.2 Following any rejection of insignificant releases, all remaining releases should be compared with those regarded as achievable in the relevant IPC Guidance Note. If they exceed those levels in the relevant IPCGN then control measures should be identified for the substances concerned.

Chimney height determination

6.5.3 Where releases occur to the atmosphere, operators should demonstrate that the current chimney height provides adequate dispersion for the pollutants produced. Guidance on the assessment of chimney heights is provided in Technical Guidance Note D1[22]. The assessment of chimney heights will also provide some information on the relative importance of different substances for control.

6.5.4 Where the calculations indicate that the current chimney height is inadequate then further calculations should be undertaken to identify the level of control required to ensure adequate dispersion through the existing stack. All options to be evaluated in the detailed assessment stage should assume that level of control and/or a stack of adequate height.

6.5.5 In so far as it is practicable to do so, vents should be combined into a single release point. Technical Guidance Note D1 or some other more appropriate analysis technique should be used to determine vent release height. A minimum vent design height of three metres above the building or structure would normally be expected.

Comparison of process contribution with EAL

6.5.6 This exercise serves two functions. Firstly, by comparison of the process contribution (PC) for each substance with its EAL the operator obtains a comparative indicator of the scale of environmental effects of each substance released to each medium. This can subsequently be used to direct attention to specific substances and media when generating options. Secondly it generates, the environmental quotients used below.

6.5.7 For all substances which have not been shown to be insignificant, the operator can calculate the PC at the relevant location in the receiving environment. The PC should be calculated as the same statistic in which the long term EAL is expressed for that substance. This is normally the annual mean concentration. The location should normally be where the PC is at its highest. For air (and deposition from air to land) it will always be at ground level and for water it will be after an appropriate mixing zone. It is up to the operator to select appropriate techniques and make appropriate assumptions in the following areas:

- choice of dispersion models for the relevant media;

- prediction of the location of highest concentration; and

- mixing zones for releases to water.

Further guidance is provided in *Released Substances and their Dispersion in the Environment*[4].

6.5.8 The PC for each substance in each medium could be divided by the relevant EAL. EALs can be found in Volume II: Technical Data, of this guidance note. This fraction is called the environmental quotient for each particular substance ($EQ_{(substance)}$). Where the PC is greater than a small fraction of the EAL for any particular substance then operators should direct attention towards techniques to prevent or minimise releases of that substance, ie that substance is a "priority for control". The Agency suggests that, as a rule of thumb, a substance should be a priority for control where the PC is greater than 2% of the EAL.

6.5.9 The EQs for all substances can be presented as a histogram to highlight which substances are priority for control.

Comparison of predicted environmental concentration with EAL

6.5.10 This exercise serves two functions. Firstly, the operator obtains a comparative indicator of the degree of environmental harm resulting from the release of each substance to each medium when

added to existing ambient concentrations relevant to the specific location. This can subsequently be used to direct attention to specific substances and media when generating options. Secondly, it shows which medium is most sensitive in the context of the "headroom" between the PEC and the EAL. This may indicate a need to give a higher priority to the effects on one particular medium and subsequently influence the operators choice of BPEO.

6.5.11 The operator should determine the ambient concentration for each of the substances in each of the media at the point where PCs have been determined. Reference should be made to any available local environmental monitoring data which may need supplementing by monitoring undertaken by the operator. For existing processes the ambient concentrations so obtained will need correcting to take account of the contribution of releases from the process to the monitoring data. Where no data are available and the operator can justify not undertaking its own environmental monitoring, then sources of data are available in *Released Substances and their Dispersion in the Environment*[3]. The annual mean is the normal statistic to be used. The predicted environmental concentrations (PECs) for each substance could be calculated by adding the PC for each substance calculated above to the corrected ambient concentration for each substance. The PEC for each substance in each medium could then be divided by the relevant EAL (see Volume II: Technical Data of this guidance note). Where the PEC approaches the EAL for any particular substance then operators should direct attention towards techniques to prevent or minimise releases of that substance, ie that substance is a "priority for control". The Agency suggests that, as a rule of thumb, a substance should be a priority for control where the PEC is greater than 80% of the EAL.

6.5.12 The ratio of PECs to EALs for all substances can be presented as a histogram to highlight which substances are priority for control.

Determination of compliance with Environmental Quality Standards

6.5.13 For substances with an Environmental Quality Standard (EQS), the operator should show whether the PEC of the substance is likely to exceed the relevant EQS for the relevant medium. Volume II: Technical Data of this guidance note lists the short term and long term EQSs that apply to each medium.

6.5.14 A comparison of PEC with EQS is relevant so that, in the option generation stage, techniques are considered which might enable compliance with the EQS. This is because the Agency must specify in an authorisation conditions that it considers appropriate for achieving compliance with EQSs. Where an EQS is, or is likely to be, breached the Agency has to come to a view as to the most appropriate manner in which environmental concentrations can be reduced.

Consideration of sensitive receptors

6.5.15 The degree of environmental harm which may result from any given concentration of substance in a particular medium will be dependent upon the nature of the pollution receptors. The obligations under the Act concerned with rendering harmless can therefore only be addressed by taking account of the site-specific pollution receptors.

6.5.16 In addition to compliance with relevant EQSs and comparison with EALs, operators should therefore consider the consequences of releases on any particularly sensitive receptors in the receiving environment. Examples of sensitive receptors may include:

- Sites of Special Scientific Interest (SSSIs);

- other industrial or commercial activities with particular environmental quality requirements (eg fish farms);

- vulnerable developments (eg hospitals); or

- particular substance/receptor combinations, such as the effects of fluoride on cattle.

6.5.17 For these types of vulnerable ecosystems, the analysis of the environmental concentration at the relevant location should be determined and a judgement made as to whether this is likely to be harmful to the sensitive receptor(s) concerned.

6.5.18 An assessment of the likely effects of the release on the receptor concerned should be undertaken and, if necessary, techniques identified to render the release harmless.

Consideration of other environmental effects from the process

6.5.19 Consideration should be given as to whether there are any other significant environmental effects from the process. Any such effects identified in section 7.8 should be included in the assessment of priority substances.

6.5.20 **If, following this stage, no substances are identified as priorities for control then detailed environmental assessment of several options is not necessary. The BPEO can be justified by reference to the identification, screening and selection of techniques undertaken in developing the preferred option.**

6.6 Identifying alternative techniques

6.6.1 Having identified priority substances, operators should consider what techniques could be used to prevent or minimise and render harmless the priority substances.

6.6.2 For new processes, a number of different techniques may have been identified when developing the preferred option and an operator may choose to re-examine those, paying particular attention to those which reduced releases of the priority substances. Sometimes new techniques may need to be generated and assessed.

6.6.3 Such a fundamental review may not have been undertaken for existing processes, and operators will be expected to generate and assess techniques which may be used to address releases of the priority substances identified above. This will involve alternative techniques for each part of the process (for example, chemical synthesis routes, process technology, abatement equipment).

6.6.4 Guidance on techniques can be found in the IPC Guidance Note (IPCGN) for the industry concerned. However, the absence of any reference in the IPCGN should not prevent the operator from selecting other techniques with which he is familiar, which are appropriate to the process at the specific location and which are available. Available in this context can be taken to mean "technically proven and commercially available with appropriate performance guarantees".

6.6.5 The IPCGNs give generic guidance only. To identify techniques for the purposes of BPEO assessment, however, the operator should take into consideration the site-specific factors which relate to preventing releases or minimising them and rendering them harmless. These site-specific factors should include the mandatory objective of EQS compliance by considering the reduction of releases of any substances which cause or contribute to the failure of an EQS. Further calculations should be undertaken at this option generation stage to identify the level of control available that would allow the EQS to be achieved. This would assist the Agency in its consideration of ways of achieving EQS compliance.

6.6.6 The following site-specific factors should also be included:

- Consideration should be given to techniques for preventing or minimising substances released where the preferred option fails to meet the achievable release levels in the relevant IPCGN(s).

- Consideration should be given to a taller stack or alternative techniques for minimising substances released via that stack where the calculations at section 6.5.4 above indicate that the chimney height of the preferred option is inadequate. Further calculations should be undertaken at this option generation stage to identify either:

> the degree of reduction of releases required to ensure adequate dispersion through the chimney height of the preferred option; and/or

> the stack height required to give adequate dispersion for the preferred option release levels.

Each option generated should achieve release levels determined by chimney height calculations appropriate to the stack height included in that option.

- Priority should be given to techniques for preventing or minimising releases of substances when a Process Contribution (PC) is more than a small fraction of the EAL. As a rule of thumb where PC $\geqslant$ 0.02 EAL. In such circumstances the options generated could focus on addressing releases to the medium where the PC is high.

- Priority should be given to techniques for preventing or minimising releases of substances when a Predicted Environmental Concentration (PEC) is high compared to the EAL. As a rule of thumb where PEC $\geqslant$ 0.8 EAL. In such circumstances the options generated could focus on addressing releases to the medium where the PEC is high.

- Consideration needs to be given to reducing releases of substances where sensitive receptors may be harmed.

6.6.7 Techniques which may be used to control and prevent fugitive releases (from storage tanks for example) should be identified as well as techniques which address the "normal" releases.

6.6.8 Operators should take account of low pollution technology, recycling rather than disposal and the implications of any cross media transfers. It is important to record the decisions for or against each alternative technique and the supporting reasons in the audit trail.

6.7 Screening of techniques

6.7.1 Individual techniques can be combined into a number of different overall process and abatement options which deal with the range of substances released to the different media as identified by the factors described above. However, where the number of permutations for process and abatement techniques for each of several substances would provide a very large number of options, then the operator may wish to reduce the number of techniques and/or permutations of techniques as discussed below. This is perhaps most relevant for chemical processes, where there are many potential chemical pathways by which any particular chemical or group of chemicals could be produced, but it may apply to other process sectors. This initial screen may reduce excessive work on options which are subsequently rejected.

6.7.2 In cases where a large number of process options might be feasible, an initial screening may be appropriate to reduce the number of techniques by the application of technical assessment, professional judgement and very limited experimentation. Factors to be considered will include:

- familiarity with particular techniques;

- technical viability;

- process development time;

- considerations of space requirements;

- possible restrictions imposed by planning legislation;

- health and safety considerations;

- excessive cost;

- other practical considerations such as fuel consumption, yield, physical space and other site-specific factors; and

- "availability" of particular techniques.

6.8 Developing feasible options to meet the objective identified in Stage 1

6.8.1 Potential techniques will have been screened to identify the most practicable for inclusion in a sensible number of feasible options for achieving the objective. Each of these options will consist of a specific configuration of techniques for carrying on the process in question. Only options which are both practicable and environmentally acceptable should be carried forward to the next stage. The Agency has followed the RCEP's suggestion that typically three to six options should be taken forward. In the case of new processes, each option taken through for BPEO assessment should meet the achievable release levels in the relevant IPCGN(s).

6.8.2 Before proceeding with the assessment stage, it may be prudent for operators to reconsider the options generated in the light of the criteria used to prioritise releases and subsequently amend options or add new ones. The criteria are:

- consideration of compliance with any statutory EQSs;

- the achievable release levels in the relevant IPCGN(s);

- an adequate chimney height;

- the Predicted Environmental Concentration (PEC) compared to the EAL (as a rule of thumb where PEC should be < 0.8 EAL);

- the Process Contribution (PC) compared to the EAL (as a rule of thumb where PC < 0.02 EAL).

Reconsidering and amending options in this way could save an operator undertaking abortive environmental assessment work on an option which subsequently turns out to be unacceptable.

6.8.3 It is important to record the decisions for and against each option and the supporting reasons in the audit trail.

7 STAGE 3: Assess the options

7.1 Introduction

7.1.1 This stage will include assessment of the environmental effects of each option. RCEP recognised that environmental assessment requires a considerable amount of data.

7.1.2 There are various measures of environmental effects that can be used. Those most relevant to IPC processes are described below but this should not preclude operators from using other techniques where justified.

7.1.3 First, the releases from each option that are not insignificant need to be identified (in a similar manner to the identification of releases from the preferred option). Second, an environmental analysis to determine the fate of those releases needs to be undertaken. Guidance on Environmental Analysis[3] is available separately. Throughout the environmental analysis stage, an audit trail should be kept and sensitivity analysis undertaken where appropriate.

7.1.4 Other relevant factors, as well as environmental effects, should be assessed. The guidance summarised in this brochure gives specific attention to the following environmental effects:

- Long Term Effects in air, water and land
- Short Term Effects (particularly in air and water)
- Global Warming
- Ozone Creation
- Waste Arisings
- Other Environmental Effects (eg odour, visible plumes, critical loads, stratospheric ozone depletion potential)

7.1.5 For existing processes where the preferred option is the existing configuration and the only available options are pollution abatement techniques, there may be scope to focus the assessment on only those environmental effects influenced by the equipment.

7.2 Identification and quantification of releases from each option

7.2.1 The first step in this particular stage of the process is to identify and quantify substances released from each option so that the environmental effects of each option can be assessed and compared.

7.2.2 All substances which may be released from each option should be identified whether prescribed or not. Guidance on which substances may be released can be found in the relevant IPC Guidance Notes. Sufficient information should be assembled by the operator to enable the extent of the releases to be quantified. For each substance identified, the following information should be assembled:

- the concentration of substance in the release;
- proposed release rate (quantity per unit time); and
- an estimate of the total annual load released.

7.2.3 The above information should cover the following:

- peak releases, which may be as a result of periodic fluctuations in the plant throughput or a consequence of start-up or shut-down operations;
- proposed normal operating conditions; and
- fugitive releases.

Mean concentrations of routine releases should be expressed as flow weighted averages.

7.2.4 In the case of releases to sewer, the above information should be assembled, together with an estimate of the final load released to the receiving water. Information on typical removal rates of the pollutant during sewage treatment can normally be obtained from the local water company. The removal rates assumed should be clearly stated in the data.

7.3 Assessment of overall long term effects of releases

7.3.1 In order to determine the long term environmental consequences of a release, a benchmark is required against which to assess harm. The Agency has developed the concept of the Environmental Assessment Level (EAL) for this purpose (see also section 3.3 above). When there is a statutory environmental quality standard (EQS) for a substance then the EAL is the EQS. In the absence of an EQS, the Agency has derived provisional EALs from data such as workplace occupational exposure limits, or from data on the toxicity of chemicals to particular species. These provisional EALs and their derivation are included in Volume II: Technical Data of this guidance note. They are not statutory standards, but are to be used as indicators of environmental quality and as an aid to prioritisation of substances released and option selection.

7.3.2 There are differences of opinion among experts about the methods by which EALs should be derived. Thus the proposed values are temporary and should be viewed with caution. For this reason a working group of experts is to be formed to comment on the methods used for determining EALs and to recommend alternatives if appropriate.

7.3.3 The Process Contribution (PC) for each substance released to air from the preferred option (see section 6.5.7 above) can be divided by the relevant long term EAL. The resulting Environmental Quotients for each substance can then be summed to produce the $EQ_{(Air)}$. Operators can then calculate the $EQ_{(Water)}$ in a similar way. To calculate the $EQ_{(Land)}$ the deposition rates should be first calculated. The deposition rates for each substance released from the preferred option can then be divided by the Maximum Deposition Rates (MDRs) for the relevant substances. (MDRs are available in Volume II: Technical Data of this guidance note). The resulting Environmental Quotients for each substance can then be summed to produce the $EQ_{(Land)}$.

7.3.4 The method is summarised by the following equations:

$$EQ_{(Substance)} = \frac{Process\ contribution}{EAL} \quad \text{...(1)}$$

$$EQ_{(Medium)} = EQ_{(a)} + EQ_{(b)} ... EQ_{(i)} \quad \text{...(2)}$$

Where:
EQ is Environmental Quotient, and
a...i are substances released to a particular medium.

7.3.5 An index of the overall environmental effect for the preferred option may also be calculated by summing the $EQ_{(Medium)}$ as follows;

$$IEI = EQ_{(Air)} + EQ_{(Water)} + EQ_{(Land)} \quad \text{...(3)}$$

Where IEI is Integrated Environmental Index.

7.3.6 The $EQ_{(Air)}$, $EQ_{(Water)}$ and $EQ_{(Land)}$ can then be calculated for each option in the same way. The $EQ_{(medium)}$ for each option may then be summed to produce IEIs for each option.

7.3.7 Aggregating the $EQ_{(media)}$ into one single index may obscure an important difference between options. In such cases, the individual $EQ_{(medium)}$ or the EQ for just the one or two most important substances, may be carried forward in the assessment as part of the consideration in ranking process options and in determining the Best Practicable Environmental Option. In all cases the operator should justify his choice of index or indices.

7.4 Assessment of short term effects of releases

7.4.1 Different process options may lead to variations in the pattern of releases, for example, a process operated intermittently may give lower annual concentrations compared to one run continuously but an increased frequency of short term peaks may be the result. Furthermore, although the long term average concentrations may have been rendered acceptable by generally good dispersion there may, on occasions, be unacceptable short term peaks. The Agency has found this is particularly true for releases to air and water. The assessment of short term releases should therefore be an integral part of the environmental assessment under IPC for both new and existing processes.

7.4.2 Detailed assessment of short term effects is often complex as the maximum process contribution and maximum ambient concentration may be separated both temporally and spatially. Information on the temporal distribution of ambient pollutant concentrations and environmental parameters is desirable but may be unavailable for a particular location. Moreover, for many substances, environmental criteria against which releases can be compared are absent, particularly for water and land. However, for releases to air a number of EC or WHO guidelines and odour thresholds are available (see Volume II). Further guidance on these values will be produced by the Agency.

7.4.3 To reduce the need for potentially extensive modelling the following screening procedure could be followed to enable those releases likely to give rise to adverse short term effects in air to be identified ie:

● To represent an extreme worst case, the value of the maximum process contribution over a short period (usually half to one hour) and maximum ambient concentration in the locality should be summed and compared with a short term EAL. If the short term PEC is less than the short term EAL then the release may be considered tolerable and unlikely to give rise to adverse short term effects.

● If the short term PEC as assessed above exceeds the short term EAL then a more detailed modelling programme should be undertaken by the operator to identify the likely frequency and magnitude of any short term effects.

Short Term EALs for air and water are given in Volume II: Technical Data. For substances with no short term EAL listed, operators could develop their own EALs in accordance with the guidance given in Volume II.

7.4.4 In following the screening procedure the peak process contribution should be identified. This may occur during periods of start up, shut down, as a result of expected but unplanned releases or under particular environmental conditions.

7.4.5 The detailed assessment of short term effects should consider the temporal pattern and magnitude of releases as well as the range of dispersion conditions. The integration of these effects is likely to require detailed computer modelling. Where this is not practical, for example, due to lack of key data, it may be possible to obtain a rough estimate by adding the maximum process contribution to the long term average ambient concentration. This value can then be compared with the adopted short term EAL.

7.4.6 For existing plant the short term effects of releases should already have been considered under previous regulatory regimes. As a result, the selection and operation of new techniques may be constrained by factors such as existing stack height, location and design of outfalls or planning requirements. However, for new processes, consideration of the short term effects of releases will be an integral part of the assessment of BATNEEC/BPEO options.

7.4.7 If the results of the more detailed assessment indicate that short term releases from one or more process options will lead to adverse effects then the operator should examine the proposed technique(s). Where short term effects are identified these should be carried forward in the assessment and taken into consideration in ranking process options and in determining the BPEO.

7.4.8 The weight that these short term effects should play in the final ranking of options and choice of BPEO should be commensurate with the significance of the effects. The operator should justify the importance he places on short term effects in justifying his decision.

7.5 Assessment of global warming effects

Introduction

7.5.1 The release of carbon dioxide, chlorofluorocarbons (CFCs), methane and nitrous oxide may lead to global warming. It is important that the release of these gases is prevented or minimised wherever possible. Due to the nature of the effects arising from these pollutants there is not currently a universally acceptable methodology

which assess them by looking at their environmental concentrations. The Agency has therefore developed a separate index called the "Global Warming Potential" (GWP).

The Method

7.5.2 All gases released from each option which have potential to contribute to radiative forcing (global warming) should be identified. The mass (in tonnes) of each gas released over a unit time (ideally one year) can then be estimated for the preferred option and other options. The direct global warming potential (GWP) (ie the warming contribution of each gas relative to an equal weight of CO_2 over a period of 100 years) of each gas is calculated from the product of the mass and the GWP index for the gas concerned. GWP indices for a number of gases are shown in Volume II: Technical Data. The total global warming potential for each option is calculated by summing the GWPs for each gas.

7.5.3 The total global warming potential may be represented by equation (4):

$$GWP_{(Total)} = \sum_{i=1}^{n} GWP_i * Mass_i \ldots (4)$$

Where:

$GWP_{(Total)}$ = sum of the global warming potentials for the substances released from the option concerned.

GWP_i = global warming potential index for substance i of n released from the process.

$Mass_i$ = mass of substance i released from process.

7.6 Assessment of potential for ozone creation

Introduction

7.6.1 Ozone is a highly reactive pollutant which may damage human health, vegetation and materials. The production of ozone in the troposphere involves the action of sunlight on hydrocarbons, usually referred to as volatile organic compounds (VOCs) and oxides of nitrogen (NO_x). The availability of NO_x downwind of a source controls the spatial extent of the area within which raised ozone concentrations may be generated. Within this area the magnitude and distribution of the pollutant is controlled by the occurrence and characteristics of the available hydrocarbons (Derwent and Jenkin, 1991)[23].

7.6.2 There is a large variation between the importance of individual VOCs in their potential for ozone generation, depending on their reactivity with hydroxyl (OH) radicals and the subsequent production of peroxy (RO_2) radicals. In order to assess the relative effect of different hydrocarbons in the episodic production of ozone and provide a basis for their control the UNECE VOC convention has proposed[17] the concept of the Photochemical Ozone Creation Potential (POCP). The POCP is defined as the change in photochemical ozone production due to a change in emission of that particular VOC. The POCP may be determined by photochemical model calculations or by laboratory experiments.

7.6.3 Estimated individual POCP values will vary both temporally and spatially depending on the VOC composition of the modelled air parcel, the assumed meteorological conditions and NO_x concentrations. However, although there is considerable uncertainty over individual POCP values the approach can be used to classify VOC species according to their importance in ozone production and average values assigned to each class of compound.

The Method

7.6.4 All substances released to air from each option which have photochemical ozone creation potential should be identified. The mass of each substance (in tonnes) released over a unit time (ideally one year) can then be estimated for each option. Where significant quantities of VOCs are released, the POCP for each substance released from each option should be calculated from the product of the mass and the individual POCP value for the gas concerned. Gases which have a potential for ozone creation are shown in Volume II: Technical Data, along with their POCP values. The POCP for each option is calculated by summing the POCP for each gas. Volume II includes a table showing the classification and average photochemical ozone creation potential (POCP) value for a range of different compounds.

7.6.5 The calculation of the total POCP of a particular process can be represented by:

$$POCP_{(Total)} = \sum_{i=1}^{n} POCP_i * Mass_i...(5)$$

Where:

$POCP_{(Total)}$ = the weighted sum of all potential ozone generating substances released from the option concerned.

$POCP_i$ = the POCP value for substance i of n substances released from the process.

$Mass_i$ = the annual mass of substance i released from the process.

7.6.6 As well as assessing the relative ozone creation potential of different process options the POCP values can be used as a basis for identifying less damaging substitutes for substances used in a process. When seeking to identify substitute compounds for those of a relatively high POCP value it is important that the properties of the proposed alternative are carefully considered. For example, although both benzene and methyl chloroform have low POCP values, benzene is a known carcinogen and methyl chloroform is relatively long lived and may persist into the stratosphere where it contributes to stratospheric ozone depletion.

7.7 Assessment of waste arisings

Introduction

7.7.1 Many processes will generate quantities of solid or liquid waste, ie material which is not released to air or water. These wastes may be treated or disposed of on-site or removed from the plant for treatment or disposal elsewhere. There are instances when waste arisings are highly relevant to the assessment of the environmental impact of a process and may be the most significant measure of environmental effects. However, incorporating such waste arisings into the calculation of an Environment Quotient or Integrated Environmental Index is less straightforward than is the case with releases to air or water. This is because their environmental effects are likely to depend on a range of more complex interactions. A separate means of comparing this aspect of different process options is required.

7.7.2 A number of hazard assessment schemes can be found in the literature. The one proposed in this document is based on that developed by the UK Government-Industry Working Group on Priority Setting and Risk Assessment[19]. The scheme is based on a number of parameters:

- toxicity (to mammals and aquatic organisms);

- potential for bioaccumulation;

- degradation (in soil/water); and

- other physical characteristics such as solubility, adsorption potential and volatility.

Each of these parameters is scored and a total score is obtained by combining the individual scores into a "unit hazard score". This represents the potential hazard for a unit quantity of the substance concerned.

7.7.3 A comparative assessment of potential environmental effects of waste arisings can be achieved by assessing each waste arising from each option on the basis of quantity of waste produced and its relative hazard potential as indicated by the unit hazard score. The unit hazard scores, together with a table showing the exposure and toxicity scores for air and water are given in Volume II: Technical Data for a range of substances along with a more detailed description of the hazard assessment scheme.

7.7.4 Section 3.5.16 above briefly described the principles behind the development of the indicator for waste arisings and explained why the environmental effects resulting from the specific method and location of disposal are not included in the indicator for waste arisings. The waste hazard index described below only considers, therefore, the "potential" effects of the waste, irrespective of its fate, but provided that it is not re-used or recycled.

The Method

7.7.5 The quantity of wastes generated per year should be determined for each option. The composition of each waste stream should then be determined to give a list of substances with their quantity for disposal in kg per year for each option. Any wastes which are re-used or recycled, or any substances in the waste stream which are extracted for re-use or recycling can be disregarded for the purposes of this assessment. Any substances present in waste streams at less than 1 kg per year may be disregarded. Any totally inert wastes can also be disregarded.

7.7.6 The hazard score for any particular substance can be calculated as a function of the annual mass for disposal of that substance and the relevant unit hazard score. Summing all the unit hazard scores for each option gives an overall hazard score for each option being considered. Different process options producing different wastes can then be ranked according to their overall hazard scores. This methodology is given by equation (6).

$$FHS = \sum \left(\log_{10}(MQD_i) * RQS_i * UHS_i \right)$$

Where:

Final hazard score (FHS) = weighted sum of the unit hazard scores for all substances arising from the process option considered.

MQD_i = the maximum quantity disposed of for substance i for any of the process options currently under consideration

UHS_i = the unit hazard score of substance i of n arising.

RQS_i = a score (1-5) which is related to the ratio of the quantity of substance (i) for disposal from the option concerned, compared to the maximum

taken across all process options. (See Volume II for further details).

7.7.7 It should be noted that no absolute quantitative meaning should be applied to these scores. All that can be inferred from them is that a waste with an overall hazard score of (say) 250 is likely to represent less of a hazard than one with a score of 350. This information can, along with the EQs, IEI and other factors, be taken into account in reaching a judgement on the option which represents the BPEO, and in ranking each practicable option considered in the assessment.

7.8 Assessment of other relevant environmental effects

Introduction

7.8.1 The factors outlined in sections 7.3 to 7.7 above are neither exhaustive nor exclusive. Other additional factors might be pertinent to any particular process at a specific location. In particular, the following factors may be relevant:

- odours;

- visible plumes;

- exceedance of critical loads (of oxides of sulphur or nitrogen);

- foreseeable but unplanned releases, for example, releases from safety valves or overflows; and

- stratospheric ozone depletion potential.

7.8.2 If operators are in doubt as to any of the above effects then they may wish to consult with the Agency over the circumstances when such environmental effects might need to be determined and how to quantify and present any such effects. Some guidance on odours and visible plumes is given below.

Odours

7.8.3 For individual odorous compounds, published odour threshold concentrations are available which define the concentration at which the human nose either detects the presence of an odour (odour detection threshold) or recognises the odour (odour recognition threshold). Predicted short term concentrations for each option can be compared to the odour detection threshold (ODT) or odour recognition threshold (ORT) to determine the potential for odour effects. Where necessary, appropriate modelling techniques should be used to predict concentrations over very short time periods. Information regarding sources of ODTs and ORTs is available in Volume II: Technical Data.

Visible plumes

7.8.4 Public perception of the effectiveness of control measures, or conversely their concerns, often relate to what they see. For that reason, an operator should, where necessary, consider techniques that provide for the avoidance of discoloration of a plume attributable to substances other than water vapour and/or the avoidance or reduction of plume visibility attributed to water vapour. The effects of visible plumes could then be assessed and compared by the operator in a qualitative manner for each option.

7.9 Assessment of costs

Introduction

7.9.1 The Agency's BPEO methodology goes beyond the scope of financial appraisal but not to the full extent of social cost benefit analysis. External effects of each option are considered in terms of appropriate environmental impacts, but comparisons are made directly rather than through the medium of money valuation of such impacts.

The need for costs to be compared

7.9.2 Balanced judgement on the control of releases needs to include consideration of the costs of abatement as well as the environmental benefits. It is only worth devoting further resources to environmental improvements as long as the social benefits exceed the costs.

The basis for comparing costs

7.9.3 The costs of options need to be presented on a basis which is comparable between different projects with different timescales. As with normal financial appraisal, this requires that capital and operating costs be reduced to a comparable basis by means of Discounted Cash Flow (DCF) techniques. DCF enables any stream of payments, receipts or costs to be reduced, or "discounted", to a single Net Present Value (NPV) in a base year.

7.9.4 DCF techniques use values which allow for inflation. These are thus 'real' or 'constant' rather than 'money' or 'current', and are expressed in terms of money of a base year (not necessarily the same as the NPV base year).

Cost estimation methodology

7.9.5 If an operator justifies a proposed process option on the grounds of avoiding excessive costs of an environmentally superior option, then the economic implications of all feasible options should be compared. Appropriate standard techniques for project appraisal should be used to compare options. This is to be done by identifying the full costs of each option, and annualizing them over the forecast period of plant operating life. The results enable comparison of options to be made in terms of the incremental equivalent annual costs of environmental improvements.

7.9.6 The Cost Estimation Methodology requires that, for each component technique of the option, estimates be made of the following.

- The capital costs of purchasing and installation, (plus interest during construction where appropriate).

- The annual operating and maintenance (O & M) costs for a typical year (or, if expected to vary, over the lifetime of the abatement technique). Allowance may be made for lost sales due to any reduction in output. Costs should be net of any relevant benefits, savings or 'recovery credits' such as reduced use or increased recycling of energy or materials inputs, saleable by-products, reduced labour requirements, enhanced production efficiency or improved product quality.

- The operating life, in years.

7.9.7 From this information a Net Present Value (NPV) for each option can be determined, with a suitable base year. This involves discounting real values (i.e. in constant terms, excluding inflation) to the base year. The appropriate real discount rate is given by the cost of capital to the operator. From the NPV, an 'annualised cost' can be determined (the value of an equal annual payment throughout the project life, which gives the same NPV). This calculation is shown in Table 1. Any sensitivity in the ranking of options to changes in the discount rate should be explored.

7.9.8 If necessary for clarity, an option should be disaggregated into its component techniques, and the annualised costs found for each element before adding them together to give the cost of the option. Annualised cost estimates should be as accurate as possible, with all assumptions made explicit. Where a margin of error is necessary, full explanation should be given. Where operator's cost forecasts appear excessive, more detailed information may be required.

7.9.9 The preferred option should be clearly defined when examining options for an existing plant. Any costs of environmental protection and pollutant abatement systems which are necessary to comply with previous requirements should be included as part of the preferred option, not added to any of the potential options.

Table 1:
Equivalent Annual Cost of Pollution Control Equipment

1. Capital Costs (£)[1] :   _____
2. Discount Rate ("r") :   _____
   (expressed as a fraction e.g. 10% = 0.10)
3. Operating Life of technique in years ("n") : _____
4. Equivalent Annual Cost factor[2] :

$$\frac{r}{(1+r)^n - 1} + r = \quad \text{_____}$$

5. Annualised Capital Costs (Multiply Line 1 by Line 4) :
6. Yearly Recurring (Operating and Maintenance) Costs[3] : _____
7. Total Annualised Project Costs (Line 5 + Line 6) : _____

[1] If spread over more than one year, reduce to present value in first year.

[2] Assumes payment at year end.

[3] Costs that recur less frequently than yearly should be pro-rated over the appropriate number of years. For example, for items that are replaced once every three years, one third of the cost should be included in each year.

Capital costs

7.9.10 Capital costs include all costs required to purchase equipment needed for the pollution control system (termed **purchased equipment** costs), the costs of labour and materials for installing that equipment (termed **direct installation** costs), costs for site preparation and buildings, and certain other costs which are termed **indirect installation** costs. Capital costs also include costs for **land, working capital, and off-site facilities**. These elements of capital investment are displayed in box 5.

7.9.11 It is important that the limits of the area or process component to be costed are described at the outset. Costs should relate to a process or activity defined by this limit. For a technique that is inherently less polluting, the limit may be the entire process or project. The cost of each major piece of equipment within the limit can be documented with data supplied by an equipment vendor or by a referenced source.

Yearly operating and maintenance costs

7.9.12 The recurring annual costs for pollution control systems consist of three elements, see box 6: direct *(variable and semi-variable) costs* (DC), indirect *(fixed) costs* (IC), and *recovery credits* (RC). These are represented by the following equation:

Yearly costs = DC + IC - RC   (7)

The appropriate time period for these costs is one year, as this allows for seasonal variations in production (and releases).

7.9.13 **Direct costs** are those which tend to be proportional or partially proportional to the quantity of releases processed by the control system per unit time or, in the case of cleaner processes, the amount of material processed or manufactured per unit time. They include costs for raw materials, utilities (steam, electricity, process and cooling water etc), waste treatment and disposal, maintenance materials, replacement parts, and operating, supervisory, and maintenance labour.

7.9.14 **Indirect**, or "fixed", annual costs are those whose values are totally independent of the release flow rate and which would in fact be incurred even if the pollution control system were shut down. They include such categories as overhead, administrative charges, insurance, and business rates.

7.9.15 Direct and indirect annual costs may be offset by **recovery credits**, taken for materials or energy recovered by the control system, which may be sold, recycled to the process, or reused elsewhere at the site. These credits, in turn, should be offset by the costs necessary for their processing, storage, transportation, and any other steps required to make the recovered materials or energy reusable or resaleable. They also include reduced labour requirements, enhanced production efficiencies or improvements to product quality.

7.9.16 The labour and materials costs of any parts which will need replacement before the end of the useful life of the main plant should be subtracted from the capital cost figure before it is multiplied by the annualization factor. Otherwise, double

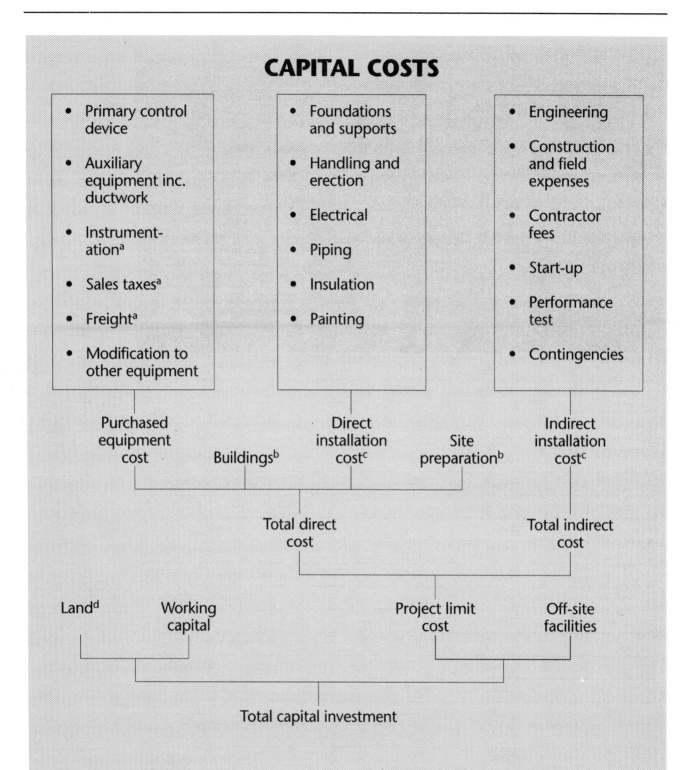

CAPITAL COSTS

- Primary control device
- Auxiliary equipment inc. ductwork
- Instrument-ation[a]
- Sales taxes[a]
- Freight[a]
- Modification to other equipment

- Foundations and supports
- Handling and erection
- Electrical
- Piping
- Insulation
- Painting

- Engineering
- Construction and field expenses
- Contractor fees
- Start-up
- Performance test
- Contingencies

Purchased equipment cost

Buildings[b]

Direct installation cost[c]

Site preparation[b]

Indirect installation cost[c]

Total direct cost

Total indirect cost

Land[d]

Working capital

Project limit cost

Off-site facilities

Total capital investment

[a] Typically factored from the sum of the primary control device and auxiliary equipment cost.

[b] Unlike the other direct and indirect costs, costs for these items are not factored from the purchased equipment cost. Rather, they are sized and costed separately.

[c] Typically factored from the purchased equipment cost.

[d] Usually only required at green field installations.

Box 5

YEARLY OPERATING AND MAINTENANCE COSTS

Direct Costs

Variable Costs

- Raw materials
- Utilities
  - Electricity
  - Fuel
  - Steam
  - Water
  - Compressed air
- Waste treatment/disposal
- Labour
  - Operating
  - Supervisory
  - Maintenance

Semi-variable costs

- Maintenance materials
- Replacement parts

Indirect Costs

- Overhead
- Rates
- Insurance
- Administrative charges
- Capital recovery

MINUS

Recovery Credits

- Recovered product
- Improved product quality
- Useful byproduct
- Reduced labour, energy & materials

Box 6

counting would occur. Costs of these parts should be accounted for in the maintenance costs.

Real values and equivalent annual values

7.9.17 Both the discount rate and all cost data should be in real, or constant, price terms rather than nominal, or cash terms. Real values are expressed in money of a specified base year. This avoids distortions due to changes in the value of money resulting from inflation. If any prices are forecast to move differently from those in the rest of the economy (eg energy), they should be identified and the source of the forecast explained.

7.9.18 Use of Equivalent Annual Values is necessary so that comparisons can be made between potential options even if they have different economic lives. This is done by reducing all financial flows for each option to an NPV in the base year. Merely comparing NPVs between options with different economic lives would be misleading: two projects could have the same NPV but one might last twice as long as the other. The solution is to establish the equivalent annual value for each option, given by the discount rate and by the option's economic life. This then allows comparison between options on an equivalent annual basis. As mentioned above, cost estimating for each option may need to be broken down into the component techniques, which are finally summed to give the cost for each option.

8 STAGE 4: Summarise and present the assessment

8.1 Introduction

8.1.1 The results of the assessment of options should be clearly presented in a transparent and consistent manner so that the Agency and others are readily able to review and audit the proposals.

8.1.2 In presenting the results of the assessment, it may be helpful to summarise the different environmental, and other relevant considerations, using qualitative and/or quantitative measures of effects as appropriate. The relative importance attached to each of the environmental factors should also be clearly stated.

8.1.3 In view of the difficulties inherent in making direct comparisons between different types of environmental effects, it is not possible or desirable to give universal guidance on how to judge the relative importance of different environmental effects.

8.1.4 If the preferred option had no priority substances requiring control, then the detailed assessment of options described above might be out of proportion to the environmental effects of the process. In such cases the summary and presentation will draw from the justification of the preferred option and the preliminary environmental assessment undertaken in stage 2.

8.2 Summarising and presenting cost data

8.2.1 When balancing the benefits and costs of further reductions in pollution, it is important to have quantitative measures of the economic costs and environmental consequences of the releases involved.

8.2.2 Information on the costs of feasible abatement options should be provided, based on standard financial appraisal methodology. It should show the costs to the operator of the option in question, by comparing the cash flow of the preferred option with that for other options. One useful comparator may be to show the cost per unit of substance abated at relevant levels of operation. This is only an intermediate factor in comparison with the cost of reducing harm to the environment, but will provide information about the techniques most likely to be worthwhile.

8.2.3 Relevant supporting material should be provided for each scenario. This should include forecasts for the following:

- itemised annualised costs;

- levels of product sales/demand; and

- levels of product price(s).

All relevant assumptions should be shown, and explanations should be provided for trends over time. This may require some assessment of the background economics and structure of the industry to support product price forecasts.

8.3 Summarising and presenting environmental effects

8.3.1 So far as quantification of environmental effects is concerned, the Environmental Quotients normally provide convenient measures of the overall pollution potential of a process to plot against costs. The Integrated Environmental Index may also be appropriate in some circumstances. However, other environmental measure(s) should also be used where the operator believes that other measure(s) of pollution potential are appropriate to the process concerned – for example:

- the quantity of individual substances removed; or

- one or more of the other measures of environmental assessment described in Section 7 above;

All assumptions made should be fully justified and clearly presented by the operator.

9 STAGE 5: Identify the Best Practicable Environmental Option

9.1 Introduction

9.1.1 The choice of the site-specific BPEO involves a consideration and assimilation of the economic and environmental information obtained in stage 3 and presented in stage 4. It will not normally be possible to make a direct comparison between abatement costs and the money value of reducing environmental harm.

9.1.2 Often, there are different environmental effects which influence the choice of BPEO, and economic (or other) considerations may also influence the choice. In such cases professional judgement should be used to identify the BPEO with appropriate justification. The work undertaken in stages 1 to 4 above will not in itself make the decision on BPEO and neither is it a substitute for professional judgement. However, by following stages 1 to 4 an auditable source of information is provided on which to base the judgement.

9.2 Comparative assessment of environmental and economic factors

9.2.1 Operators should reach their own view as to which of the potential options constitutes the site-specific BPEO by considering the trade-off between costs of options and the extra benefits of pollution reduction or prevention.

9.2.2 Three main techniques can be used to identify the trade-off between the cost and benefits of options.

- *Actual cost comparison*: Annualized costs of each option can be compared with an index of environmental effects.

- *Incremental costs compared to incremental environmental effects*: Incremental annualized costs of each process option can be compared with the incremental change in an index of environmental effects of the next more environmentally harmful option to show the cost for each option per reduction in environmental effects compared to the next more environmentally harmful option. This can be expressed as:

$$\frac{Cost\ (c) - Cost\ (b)}{Pollution\ Potential\ (b)\ -\ Pollution\ Potential\ (c)}...(8)$$

- *Incremental costs over and above the option with greatest environmental effects*: The annualised costs of each option over and above the costs of the option with greatest environmental effect can be

compared with the incremental change in an index of environmental effects to show the cost for each option per reduction in environmental effects. This can be expressed as:

$$\frac{Cost\ (x) - Cost\ (a)}{Pollution\ Potential\ (a)\ -\ Pollution\ Potential\ (x)}...(9)$$

9.2.3 Correctly identifying the assumptions on which costs are defined are important considerations in addressing the costs. When using the actual cost comparison (as described at the first indent above) for an existing process, previously-incurred costs of, and any existing commitment to, environmental protection and pollutant abatement systems should be included in the preferred option, and should not be added to any of the other options (unless any options also include those very same environmental protection and pollutant abatement systems). Similarly, where an operator compares incremental costs and benefits (as in the second and third indent above) then it is only the incremental costs of installing and operating additional techniques that are relevant for such comparisons.

9.2.4 The application of the above techniques would assist the operator in the following ways:

- *Actual cost comparison* allows a trade off to be made between options. The optimal (best) option may be considered as the one for which the value of incremental environmental benefits is broadly equivalent to the incremental cost of pollution control.

- *Incremental costs compared to incremental environmental effects* allows the costs of achieving more stringent levels of pollution control to be shown. This information will illustrate any significant 'break point' beyond which reductions in pollution can only be achieved at much greater incremental cost.

- *Incremental costs over and above the option with greatest environmental effects* establishes the magnitude of the incremental costs and environmental effects between each option and the option with greatest environmental effects.

9.2.5 The Agency normally needs to see the financial information on which an operator is basing his statement of the appropriate trade-off between incremental levels of expenditure and incremental environmental improvements. In cases where an assessment examines an option which represents a significant cost saving to the operator with no significant environmental effects (ie there is no trade-off between the costs of the technique and the environmental quality), the Agency still needs to establish the extent of the benefit to the operator. This is because a significant cost saving could result in a different site-specific BPEO. The Agency needs financial information as part of the procedure of establishing the new BPEO and thus how much additional abatement can be afforded before excessive cost is encountered.

9.2.6 The operator may feel that more than one measure of environmental effects should be used to plot against costs to determine the BPEO. If the BPEO turns out to vary according to the environmental effect used, then the operator should either justify his final choice with reference to the most important effect, or combine relevant techniques from each potential BPEO to produce an option that would be the BPEO with respect to all environmental effects.

9.3 Justification of BPEO

9.3.1 The assessment of the various environmental factors is complex and must inevitably rely on professional judgement to identify the BPEO. Whichever option the operator believes is the BPEO and however that decision has been arrived at, that decision should be justified by clearly setting out the environmental factors that were most important and showing how the final ranking of the options and the choice of BPEO was made.

9.3.2 It should be remembered that the objective for the methodology is that set out in section 7(7) of the Act. Hence the requirement is to ensure

"that the BATNEEC will be used for minimising the pollution which may be caused to the environment as a whole by the releases having regard to the BPEO available". The BPEO can thus be considered as the option which provides the most benefit or least damage to the environment as a whole, in the long term as well as the short term, at a cost that is not excessive.

9.3.3 In a practical sense, the option which is the BPEO could be regarded as at the "break point" (if one is clearly identifiable) where the marginal costs of further reductions in pollution potential start to rise significantly. However, where the magnitude of incremental costs between options is low then it would be difficult to justify the BPEO as other than the best environmental option. Alternatively, where the incremental costs for environmental improvement is high then the BPEO may be below the break point.

9.3.4 An audit trail listing the sources of information, methods of calculation and any assumptions made, should be provided by the operator.

9.3.5 By reference to this methodology and by the application of professional judgement, the Agency believes that operators should be able to identify and justify the BPEO. It should be noted however, that this methodology is not meant to supplant or override the need to meet other legal requirements, in particular the objectives in section 7(2) of the Act (for example to use BATNEEC to prevent or where that is not possible to minimise the releases of prescribed substance). The process that is ultimately authorised should meet all the objectives of section 7 of the Act.

10 STAGE 6: Review the Best Practicable Environmental Option

10.1 Having come to a conclusion over the BPEO, an operator should review the data used, the information obtained and decisions taken. There may be benefit in carrying out some degree of sensitivity analysis to see if the final decision would be altered by changes to any of the data. It may be necessary to revisit certain stages of the assessment in the light of information obtained at later stages.

10.2 Throughout the assessment, uncertainties about many of the assumptions made could influence the results of the assessment. This does not necessarily invalidate the methodology used to undertake the assessment, but highlights the importance of sensitivity analysis as a technique to explore the importance of any uncertainties. Sensitivity analysis involves varying the values of parameters used in the assessment within reasonably expected bounds and analysing how alternative assumptions could change the results of the assessment. Such a technique might need to be used at various stages of the assessment, including, for example, the identification of significant releases, where assumptions about the amount of substances released could be important, as well as the assessment of the environmental and economic effects of the various options, to test the robustness of the results to possible alternative assumptions.

10.3 Throughout all the stages in an assessment an audit trail should be kept. Indeed RCEP stated that "The presentation of information, opinions and conclusions reached at different stages of the BPEO study is clearly important. The decision maker, and other persons, should be able to see separately the data or scores relating to each aspect of the decision for each option".

10.4 The Agency will review the BPEO assessment, and may ask for further information. Members of the public may also undertake their own reviews of BPEO assessments on the public register. It is therefore in the operators own interests to have a justified case which has taken into account all the relevant information.

11 Conclusions

11.1 Integrated Pollution Control has various objectives which can, to a certain degree, be addressed separately. However, the final decision over how the process should be configured and operated should take account of all those objectives.

11.2 The guidelines in this document addresses just one of the objectives, namely how operators should undertake BPEO assessments to justify, in particular, that they are using BATNEEC to minimise pollution to the environment as a whole having regard to BPEO. This methodology sets out a structured approach which concentrates on the BPEO while recognising the other objectives of IPC.

The methodology is intended to be a framework which can be applied flexibly to different circumstances rather than a prescriptive approach to be used by all operators. It takes account of the views of the Royal Commission on Environmental Pollution, but is specifically aimed at IPC processes regulated by the Agency.

11.3 The Agency believes the methodology set out in the guidance strikes a workable balance between the complexities of representing the impacts of releases of polluting substances on the environment and the need for a practical approach which any operator can follow.

References

1 Best Practicable Environmental Option
Royal Commission on Environmental Pollution
(1988) Twelfth Report HMSO

2 Environmental, Economic and BPEO Assessment Principles
for Integrated Pollution Control
HMIP Consultation Document, April 1994

3 Released Substances and their Dispersion in the
Environment: Guidance for Applicants for Process
Authorisation under Integrated Pollution Control
Environmental Analysis Co-operative
Development Project (1996) HMSO March
1996 ISBN 0-11-702010-9

4 Chief Inspector's Guidance Notes (since 1 April
1996 they are called "IPC Guidance Notes")
see associated publications list at the end of
this document HMSO

5 Good Practice Guide for conducting BPEO Assessments:
chemical industry (batch processing)
Environmental Agency (not published at time
of writing)

6 The Environmental Protection (Prescribed Processes and
Substances) Regulations 1991
SI 1991 No 472 (as amended: 1991
onwards), ISBN 0-11-013472-9

7 The Environmental Protection (Applications, Appeals and
Registers) Regulations 1991, Statutory Instrument 1991
No. 507 (as amended), HMSO, London.

8 The United Kingdom's Programme and National Plan for
Reducing Emissions of Sulphur Dioxide and Oxides of
Nitrogen from Existing Large Combustion Plant.
Department of the Environment and the Welsh
Office, 20 December 1990.

9 Integrated Pollution Control: A Practical Guide
Guidance issued by the Department of the
Environment and the Welsh Office. DOE
January 1997 ISBN 1-85112-021-1

10 EC Directive laying down the principles for the assessment
of risks to man and the environment of substances notified
in accordance with Council Directive 67/548/EEC
93/67/EC (OJL227, 20/7/93)

11 Technical Guidance Documents in Support of
the Risk Assessment Directive (93/67/EEC)
for New Substances Notified in Accordance
with the Requirements of Council Directive
(67/548/EEC)
EC Brussels

12 EC Regulation on the evaluation and control of the
environmental risks of existing substances
93/793/EC(OJL84, 23/3/93)

13 Technical Guidance Document on Risk Assessment of
Existing Substances Document No XI/919/94-EN
EC, Brussels

14 Uniform System for the Evaluation of Substances (USES)
Version 1.0. 1994
RIVM, VROM, WVC, The Hague, Netherlands

15 VERIS: Computer System for Evaluation of Risk to the
Surface Water from Chemical Sites
Version 1.0. 1992 SoLOGIC, Delft
Ministry of Housing, Physical Planning and
the Environment, The Netherlands

16 Climate Change 1992
Supplementary Report to the IPCC Scientific
Assessment
Houghton, J T, Callendar, B A and Varney, S K
(eds) (1992)
The Cambridge University Press, Cambridge

17 Protocol to the 1979 convention on long-range
transboundary air pollution concerning the control of
emissions of organic compounds or their transboundary
fluxes
United Nations Economic Commission for
Europe (1991)

18 A Conceptual Framework for Life-Cycle Impact
Assessment
Workshop Report, February 1–7, 1992,
Sandestin, Florida, USA
SETAC Foundation for Environmental
Education Inc., Pensacola, Florida

19 An Environmental Priority Setting Scheme for Existing
Chemicals
Department of the Environment – draft for
comment 1991

20 Economic Appraisal in Central Government: A Technical
Guide for Government Departments
HM Treasury, London 1991
HMSO

21 Policy Appraisal and the Environment
Department of the Environment, London 1991

22 Guidelines on discharge stack heights for polluting
emissions
HMIP Technical Guidance Note (Dispersion)
D1
(HMSO) June 1993, ISBN 0-11-752794-7

23 Hydrocarbons and the Long Range Transport of Ozone and
PAN across Europe
Atmospheric Environment, 25A (8) 1661–
1678
Derwent R.G. and Jenkin M.E. (1991)

Best Practicable Environmental Option Assessments for Integrated Pollution Control

Volume II: TECHNICAL DATA

For Consultation

Contents

1 Introduction

1.1 Part I of the Environmental Protection Act 1990 introduced a new system of Integrated Pollution Control (IPC) which provided the framework for controlling releases from certain prescribed industrial processes and ensuring compliance with relevant EC Directives on pollution control. The Agency is responsible for regulating prescribed processes in accordance with IPC.

1.2 Section 4.2 of the Act states that the functions of the Agency under Part I of the Act are to be exercisable for the purpose of preventing or minimising pollution of the environment due to the release of substances into any environmental medium. The Environment Act 1995 also contains a range of new powers and duties for the Agency.

1.3 Under section 6 of the 1990 Act no process prescribed for control by the central authority (Agency) may be operated without an authorisation from the Agency. In determining an authorisation, section 7 of the Act requires the Agency to include conditions for achieving the objectives set out in section 7(2). These objectives are to ensure that in carrying out a prescribed process the Best Available Techniques Not Entailing Excessive Cost (BATNEEC) will be used.

- for preventing the release of substances prescribed for any environmental medium into that medium, or where that is not practicable by such means, for reducing the releases of such substances to a minimum and for rendering harmless any substances which are so released; and

- for rendering harmless any other substances which might cause harm if released into any environmental medium.

1.4 Furthermore, where the process is designated for control by the Agency and is likely to involve the release of substances into more than one environmental medium, section 7(7) of the Act requires that BATNEEC will be used:

"for minimising the pollution which may be caused to the environment taken as a whole by the releases having regard to the Best Practicable Environmental Option (BPEO) available as respects the substances which may be released".

1.5 In addition, section 7(2) requires that conditions should be placed within an authorisation to ensure the objectives of compliance with:

- any direction given by the Secretary of State to implement European Community or international obligations relating to environmental protection;

- any statutory environmental quality standards or objectives or other statutory limits or requirements;

- any plan made by the Secretary of State under section 3(5) of the Act (eg the National Plan for Reducing Emissions of SO_2 and NO_x).

1.6 This guidance note (E1) describes a methodology for undertaking BPEO assessments for IPC in a consistent manner which is compatible with the requirements of the Environmental Protection Act. It is published as a single publication in two volumes:

- Volume I: Principles and Methodology

- Volume II: Technical Data (for consultation)

1.7 Volume I includes all the guidance on the methodology and its application. Volume II contains data that the Agency has put together to support the methodology. However there are differences of opinion amongst experts about the methods by which Environmental Assessment Levels (EALs), in particular, should be derived. For this reason a working group of experts from industry and academia is being set up by the Agency to comment on the methods used for determining EALs etc and to recommend alternatives if appropriate. Thus Volume II is a consultative draft and feedback from users of the methodology is encouraged. The values therein are temporary and should be viewed with caution. There is a possibility that, as a result of the deliberations of the working group, some values could be increased as well as others being decreased.

1.8 This volume, Volume II provides some of the technical information assembled by the Agency which should assist in the production of BPEO assessments under Part 1 of the Act. Information is provided on:

- statutory Environmental Quality Standards (EQSs);

- the derivation and value of Environmental Assessment Levels (EALs);

- sources of information on ambient environmental quality data;

- methodology for test of insignificance and significant release rates;

- Global Warming Potentials (GWP);

- Photochemical Ozone Creation Potential (POCP);

- waste hazard scores; and

- the assessment of odours.

The information provided in this volume is intended only for use in conjunction with the assessment methodology described in Volume I of this guidance note and the user should refer to Volume I for more detail on the application of the methodology. Guidance on the assessment of costs is not provided in this volume and the user should refer to Volume I: Principles and Methodology, for more information in this area.

1.9 It is intended that the data and approaches outlined here will always be kept under active review and updated as necessary in the light of research and technical developments. Initially the Working Group is likely to focus on two main areas, the derivation of Environmental Assessment Levels (EALs) and the assessment of wastes arising from prescribed processes.

1.10 The review of EALs will deal principally with substances released to air and land (via deposition). For many substances released to air, environmental criteria have been derived from Occupational Exposure Standards. It is intended to review these substances and identify and prioritise those substances for which this method may be inappropriate. Alternative values will then be proposed based on a review of the available literature.

1.11 With regard to deposition criteria, it is recognised that the use of environmental criteria from different sources may lead to inconsistencies in the approach and therefore it is proposed to review the methodology by which these values are derived.

1.12 It is also proposed to review the methodology used to assess the disposal of wastes from prescribed processes to take account of the different treatment and disposal routes available. However, it is believed that the current methods described in this report will if followed, enable decisions on BATNEEC and BPEO to be taken in a robust, transparent and objective manner.

1.13 The guidance provided by Volumes I & II of this note (E1) is complemented by that prepared by a consortium of regulators (including the Agency), operators and environmental groups (EACDP 1996). Their guidance provides information on the use and availability of tools, such as predictive mathematical models and databases, which might be applied in environmental analyses. Applicants for authorisation under IPC should find it helpful to refer to this document in preparing their application.

2 Environmental Quality Standards and Environmental Assessment Levels for releases to air

2.1 Environmental Quality Standards for releases to air

2.1.1 An Environmental Quality Standard (EQS) can be defined as the concentration of a substance in the receiving environment which must not be exceeded if the environment is to be suitable for a particular purpose or use, or to achieve a given level of protection for a particular receptor(s).

2.1.2 For the purposes of BPEO assessments undertaken for IPC the term EQS has been applied only to limits prescribed by the Secretary of State either through appropriate regulations or direction to the relevant competent authority. Section 7 of the Environmental Protection Act 1990 requires the Agency to set in an authorisation conditions that it considers appropriate for achieving compliance with EQSs.

2.1.3 Relevant EQSs for air are shown in Annex A Table A1. Where different uses for a medium spatially overlap, more than one EQS may apply; under these circumstances the most stringent value must be used.

2.2 Environmental Assessment Levels for releases to air

Derivation of Environmental Assessment Levels

2.2.1 For many substances which are released to air EQSs have not been defined. Where the necessary criteria are absent then interim values known as Environmental Assessment Levels (EALs) have been adopted by the Agency. The EAL is the concentration of a substance which in a particular environmental medium the Agency regards as a comparator value to enable a comparison to be made between the environmental effects of different substances in that medium and between environmental effects in different media and to enable the summation of those effects.

2.2.2 Ideally EALs to fulfil this objective would be defined for each pollutant:

- based on the sensitivity of particular habitats or receptors (in particular three main types of receptor should be considered, protection of human health, protection of natural ecosystems and protection of specific sensitive receptors eg materials, commercial activities requiring a particular environmental quality;

- be produced according to a standardised protocol to ensure that they are consistent, reproducible and readily understood;

- provide similar measure of protection for different receptors both within and between media;

- take account of habitat specific environmental factors such as pH, nutrient status, bioaccumulation, transfer and transformation processes where necessary.

2.2.3 A suite of EALs derived in this consistent manner is not currently available, therefore, interim values based on published information have been adopted. Table 2.1 shows the sources from which information has been obtained. For consistency, risk based values proposed by the World Health Organisation or given in the IRIS data base have been excluded.

2.2.4 Currently some 460 substances or groups of substances are authorised by the Agency for release to the environment and many of these may be released to air. However, established environmental criteria (other than a limited number of EQSs) are available for only a small fraction of this number. For example, in the case of releases to air, EPAQS have produced guideline values for only six substances (ozone, benzene, carbon monoxide, sulphur dioxide, particles and 1,3 butadiene) although values for a further three pollutants are planned (nitrogen dioxide, PAHs and lead) and the WHO Air Quality Guidelines contain values for 27 substances.

Table 2.1:
Sources of information used for setting interim Environmental Assessment Levels for releases to air

Information source
Expert Panel on Air Quality Standards (EPAQS)
EC Air Quality Directives - limit values and guidelines
World Health Organisation Air Quality Guidelines for Europe (1987, 1995)
Other International Organisations (eg United Nations Economic Commission for Europe)
Other National Organisations (eg US IRIS data base)
Health and Safety occupational exposure limits
Expert judgement

2.2.5 Ideally EALs for those substances where there are no existing criteria would be derived direct from toxicological data on the effects of the pollutant on a particular receptor. However, an assessment of this type would be a very substantial undertaking which could only be considered over an extended timescale. One approach to overcoming this problem is to make use of occupational exposure limits which provide an assessment for a specific receptor (ie adult human workforce) of the toxicological effects of a pollutant. These values might then be progressively revised as further information and resources allow. Indeed a similar approach to this was followed by the then Factory Inspectorate in 1968 when a large number of occupational standards were adopted from the American Conference of Governmental Industrial Hygienists (HMSO 1968) which have since been progressively revised by the Health and Safety Executive on the basis of new information and UK experience.

2.2.6 The practice of using occupational exposure limits in regulatory decisions is well established in the UK, for example, in the approaches recommended by Mahler (1967), Ireland (1970) or more recently HMSO (1993) to undertaking stack height determinations. Occupational exposure limits have also been used to provide appropriate environmental criteria where there are no other sources of information in Environmental Statements prepared under the Town and Country Planning (Assessment of Environmental Effects) Regulations 1988, Statutory Instrument 1988 No 1199. For example, Cory Environmental (1991), Coca Cola and Schweppes Beverages Ltd (1991), Leigh Environmental (1990) and Cleveland Fuels (1992) have derived air quality criteria from 8 hour time weighted occupational exposure standards (OES) by dividing the OES by a suitable safety factor (typically in the range of 30-100).

2.2.7 Occupational exposure limits are intended to set a level of exposure based on 8 hours per day, 5 days per week during a normal employment lifetime below which adverse effects are unlikely to arise for the majority of the working population who may be exposed. Occupational limit values may be derived from either actual data on workers or animal toxicity data, in addition, factors such as the ability to achieve or measure the proposed limit may also be taken into consideration. Consequently, the precise basis on which limit values have been set is difficult to determine and a cautious approach needs to be taken in deriving EALs from occupational exposure limits.

2.2.8 In deriving EALs for long term exposure from occupational limits two factors need to be taken into consideration: the duration of exposure

of the general population compared with the workforce and the sensitivity of the group at risk. The weekly exposure of the local population could be up to 168 hours per week (7*24 hrs) rather than the 40 hours (5*8 hrs) which might be expected for the workforce. Moreover, exposure for the general population may extend to 52 weeks compared with an average working year of 44 weeks. On this basis the minimum safety factor would be 4.96 (ie (168/40 * 52/44). In addition, since there may be no recovery period between exposure sessions and exposure could be for a lifetime a further safety factor of 2 could be introduced giving a total safety factor of 10.

2.2.9 It might also be expected that the general population will contain more sensitive individuals, for example, children, the elderly or those with diseases such as asthma, than workers who are typically between the ages of 16 and 65. In the absence of other information a factor of 10 is normally used to allow for differences between the population mean and the response of sensitive individuals (WHO 1994). This is likely to be over conservative since in setting occupational limit values some allowance will have been made for variation in the sensitivity of the workforce to the pollutant concerned. Combining the safety factors for exposure and sensitivity of the general population gives a long term air quality standard of 1/100th of the 8 hour occupational exposure limit.

2.2.10 In the UK the Health and Safety Executive distinguish two types of long term occupational exposure limits, occupational exposure standards (OESs) and maximum exposure limits (MELs). MELs are set for chemicals where there is particular concern, for example carcinogens, or doubt over the actual no effect level and for occupational health purposes it is an offence to exceed an MEL. Within the workplace this leads to an emphasis on reducing average levels of exposure of the chemical to ensure that the MEL is not exceeded. In practice this leads to an additional safety margin of up to 5 for chemicals which have MELs over those which have OES values. Effectively therefore, an additional factor of up to 5 is achieved in the workplace by setting an MEL and this factor has been incorporated in determining an EAL for those chemicals listed as having an MEL in HSE Guidance Note EH40/95 – ie a safety factor of 500 (10*10*5) is used to set the long term EAL for such substances. Long term EALs derived through this approach are shown in Annex A, Table A2.

2.2.11 Where no short term environmental criteria have been identified in the literature a similar approach to their derivation from occupational exposure limits can be adopted to that described above for long term EALs. However, in this instance it would be more appropriate to calculate values based on the short term exposure limits (STELs) set by HSE. Where STELs are not listed then a value of 3 times the 8 hour time weighted average occupational exposure limit may be used (HSE 1995).

2.2.12 Since STELs are by definition appropriate for consideration of short term impacts there is no need for additional safety factors relating to the duration of exposure as suggested for the derivation of long term EALs. Moreover, as STELs already incorporate a limited safety margin for variation in the sensitivity of the workforce an additional factor of 10 is likely to be adequate to account for the increased sensitivity of the general population (WHO 1994). However, since many atmospheric dispersion models are only able to produce estimates for time averaging periods in the order of 1 hour it would be convenient for the short term EALs also to be expressed on this basis. Typically ratios between concentrations measured over a 15 minute averaging period and those taken over an hour may be between 1.3 - 2.3 (Turner 1994). Given this relatively small range and the likely overestimate of the safety factor representing variation in human sensitivity it is proposed to adopt a value of 1/10th of the STEL as the short term EAL.

2.2.13 Where the substance attracts a maximum exposure limit value then an additional safety factor of 5 can be included on a similar basis to that described for the derivation of long term EALs. The safety factors used in deriving long and short term EALs are summarised in Table 2.2. Short term EALs derived by this approach are given in Annex A, Table A2.

2.2.14 It is recognised that the safety factors shown in Table 2.2 have been derived largely on the basis of experience and that for some substances the 'true' EAL derived from a more fundamental study of the toxicological data may be very different. EALs derived in this manner need therefore to be treated with caution and where necessary further work undertaken to assess the implication of any actual or potential breaches. However, some comfort in the use of these safety factors may be gained from the fact that they have been applied in a number of recent high profile planning enquiries (DoE 1992a, DoE 1992b, Thames Water 1991a, Thames Water 1991b) and therefore have been subjected to considerable public scrutiny.

2.3 Environmental Assessment Levels for other substances

2.3.1. Annex A, Table A2 includes a large number of substances but there will be times when EALs for other substances are needed. In these cases it is suggested that the operator should discuss the requirement with the site inspector who, if necessary, can obtain appropriate advice.

2.4 Critical levels for the assessment of sensitive receptors

2.4.1 There are many areas in England and Wales which have been designated by a variety of UK and international bodies as being worthy of protection. For example, Sites of Special Scientific Interest (SSSIs), Ramsar Sites and World Heritage Sites. It is likely that these sites will contain species, communities or other receptors which will be sensitive to pollution. In addition, material or industrial/ commercial activities may have particular environmental requirements.

2.4.2 The presence, location, size and characteristics of any potentially sensitive receptors within the area of impact (or 'footprint') of the process should be identified by the operator. Where the site has been designated on the basis of its vegetation then the critical levels for SO_2, NO_x and NH_3 as shown in Table A3 should be applied as the EAL. Since both sulphur and nitrogen oxides possess statutory EQSs the ambient concentration should first be compared with these higher values to determine whether there may be a breach of the EQS. The critical levels should then be used in the subsequent BPEO assessment.

Table 2.2:
Safety factors for use in deriving long and short term EALs from occupational exposure limits.

	Long term EAL (as an annual average)	Short term EAL (as a 1 hour average)
OES 8 hour time weighted average.	$\frac{OES}{100}$	-
MEL 8 hour time weighted average	$\frac{MEL}{500}$	-
OES STEL 15 minute average[1]	-	$\frac{OES\ STEL}{10}$
MEL STEL 15 minute average[1]	-	$\frac{MEL\ STEL}{50}$

(1) For those substances for which a STEL is not listed a figure of 3 times the 8hr time weighted average may be used.

3 Environmental Quality Standards and Environmental Assessment Levels for releases to water

3.1 Environmental Quality Standards for water

3.1.1 The definition and purpose of Environmental Quality Standards is discussed in Section 2.1 with respect to air, however, the same principles can be applied to water. The Framework Directive 76/464/EEC on pollution caused by certain dangerous substances discharged into the aquatic environment of the Community provides the basis for setting statutory EQSs in the UK. The annex to the Directive identifies two types of substance, List I and List II substances .

3.1.2 List I comprises substances which require particularly stringent control. However, a particular substance is not confirmed as List I until a daughter directive setting Community limit values has been agreed. In England and Wales these limit values have been implemented through the Surface Waters (Dangerous Substances) (Classification) Regulations 1989, Statutory Instrument 1989 No. 2286 and Surface Waters (Dangerous Substances) (Classification) Regulations 1992, Statutory Instrument 1992 No. 337. These regulations establish a classification system for all surface waters in England and Wales and a Direction issued by the Secretary of State requires the appropriate authority to ensure compliance with the specified limit values. Statutory EQSs for releases to water are shown in Annex B Table B1.

3.1.3 All substances that belong to those groups detailed under List I but for which limit values and quality standards have not been agreed by the Community are treated as List II substances. For List II substances the Directive requires quality standards to be set at national level. For the purposes of the BPEO assessment methodology UK quality standards for List II substances are considered to be EALs. As with Statutory EQSs for List I substances, these EALs should be considered as upper limits of acceptability, and their application must not lead, either directly or indirectly, to increased pollution.

3.1.4 A number of other regulations setting out classification schemes for surface waters in the UK have also been produced (ie The Surface Waters (Classification) Regulations 1989, Statutory Instrument 1989 No 1148 and The Surface Waters (River Ecosystem) (Classification) Regulations 1994, Statutory Instrument 1994 No. 1057). However, no Directions have yet been issued to

implement these regulations, and therefore it has been considered inappropriate to base EALs on the values listed within them.

3.2 Environmental Assessment Levels for releases to water

3.2.1 The purpose and characteristics of Environmental Assessment Levels (EALs) for releases to water are similar to those described for releases to air as discussed in Section 2.2 above. Similarly, a consistent suite of EALs derived in this manner are not available and values based on published criteria have been adopted.

3.2.2 Table 3.1 indicates that a variety of information sources are available from which the EALs set out in Annex B Table B2 have been derived. In general the EALs are based on the European Directives, UK National Environmental Quality Standards and UK Proposed National EQSs which are undergoing public consultation (via DoE 1991 or published technical documents). As indicated in Annex B Table B2, certain other values are also under review and therefore may be subject to revision in the future. Environmental criteria for a range of other substances are being developed but since these values are yet to be agreed by consultation it would be inappropriate to publish them at this stage.

Table 3.1:
Sources of information used for setting Environmental Assessment Levels for releases to water

Information source
European Directives (other than those implemented through UK Regulations)
UK National Environmental Quality Standards
UK Proposed National Environmental Quality Standards
Relevant national or international organisations (eg US EPA, WHO)
Expert judgement

3.2.3 In selecting an EAL from Annex B, Table B2 the user should first consider the type of receiving water, ie whether it is inland, estuarine or coastal. Estuaries are considered to extend as far upstream as the tidal limit. If the receiving water is inland then the appropriate 'use' should be selected, ie either 'salmonid' or 'cyprinid'. Environmental criteria listed under 'salmonid' are intended to provide protection to sensitive aquatic life, for example salmonid fish, although in some cases more stringent criteria may be appropriate locally to protect particularly sensitive flora or fauna. The 'cyprinid' criteria are intended to provide protection for other aquatic life, eg cyprinid fish. For some substances EALs are available as annual average concentrations and 95 percentile or maximum admissible concentrations (MAC). For reasons of consistency, annual average criteria should be used for calculating the Integrated Environmental Index. Where appropriate information on the flow regime and ambient pollutant concentrations in receiving water is available then the 95 percentile and MAC criteria may be used to assess the short-term impact of releases.

3.2.4 Where the receiving water is a designated fishery under the terms of the EC fisheries directive (78/659/EEC) then, and only then, the criteria listed in columns 2 and 3 of Table B2 (Annex B) should be applied. Where more than one requirement might be applied to a particular stretch of water, the most stringent should be used.

3.3 Environmental Assessment Levels for other substances

3.3.1 Annex B, Table B2 includes a number of substances but there will be times when EALs for other substances are needed. In these cases it is suggested that the operator should discuss the requirement with the site inspector who, if necessary, can obtain appropriate advice.

4 Environmental Quality Standards and Environmental Assessment Levels for releases to land (via deposition)

4.1 Environmental Quality Standards for releases to land

4.1.1 There are no Environmental Quality Standards in the UK for releases to land by deposition.

4.2 Environmental Assessment Levels for releases to land

4.2.1 Setting environmental criteria for soils is a complex process which is likely to involve consideration of a number of factors, including soil type, potential land use and underlying geology. Where this has been undertaken in any detail, for example, in establishing critical loads for sulphur and nitrogen then this has taken many years of scientific effort over a considerable period of time. To overcome these problems a pragmatic approach has been adopted using existing (limited) soil quality criteria from a number of sources and back calculating a maximum deposition rate (MDR) which would result in the criteria being met over an extended period. The following sources of information are available for deriving EALs for land:

- UK DoE Sewage Sludge Disposal Code of Practice;

- MAFF recommendations;

- international guidelines;

- other overseas national guidelines;

- expert judgement.

4.2.2 It is recognised that many of the soil criteria available in these sources have been developed for a particular purpose and may not be directly applicable to the assessment of deposition from industrial processes. However, until further information becomes available, these sources provide practically the only information from which EALs can be derived. The development of a more robust suite of EALs is being given high priority within the Agency's research programme.

4.2.3 The maximum deposition rate (MDR) is the quantity of pollutant which can be added to the soil daily over 50 years before the selected soil quality criteria are exceeded. For inorganic compounds the soil quality criteria were corrected for the median ambient soil concentration and no allowance was made for degradation or other removal processes. For organic pollutants it was assumed that the ambient soil concentration was zero and that soil concentrations declined according to a first order decay rate. Environmental Assessment Levels (EALs) for releases to land (via atmospheric deposition) are shown in Annex C, Table C1.

4.2.4 The provisional MDR for inorganic compounds was calculated from:

$$MDR = \frac{(SQC - AMB_s) * D_s * d_s}{T}$$

and the MDR taking into account the ½ life of the organic compounds concerned was calculated from:

$$MDR = \frac{SQC * \lambda * D_s * d_s}{(1 - e^{-\lambda T})}$$

Where   MDR is the provisional maximum deposition rate ($mg/m^2/day$);
SQC is the selected soil quality criteria (mg/kg dry soil);
AMB_s is the median soil pollutant concentration;
D_s is the soil density ($1000\ kg/m^3$);
d_s is the mixing depth for the pollutant concerned ($7.5\ cm$);
T is the evaluation period over which deposition occurs (50 years); and
λ is the disappearance rate of the chemical in soil and is related to the half life ($t_{0.5}$) by ($\ln 2/t_{0.5}$).

4.2.5 Ambient soil metal concentrations have been derived from Davis (1980) and McGraph and Loveland (1992).

4.3 Environmental Assessment Levels for other substances

4.3.1 Annex C, Table C1 includes a number of substances but there will be times when EALs for other substances are needed. In these cases it is suggested that the operator should discuss the requirement with the site inspector who, if necessary, can obtain appropriate advice.

5 Sources of information on ambient environmental quality

5.1 Introduction

5.1.1 For substances which have not been identified as potentially environmentally 'insignificant' using the methodology outlined in Section 6.4 of Volume I and Section 6 of this Volume, the operator should provide an assessment of ambient pollutant concentrations. In general the assessment should cover both long term (annual average) and short term (generally < 24 hours) time averaging periods. In practice the extent and quality of the data which can be provided will be determined by the availability of suitable monitoring information, the requirements of any modelling studies undertaken and the need for consistency with relevant environmental criteria. Additional guidance on the sources and handling of ambient environmental quality data is provided by EACDP (1996) to which the reader may wish to refer.

5.1.2 The availability of monitoring data for substances of interest varies from reasonably abundant quality assured measurements for a few substances (eg SO_2 and NO_x) to almost non existent for some pollutants, particularly organic compounds. Inevitably, for some pollutants, resort will need to be made to 'typical' values published in the literature. Guidance on sources of information on existing monitoring programmes is provided in Section 5.3 for ambient air quality, 5.4 for water quality and 5.5 for land.

5.1.3 In selecting ambient data for use in the assessment preference should be given to measured, quality assured values where these are available. In deciding whether the measurements are appropriate consideration should be given to the sampling, analytical and data handling methods employed, the nature of the sampling regime, for example, whether it is continuous or discrete, the location of the sample point in relation to the process, geographic area of concern and other sources of pollution, the sampling period and any seasonal or diurnal variation which may influence the final measurements.

5.1.4 Where appropriate data on ambient concentrations of pollutants are unavailable from existing monitoring programmes, consideration should be given by the operator to the need to undertake site-specific measurements. Given the variety of situations which are likely to be encountered it is not possible to identify the circumstances when site-specific monitoring would be required. However, site-specific measurements

are likely to be appropriate, at least, in conditions where the pollutant does not form an insignificant component of the releases from the process, where it is likely to be a major contributor to the local ambient pollutant load or there is concern over potential breaches of environmental criteria or impacts on a particular receptor.

5.1.5 It is beyond the scope of this document to provide detailed guidance on how site-specific monitoring should be undertaken and it is suggested that any proposals are discussed with the Agency prior to their implementation. In designing a study, modelling studies may provide a cost effective means of identifying sampling locations and regimes and consideration should be given to quality control measures for sampling, analysis and data handling.

5.1.6 Where it is believed (initially at least) that the assessment of releases does not warrant site-specific monitoring of ambient pollutant concentrations then 'typical' values from literature sources may be used. The source reference should be clearly stated and preference should be given to values appropriate to UK conditions and where the sampling, analytical and data handling techniques are identified. It is also important that the values chosen are compatible with the process or receptor being considered. For example, urban values should be selected where the plant and area of interest is located in an urban area. However, for a remote receptor in a rural location, rural values are likely to be more appropriate.

5.1.7 For many substances a range of possible 'typical' values may be found and under these circumstances sensitivity analyses could be undertaken to determine whether the choice of any particular value(s) lead to changes in the overall conclusions of the study. Where this occurs, or for some other reason it is found that more information on a particular pollutant is required then additional site-specific monitoring may need to be undertaken.

5.2 Interpolation of ambient pollutant concentrations and 'correction' for the contribution from existing processes

5.2.1 Where monitoring data have been used to provide an assessment of ambient pollutant concentrations it is likely that measurements will have been made at points which do not coincide with the principal area of interest. Moreover, for existing plant they are likely to include some unknown contribution from the process concerned. This situation gives rise to two related problems, how to determine the ambient pollutant concentration at the point of interest and secondly how to assess the process contribution to these values.

5.2.2 There are a number of general approaches which might be applied to the problem of infilling data:

- interpolation or extrapolation from measurement points;

- curve or surface fitting methods which provide only an approximation of the concentration at the measurement points;

- upscaling where data are required at a lower resolution than originally measured; and

- subjective assessment, which may be the only solution where there is insufficient data to warrant the use of other methods.

Within these general approaches a large number of mathematical techniques have been proposed. There is no single ideal method of interpolation or purely quantitative means of determining the 'correct' form of interpolant. The selection needs to be based on a detailed knowledge of the characteristics of the existing data and the factors affecting its spatial and temporal distribution. Each pollutant therefore needs to be considered on its merits.

5.2.3 Given the complexity of this issue it is suggested that in the first instance a subjective assessment of the ambient pollutant concentration at the point of interest is made based on data from nearby monitoring stations. This will often involve the assumption that data at the monitoring site are representative of the wider area as a whole. Where such assumptions are made they should be clearly stated.

5.2.4 It is recognised that on occasion it may be important to be able to estimate the concentration at a point with greater certainty, perhaps as part of an evaluation of the need for further monitoring. Under these circumstances the reasons for the selection of a particular method of interpolation should be clearly presented.

5.2.5 The evaluation of the contribution made by an existing process to a measured ambient pollutant concentration is complex and would normally require detailed spatial and temporal modelling of the process contribution at the monitoring location, together with a knowledge of the statistical relationships with other contributors in the area. In addition, there are likely to be significant

uncertainties in the modelled values. Typically for gaussian air dispersion models the uncertainty may be a factor of 2 on annual average concentrations and 5 or more for shorter time periods. Difficulties will also occur in ensuring temporal and spatial compatibility between parameters used in modelling and observed values from the monitoring station.

5.2.6 Therefore, in order to simplify the assessment it would generally be acceptable to make the conservative assumption that the measured contribution excludes any contribution from the process concerned. It is recognised, however, that there may be occasions, for example, where breaches of an EQS or EAL may occur or the process makes a major contribution to the local pollution climate, that it is necessary to calculate a 'corrected' ambient concentration which excludes the process contribution. On these occasions the methods by which a 'corrected' value has been estimated should be set out and should indicate how the factors mentioned in Section 5.2.5 have been taken into consideration.

5.3 Air

5.3.1 Air quality monitoring in the UK is undertaken by contractors and some local authorities on behalf of the Department of Environment (DOE). A number of other local authorities also maintain air pollution monitoring sites which are not part of the government network.

5.3.2 Two types of monitoring are carried out on behalf of the DoE, continuous monitoring which provides instantaneous measurements of air pollutants and secondly non automatic which provide concentrations over longer time averaging periods, for example daily or monthly. Periodic surveys of substances, for example NO_x may also be undertaken.

5.3.3 Thirty eight automatic (continuous) monitoring stations are currently operational in England and Wales measuring one or more of the following pollutants: ozone, oxides of nitrogen, carbon monoxide, sulphur dioxide, PM_{10} and a variety of volatile organic compounds (VOCs). The location and pollutants measured at continuous air quality monitoring sites are shown in Table 5.1. Expansion of the networks is planned in future years and an increasing number of local authority funded sites are being affiliated to the programme. VOC species monitored are shown in Table 5.2.

Table 5.1:
Department of Environment Continuous Monitoring Sites (September 1994 Willis 1994)

County	Site name	Pollutants	Start date
Avon	Bristol Centre	O_3, NO_x, CO, SO_2, PM_{10}	04/01/93
	Bristol East	VOCs	01/04/94
Cheshire	Glazebury	O_3	01/04/88
Cleveland	Billingham	NO_x	01/01/87
	Middlesbrough	O_3, NO_x, CO, SO_2, PM_{10}, VOCs	01/01/92
Cumbria	Great Dun Fell	O_3	09/05/86
	Wharleycroft	O_3	08/05/85
Derbyshire	Ladybower	O_3, NO_x, SO_2	15/07/88
Devon	Yarner Wood	O_3	26/06/87
East Sussex	Lullington Heath	O_3, NO_x, SO_2	04/10/86
Greater London	London Victoria	O_3, NO_x, CO, SO_2	01/07/72
	Bexley	O_3, NO_x, CO, SO_2, PM_{10}	01/05/94
	Cromwell Road	NO_x, CO, SO_2	22/02/73
	West London	NO_x, CO	01/01/87
	London Bloomsbury	O_3, NO_x, CO, SO_2, PM_{10}	23/01/92
	London UCL	VOCs	01/12/92
	London Eltham	VOCs	01/03/93
Greater Manchester	Manchester	NO_x, CO	22/01/87
Hampshire	Southampton Centre	O_3, NO_x, CO, SO_2, PM_{10}	04/01/94
Hertfordshire	Stevenage (closed during 1994)	O_3, NO_x, CO, SO_2	22/06/76
Humberside	Hull Centre	O_3, NO_x, CO, SO_2, PM_{10}	04/01/94
Leicestershire	Leicester Centre	O_3, NO_x, CO, SO_2, PM_{10}	04/01/94
Merseyside	Liverpool Centre	O_3, NO_x, CO, SO_2, PM_{10}	23/03/93
North Yorkshire	High Muffles	O_3	16/07/87
Nottinghamshire	Bottesford	O_3	01/10/77
Oxfordshire	Harwell	O_3	22/06/76
Powys	Aston Hill	O_3	26/06/86
South Glamorgan	Cardiff Centre	O_3, NO_x, CO, SO_2, PM_{10}	12/05/92
	Cardiff East	VOCs	01/11/93
South Yorkshire	Sheffield	NO_x, CO	28/11/90
	Barnsley	SO_2	14/03/91
Suffolk	Sibton	O_3	01/07/73
Tyne and Wear	Sunderland	SO_2	06/10/92
	Newcastle Centre	O_3, NO_x, CO, SO_2, PM_{10}	08/03/92
West Glamorgan	Swansea Centre	O_3, NO_x, CO, SO_2, PM_{10}	01/12/94

County	Site name	Pollutants	Start date
West Midlands	Walsall	NO_x	05/03/87
	Birmingham Centre	O_3, NO_x, CO, SO_2, PM_{10}	18/03/92
	Birmingham East (2 stages)	O_3, NO_x, CO, SO_2, PM_{10} and VOCs	01/08/93 & 01/12/93
West Yorkshire	Leeds Centre	O_3, NO_x, CO, SO_2, PM_{10}	04/01/93
	Leeds Potternewton	VOCs	22/12/94

Table 5.2:
Species of Volatile Organic Compounds monitored at continuous monitoring sites

Ethane	cis-2-butene	n-Heptane	Ethylene
n-Pentane	Benzene	Acetylene	i-Pentane
Toluene	Propane	trans-2-Pentene	Ethyl Benzene
Propene	cis-2-Pentene	o-xylene	n-Butane
Isoprene	m-xylene	i-Butane	n-Hexane
1,2,4 Trimethyl benzene	i-Butene	2-Methyl pentane	1,3,5 Trimethyl benzene
trans-2-Butene	3-Methyl pentane	1,3 Butadiene	

Table 5.3:
Non automatic monitoring networks in England and Wales

Network	Purpose	Number of sites	Pollutants measured
Acid Deposition	Assessment of acid deposition	21 (32 in UK)	Precipitation analyzed for: conductivity, pH, NH_4^+, Na^+, K^+, Ca^{2+}, Mg^{2+}, NO_3^-, Cl^-, SO_4^{2-}, PO_4^{3-}. NO_2 monthly samples
Rural SO_2	Estimation of dry deposition (calculated from ambient SO_2 measurements)	25 (38 in UK)	SO_2
Smoke and SO_2. (Two networks Basic Urban Network, EC Directive Network)	Monitoring for compliance with EC Directive on smoke and SO_2 and assessment of long term trends.	252 sites in UK (Some sites belong to both networks)	Smoke and SO_2
Multi element and lead	Long term monitoring of urban metal concentrations	5 in UK (Lead also is measured by a number of other networks giving a total of 26 sites)	Cd, Co, Cr, Cu, Fe, Mn, Ni, Pb, V and Zn.
NO_x diffusion tube survey	Identification of areas which may require additional monitoring to ensure compliance with EC Directive on NO_x; determination of NO_x trends	Over 1100 in UK	NO_x
Toxic Organic Micropollutants (TOMPS)	Monitoring of toxic organic micropollutants in the atmosphere and in deposition.	5	17 polychlorinated dioxin and furan congeners, range of PAHs (varies between sites) and range PCBs

5.3.4 In addition to the continuous monitoring networks in Tables 5.1 and 5.2 there are also a number of non automatic networks and these are shown in Table 5.3. Diffusion tube surveys of NO_2 have been undertaken at over 360 measurement sites in 1986 and 1991 and at over 1100 sites in 1993.

5.3.5 The results of monitoring undertaken through these networks are published by the DoE and their contractors in a variety of forms including the Digest of Environmental Statistics (HMSO 1995) which is produced annually. Site-specific information can be obtained direct from the National Environmental Technology Centre (NETCEN) at AEA Technology, Culham, Oxfordshire.

5.4   Water

5.4.1 Responsibility for monitoring ambient pollutant concentrations rests largely with the Environment Agency for inland, estuarial and coastal waters. Additional information on coastal pollutant concentrations may be available from the Ministry of Agriculture Fisheries and Food (MAFF).

5.4.2 Monitoring takes place for a wide variety of determinands including: inorganics (other than heavy metals), heavy metals, pesticides and other organics at over 6000 sites in the UK. The pollutants sampled and the sampling frequency will vary from site to site depending on the purpose for which the monitoring point has been selected. It is therefore not possible to provide any more detailed guidance on the availability of data for pollutant concentrations in water.

5.4.3 Each region maintains a water quality archive for waters in its area and can be contacted for more detailed site-specific information.

5.5   Land

5.5.1 With a limited number of exceptions there is little information available on the distribution and concentration of pollutants in UK soils. The principal source of data is likely to be the National Soil Inventory maintained by the Soil Survey and Land Research Centre, Silsoe. Soil Samples were taken at points on a 5 km grid throughout the UK and the topsoil (0-15cm depth) analysed for the parameters shown in Table 5.4. The results of the National Soil Inventory Survey have been published by McGraph and Loveland (1992). Information on other pollutants may be available on a site-specific basis.

5.5.2 A number of other surveys have been undertaken which may provide some additional information for a limited range of pollutants and these are summarised in Table 5.5.

Table 5.4:
National Soil Inventory Determinands

'Extractable' analyses	'Total' analyses	Other
P, K, Mg, Cd, Co, Cu, Pb, Mn, Ni, Zn.	P, K, Mg, Al, Ba, Cd, Ca, Cr, Co, Cu, Fe, Pb, Mn, Ni, Na, Sr, Zn.	pH, organic carbon.

Table 5.5:
Other major soil quality surveys

Survey	Outline description	Pollutants measured	Reference
Welsh soils	Conducted at the same time as the National Soil Inventory but some differences in sample collection and analysis.	pH, organic matter, Pb, Zn, Cu, Cd, Co, Ni.	Davies (1985)
Urban soils	Garden soils were sampled at over 100 locations in 53 UK towns. Measurements of house dust, road dust, playground dust, vegetable plot soil and public garden soils were also made.	Pb, Cd, Zn, Cu	Culbard et al (1988)
Organic pollutants	Two surveys: i) Samples collected on a 50km grid across England, Wales, Northern Ireland and part of Scotland. ii) Selective sampling in urban areas and around potential emission sources.	PCBs, Polychlorinated dibenzo-p-dioxins, Polychlorinated dibenzo-p-furans.	HMIP (1989), HMIP (1995a)

6 Test of insignificance

6.1 Objective

6.1.1 In general terms it is unlikely that the release of a very small quantity of a pollutant will lead to significant environmental effects. Under these circumstances significant expenditure of assessment resources would not be warranted unless there was great uncertainty over the level of release, its environmental behaviour or the susceptibility of the environment to the pollutant concerned. Therefore, it might be considered that the level of assessment effort deployed should be related to the potential impact of the release and the certainty with which the environmental consequences can be predicted.

6.1.2 Section 6.4 of Volume I: Principles and Methodology describes a simple test of insignificance to identify those releases for which a more detailed environmental assessment is not required. The objective of the methodology is to enable more effective use to be made of limited resources which can be devoted to environmental assessment. EACDP (1996) provides additional helpful guidance on identifying insignificant releases.

6.2 Approach

6.2.1 The data and methods for a suitable test of insignificance should strike a balance between two competing considerations:

- the requirement that the methods chosen are relatively simple in order to ensure minimum use of resources;

- the requirement for sufficiently detailed methods to enable a robust judgement to be made, particularly, since by definition, 'screened out' releases will not be considered further.

6.2.2 A practical balance between these considerations can be achieved by using basic, readily available data on a release together with simple methods of calculation. In this context 'simple' is intended to imply methods which can be implemented through the use of calculators, nomograms or a standard spreadsheet.

6.2.3 Conceptually, there are a number of ways in which such a test of insignificance could be defined, for example:

i) It might be considered that ecosystems are in equilibrium with background levels of a substance and are able to tolerate fluctuations in these levels as a result of 'natural' seasonal or yearly variations. For example, factors of 2-3 may separate the annual average flow rates of individual rivers, and for air, year on year annual substance concentrations may differ by 20-30% purely as a result of meteorological variation. A knowledge of variations of this type could be used to suggest the fluctuations in substance level which could be tolerated on an annual basis and similar calculations could be undertaken using short term seasonal fluctuations. This approach requires a knowledge of background concentrations and loadings for each pollutant and the magnitude of seasonal and yearly environmental variations.

ii) An alternative approach would be to use the concept of an environmental no observed effect concentration (NOEC). In simple terms, concentrations above this level may cause 'harm' to the environment whilst below, no effects are apparent. Any release which potentially could lead to a breach in the NOEC would require further assessment. The possibility of a breach in the NOEC is related to the existing ambient concentration and the likely seasonal variation as discussed in point (i) above. This approach requires a fundamental understanding of the dose response curve for the substance, a knowledge of the ambient pollutant concentration, together with the statistical relationships between contributions from different sources and an appreciation of the seasonal and yearly environmental variation.

6.2.4 Whilst knowledge of this type can probably be compiled for a number of substances, detailed information on ambient or background levels for the wide range of pollutants which would need to be considered for the UK environment is at present unavailable. Moreover, these approaches define the total capacity of the environment to tolerate changes in concentration and give no guidance as to how this might be allocated between individual processes or between natural and anthropogenic variations.

6.2.5 Given the shortage of suitable data on which to base a rigorous approach a more pragmatic method should be devised. One approach is to assume simply that changes in environmental concentration which are small (say 0.2%) in relation to an appropriate environmental criterion are unlikely to result in significant effects. Any release which makes a greater contribution than 0.2% would then be subject to a more detailed review. The choice of the 0.2% criterion is arbitrary but has been chosen to provide a factor of 10 difference compared with the requirement to prioritise a release for control (see Volume I, Section 3.4).

6.3 Assessment of insignificance

6.3.1 Each substance released from the process should be subjected to the test of insignificance. Where a substance is not identified as insignificant for a particular medium the environmental consequences arising from the release should be assessed in more detail as outlined in Volume I: Principles and Methodology of this guidance note.

6.3.2 <u>Insignificant</u> substances are those where:

- the long term PC in air is less than 0.2% of the long term EAL for air;

- the long term PC in water is less than 0.2% of the long term EAL for water;

- the deposition rate on land is less then 0.2% of the MDR for land;

- the short term PC in air is less than 0.2% of the short term EAL for air; or

- the short term PC in water is less than 0.2% of the short term EAL for water

Where:

PC = estimated process contribution in the medium concerned arising from the release; and

MDR = maximum deposition rate.

6.3.3 A substance can be insignificant for one medium but not for another. Similarly a substance can be released in insignificant quantities with respect to long term effects but not short term and vice versa.

6.3.4 The assessment of insignificance could be carried out as described in the following manner:

- For each substance identify release points, the rate of release (g/s) and receiving medium (air, water or land). In the case of releases to air, the effective height of release (see Section 6.4) should also be recorded and for water, whether the discharge is via sewer or direct to the receiving water. If discharge is via sewer, the release rates should be corrected to allow for any removal or degradation of the substance which may occur at the treatment works (see Section 6.5).

- Where there is a single release point for a substance to a particular medium or multiple releases occur under similar release conditions (for example, at the same effective height of release) then the release rates can be summed and compared with the critical values given in Annex D. Substances where the release rates are less than those shown in Annex D may be

considered insignificant. The release rates shown in Annex D have been calculated using the simple methods described in Section 6.6 below and assuming the most stringent EAL and dispersion characteristics.

- Where these simple methods of estimating the process contribution are felt to be inappropriate or the release of a substance cannot effectively be considered to take place from a single point, for example, where the effective height of releases are different or discharges take place to both sewer and direct to the watercourse, then the total process contribution could be estimated by summing the process contributions from individual release points. The total process contribution can then be compared with 0.2% of the EAL to assess the insignificance of the substance concerned.

- The process contribution arising from an individual release can be estimated using the simple methods described in Section 6.6 or derived from previous modelling or other studies where they exist.

6.4 Estimation of effective height of release for discharges to air (for the purpose of assessing insignificance of releases only)

6.4.1 In determining the effective height of release for a substance, any plume rise or momentum effects are ignored and the release is assumed to occur at the point of discharge into the atmosphere unless:

- the point of discharge is less than 3m above the ground or building on which it is located or is less than the height of any building which is within the equivalent of 5 'stack heights' horizontal distance of the release point. Under these conditions the release may become entrained in the building wake cavity and therefore the effective height of release could be considered as zero.

- the height of release is greater than 3m above the ground or building on which it is located but less than 2½ times the height of the tallest building then the effective height of release could be estimated from:

$$U_{eff} = 1.66H\left(\frac{U_{act}}{H} - 1\right)$$

Where:

H = height (m) of the tallest building within 5 stack heights;

U_{act} = actual height of release (m), and

U_{eff} = effective height of release (m).

Table 6.1:
Removal of substances during sewage treatment

Substance	Sewage treatment reduction factor (STRF)
Substances unattenuated during sewage treatment (eg. Cl, K, Na)	1 (ie no reduction)
Other pollutants (eg biodegradable organics, insoluble metals)	0.6

6.4.2 The above equation is based on that given in the third edition of the Clean Air Act Memorandum (DoE 1981) and is effectively a back calculation of the uncorrected stack height allowing for downwash effects. Although more suited to low wide buildings (by far the most common type) the equation is conservative for tall narrow buildings and is simpler to apply than more sophisticated versions given in later guidance on stack height determinations such as HMIP Technical Guidance Note D1 (HMSO 1993).

6.4.3 The effective height of release can then be used to estimate the critical release rates for air long term, and short term, and deposition to land, or alternatively used to calculate a specific process contribution as discussed in Section 6.6 below.

6.5 Calculation of corrected release rate for discharges to sewer

6.5.1 Where a release takes place first to sewer and is then treated at an inland sewage treatment works the release rate could be modified to take account of pollutants removed during treatment.

$$RR_{corr} = RR_{act} * STRF$$

Where:

STRF = sewage treatment reduction factor and represents the remaining proportion of the pollutant in the effluent following treatment.
RR_{act} = actual release rate of pollutants discharged to sewer (g/s); and
RR_{corr} = corrected release rate allowing for any attenuation of pollutant during sewage treatment.

6.5.2 During sewage treatment the pollutant may undergo physical, chemical and biological changes which affect its form and concentration in the effluent and subsequent environmental impact on the receiving water. The extent of removal during sewage treatment will depend on the interaction between the properties of the substance, the degree of treatment and operational characteristics of the receiving works.

6.5.3 A review of the available literature (HMIP 1995b) indicated that where data were available

and, apart from some highly soluble ionic species, removal efficiencies were only occasionally less than 40% and often greater than 80-90%. For the purposes of this screening procedure values for the sewage treatment reduction factor are shown in Table 6.1.

6.6 Simple methods for the estimation of process contributions to air, water and land

6.6.1 The calculation of process contributions to different media are based on the procedures developed for use in the environmental evaluation of achievable releases in Chief Inspector's Guidance Notes (HMIP 1995b – now termed IPC Guidance Notes (IPCGNs)).

Air: Annual Average Concentration

6.6.2 The process contribution can be estimated from:

$$PC = MAA * RR$$

Where:

PC = process contribution ($\mu g/m^3$)
MAA = maximum annual average ground level concentration for unit mass release rate ($\mu g/m^3/g/s$). For typical values see Table 6.2; and
RR = release rate (g/s).

6.6.3 The values of MAA relate to Pasquill category D stability conditions for 60% of the time, and are derived from Clarke (1979). No allowance is made for thermal or momentum plume rise effects.

Table 6.2:
Maximum annual average ground level concentration for unit mass emission rate

Effective height of release (m)	Maximum annual average ground level concentration for unit mass emission rate ($\mu g/m^3/g/s$)
0	60 (At 100 m from stack)
10	15
20	2.7
30	0.9
50	0.27
70	0.11
100	0.044
150	0.015
200	0.0065

Air: Short term assessment

6.6.4 The process contribution can be estimated from:

$$PC = MAA * RR$$

Where:

PC = proces contribution ($\mu g/m^3$)
MAA = maximum 60 minute average ground level concentration for unit mass release rate ($\mu g/m^3/g/s$). For typical values see Table 6.3; and
RR = release rate (g/s).

6.6.5 For the assessment of short term concentrations the calculation of 60 min average ground level concentrations are derived from Clarke (1979) and relate to Pasquill stability category F for ground level releases and category B stability conditions for elevated sources.

Land: Assessment of Deposition

6.6.6 The process contribution is estimated from:

$$PC = \frac{MAA * RR * DV * 3 * 86400}{1000}$$

Where:

PC = process contribution ($mg/m^2/d$)
MAA = maximum annual average ground level concentration for unit mass release rate ($\mu g/m^3/g/s$). For typical values see Table 6.2
RR = release rate (g/s).
DV = deposition velocity (taken as 0.01 m.s^{-1}).
The value of 3 is a nominal factor to convert dry deposition to total deposition. (HMIP 1995b)

Table 6.3:
Maximum 60 minute average ground level concentrations for unit mass release

Effective height of release (m)	Maximum 60 minute average ground level concentration for unit mass emission rate ($\mu g/m^3/g/s$)
0	4070 (at 100 m from the release point)
10	450 (at 100 m from the release point)
20	200
30	81
50	27
70	13.5
100	6.2
150	2.8
200	1.5

6.6.7 Dry deposition is affected by a variety of factors including the characteristics of the atmosphere, the nature of the receiving surface and depositing material. The resistance to transfer from the atmosphere to receiving surface in the lowest layers of the atmosphere imposes an upper limit on the value of the deposition velocity. In stable conditions this is of the order of 0.01 m/s (Jones 1983) and this value could be used to calculate the PC. A deposition velocity of this magnitude is generally appropriate for particles of less than 10 mm and will be conservative for particles smaller than this.

Water: Rivers

6.6.8 The process contribution for a direct discharge to an inland river can be estimated from:

$$PC = \frac{EFR * RC}{EFR + RFR}$$

Where:

PC = Process contribution (μg/l)
EFR = Effluent flow rate (m^3/s)
RFR = River flow rate (m^3/s)
RC = Concentration of pollutant in the effluent (μg/l)

6.6.9 Where available, site-specific values for river flow should be used. However, where these data are unknown, an appropriate value from those shown in Table 6.4 may be used.

6.6.10 Where a release takes place to sewer and is then treated at an inland sewage treatment works the estimated release rate (ie EFR * RC) should be modified to take account of any pollutant removal during sewage treatment by the use of the factor STRF, as described in Section 6.5, and shown in Table 6.1.

Water: Estuary

6.6.11 The dispersion of substances within the estuary environment is complex and will be highly site-specific. However, for the purposes of this screening procedure it has been assumed that estuaries are of two types, those dominated by

freshwater flows and those which are predominantly saline. In the case of freshwater estuaries, dispersion is assumed to occur mainly as a result of the effects of current. However, for saline dominated estuaries dispersion may occur either through buoyancy (assuming the release is freshwater) or current effects. Saline estuaries in England and Wales are typically current dominated.

6.6.12 The process contribution to waters where dispersion is current dominated may be estimated from:

$$PC = \frac{EFR * RC}{DR}$$

and:

$$DR = C_3 * ACS * DD^2$$

Where:

PC = process contribution (μg/l);
EFR = effluent flow rate (m^3/s);
DR = dispersion rate (m^3/s);
RC = concentration of pollutant in the effluent (μg/l)
C_3 = constant (0.11 for 95%ile values; 0.27 for median values; and 0.32 for mean values);
ACS = ambient current speed (m/s);
DD = depth of discharge (m).

6.6.13 For current dominated dilution to apply, the following must be satisfied:

$$\frac{DD * ACS^3}{EFR * D * G} > 5$$

Where:

D = ratio of the density difference between the receiving water and the effluent to the density of the receiving water ($\rho_{rec} - \rho_{eff}$)/ρ_{rec} [0.01 for freshwater and 0.029 for salt water];
G = acceleration due to gravity (m/s^2).

If this criterion is not satisfied, then buoyancy dominated dilution applies and the details are as for coastal waters.

6.6.14 Where available, site specific values for dispersion rate should be used. However, where these data are unknown, an appropriate value from

Table 6.4:
Typical annual average river flow rates

Nominal flow regime	Typical upstream catchment area (km^2)	Average flow rate (m^3/s)
High	>400	19.0
Medium	80-400	2.0
Low	<80	0.4

Table 6.5:
Estimated dispersion rates for a release to an estuary (HMIP 1995b)

Estuary type	Nominal dilution conditions	Dispersion rate (m³/s)
Freshwater	Low	2.4
	Medium	5
	High	10
Saline	Low	2.4
	Medium	5
	High	15

those shown in Table 6.5 may be used. The values shown have been selected as representative of typical conditions in UK estuaries. This approach does not take into account the flushing time of the estuary, negatively buoyant plumes and changes in dispersion during the tidal cycle.

6.6.15 In the UK a significant proportion of estuary or coastal sewerage systems discharge direct to the receiving water via a long outfall with little treatment beyond screening or primary sedimentation. However, in advance of the implementation of the Urban Waste Water Directive, UK water companies have initiated a major capital programme which in many cases will provide full treatment for estuary and coastal sewage discharges. If the extent of any sewage treatment measures are unknown it could be assumed that there is no further reduction in pollutant concentration where a release takes place to sewer. However, if full treatment is known to occur then the approach suggested for releases to inland sewers can be adopted and the release rate modified accordingly.

Water: Coastal

6.6.16 In coastal waters dispersion may be dominated by either buoyancy or current effects, the latter being derived mainly from tidal flows. For the purposes of this screening procedure it has been assumed that dispersion is dominated by buoyancy effects, a situation most likely to occur in bays with limited tidal circulation. The process

contribution to coastal waters can be estimated from:

$$PC = \frac{EFR^{2/3} * RC}{DR}$$

and:

$$DR = C_1 * D^{1/3} * G^{1/3} * DD^{5/3}$$

Where:

PC = process contribution (μg/l);

EFR = effluent flow rate (m³/s);

DR = dispersion rate (m²/s$^{2/3}$);

RC = concentration of pollutant in the effluent (μg/l);

C_1 = constant (0.16 for 95%ile values; 0.27 for median values; and 0.34 for mean values);

D = ratio of the density difference between the receiving water and the effluent to the density of the receiving water $(\rho_{rec} - \rho_{eff})/\rho_{rec}$ [0.01 for freshwater and 0.029 for salt water];

G = acceleration due to gravity (m/s²);

DD = depth of discharge (m).

6.6.17 For buoyancy dominated dilution to apply, the following must be satisfied:

$$\frac{DD * ACS^3}{EFR * D * G} < 5$$

Where:

ACS = ambient current speed (m/s)

Table 6.6:
Estimated dispersion rates for coastal releases (HMIP 1995b)

Nominal dilution characteristics	Dispersion rate (m²/s$^{2/3}$)
Low	2.5
Medium	8.0
High	25

If this criterion is not satisfied, then current dominated dilution applies and the details are as for estuarial waters.

6.6.18 Where available, site-specific values for dispersion rates should be used. However, where these data are unknown, an appropriate dispersion rate from those given in Table 6.6 may be used. These represent the initial dilution which takes place between the point of discharge at depth (5-20m) and the water surface. No allowance has been made for any subsequent dispersion.

6.6.19 Where a release takes place to a coastal sewerage system then similar considerations to those described for discharges to estuaries apply.

7 Assessment of Global Warming Potential (GWP) of releases

7.1 The release of carbon dioxide, methane, nitrous oxide, chlorofluorocarbons (CFCs), and other halocarbons may lead to global warming. In addition, ozone which is present in both the stratosphere and the troposphere, also acts as a greenhouse gas. However, the net effects of declining stratospheric ozone but increasing tropospheric concentrations are uncertain and are still under review. Other pollutants such as nitrogen oxides and carbon monoxide, although not important greenhouse gases in their own right can influence the concentration of other greenhouse gases and in particular, ozone. Atmospheric aerosols arising from direct emissions or chemical reactions in the atmosphere appear to have a negative radiative forcing effect; however, the magnitude of this is not yet clear. A more detailed summary of the relative effects of different pollutants can be found in the reports published by the Intergovernmental Panel on Climate Change (IPCC 1994 and IPCC 1996).

7.2 It is important that the release of gases which contribute to global warming is minimised

Table 7.1:
Net Global Warming Potentials relative to CO_2 over 100 years. (Typical uncertainty 35% relative to CO_2, Source: IPCC 1996)

Substance	Chemical formula	Atmospheric lifetime (yrs)	Global warming potential (GWP)
Carbon dioxide	CO_2	variable	1
Methane	CH_4	123	21
Nitrous oxide	N_2O	120	310
Others			
HFC-23	CHF_3	264	11700
HFC-32	CH_2F_2	5.6	650
HFC-41	CH_3F	3.7	150
HFC-43-10mee	$C_4H_2F_{10}$	17.1	1300
HFC-125	C_2HF_5	32.6	2800
HFC-134	$C_2H_2F_4$	10.6	1200
HFC-134a	CH_2FCF_3	14.6	1300
HFC-152a	$C_2H_4F_2$	1.5	140
HFC-143	$C_2H_3F_3$	3.8	300
HFC-143a	$C_2H_3F_3$	48.3	3800
HFC-227ea	C_3HF_7	36.5	2900
HFC-236fa	$C_3H_2F_6$	209	6300
HFC-245ca	$C_3H_3F_5$	6.6	560
Chloroform	$CHCl_3$	0.51	4
Methylene chloride	CH_2Cl_2	0.46	9
Sulphur hexafluoride	SF_6	3200	23900
Perfluoromethane	CF_4	50000	6500
Perfluoroethane	C_2F_6	10000	9200
Perfluorocyclo-butane	$C-C_4F_8$	3200	8700
Perfluoropentane	C_5F_{12}	4100	7500
Perfluorohexane	C_6F_{14}	3200	7400

Table 7.2:
Direct Global Warming Potentials relative to CO_2 over 100 years. (Typical uncertainty 35% relative to CO_2, Source: IPCC 1994)

Substance	Chemical formula	Atmospheric lifetime (yrs)	Global warming potential (GWP)
Carbon tetrachloride	CCl_4	42	1400
Methyl chloroform	CH_3CCl_3	5.4 ± 0.6	110
CFCs			
CFC-11	$CFCl_3$	50 ± 5	4000
CFC-12	CF_2Cl_3	102	85000
CFC-13	$CClF_3$	640	11700
CFC-113	$C_2F_3Cl_3$	85	5000
CFC-114	$C_2F_4Cl_2$	300	9300
CFC-115	C_2F_5Cl	1700	9300
HCFCs			
HCFFC-22	CF_2HCl	13.3	1700
HCFC-123	$C_2F_3HCl_2$	1.4	93
HCFC-124	C_2F_4HCl	5.9	480
HCFC-141b	$C_2FH_3Cl_2$	9.4	630
HCFC-142b	$C_2F_2H_3Cl$	19.5	2000
HCFC-225ca	$C_3F_5HCl_2$	2.5	170
HCFC-225cb	$C_3F_5Cl_2$	6.6	530
Bromocarbons			
H-1301	CF_3Br	65	5600

wherever possible. Due to the nature of the effects arising from these pollutants it is not possible to incorporate them directly in the Environmental Index proposed in Volume I. Instead, process options could be ranked according to their potential to contribute to radiative forcing (global warming). The Global Warming Potential (GWP) provides a measure of the future commitment to global warming arising from current emissions. The GWP is defined as the cumulative radiative forcing between the present and a future time 'horizon' caused by a unit release relative to some reference gas, in this case CO_2 (IPCC 1996). The total global warming potential for a particular process option may be represented by the following equation:

$$GWP_{(Total)} = \sum_{i=1}^{n} GWP_i * Mass_i$$

Where:

$GWP_{(Total)}$ = the weighed sum of the global warming potentials for the substances released from the process option being considered;

GWP_i = global warming potential for substance i of n released from the process option;

$Mass_i$ = mass of substance i released from process option (tonnes/annum).

7.3 Ideally the GWPs would take into account any indirect effects arising from the gas, for example, the production or removal of other greenhouse gases. The global warming potentials (ie the warming contribution of each gas relative to an equal weight of CO_2 over a period of 100 years) for a number of different pollutants are shown in Table 7.1. The values in the table relate to the net GWPs including the direct 'warming' and indirect 'cooling' effects which have now been estimated (IPCC 1996) for most greenhouse gases. However, as the net GWP values for CFCs and HCFCs are still currently being updated, the direct GWPs for these gases are presented in Table 7.2 (IPCC 1994).

7.4 There may be times when it is appropriate to consider a GWP for a substance not included in Table 7.1 or Table 7.2. On these occasions it is suggested that the operator should discuss the requirement with the site inspector who, if necessary, can obtain further advice.

8 Assessment of the potential for ozone generation

8.1 Production of ozone

8.1.1 Ozone is a highly reactive pollutant present in the atmosphere up to heights of 50km with concentrations tailing off rapidly above this level. Ozone is produced naturally in the upper layers of the atmosphere some 10-50 km above the surface by the action of ultraviolet light on oxygen and at this height is known as the stratospheric ozone layer. At this level in the atmosphere ozone helps provide protection against ultraviolet radiation which may otherwise damage living organisms including man.

8.1.2 Below the stratosphere is the troposphere which extends from the surface to about 8 km in polar regions and up to 13km in the tropics. Ozone in this area has three main sources:

- from the stratosphere, on occasion naturally occurring processes may bring ozone down into the troposphere;

- as a result of the oxidation of man-made and natural methane and carbon monoxide, which gives rise to a background level of ozone throughout the year.

- as a result of photochemical action on hydrocarbons and oxides of nitrogen.

8.1.3 In unpolluted air ozone is continually being created by the action of sunlight on nitrogen dioxide. The ozone generated by this method may react with nitric oxide to reform nitrogen dioxide and during sunlight hours a photochemical steady state can be achieved. During the night reformation of nitrogen dioxide will predominate and ozone concentrations have been observed to decline . In addition, naturally occurring excursions of ozone from the stratosphere give rise to background ambient concentrations of about 10ppb of ozone. However, there is now convincing evidence that pollution has more than doubled background ozone levels to an average in the northern hemisphere of 20-30ppb, a factor of only 2-3 smaller than the threshold of effects for humans and materials. Moreover peak concentrations frequently exceed internationally recognised air quality guidelines and standards set to protect human health. Ozone may lead to vegetation damage where cumulative exposure exceeds 300 ppb hours above a 40 ppb threshold, ie cumulative exposure = (measured conc. - 40 ppb) * time (hrs) above 40 ppb threshold (Ashmore and Wilson 1992). In addition, effects on materials, particularly organics may occur at concentrations as low as 20 ppb (UNECE 1993). Ozone is also a greenhouse gas.

8.1.4 In polluted air containing hydrocarbons and nitrogen oxides, peroxyradicals (RO_2) are generated by the action of hydroxyl radicals on the hydrocarbons. The peroxyradical then acts through a series of chemical reactions with the oxides of nitrogen to form ozone. A more detailed description of the atmospheric chemistry of these pollutants is given by the Photochemical Oxidants Review Group (PORG (1993)). These chemical reactions take time to form ozone and this means that elevated concentrations may occur away from the original sources of the precursors. Given the importance of sunlight to these reactions it can be understood that ozone pollution occurs more in summer than in winter and in southern rather than northern areas of the UK (EPAQS 1994).

8.1.5 At night ozone may be removed by reaction with nitric oxide to reform NO_2 and by dry deposition. The dry deposition process is controlled by stomatal uptake by vegetation and therefore shows marked diurnal and seasonal cycles.

8.2 Control of ozone

8.2.1 Since the main source of ozone is not direct emissions but the result of an interaction between hydrocarbons and nitrogen oxides then control strategies should focus on these substances and in particular hydrocarbons since these are the source of the peroxyradical which initiates ozone formation in polluted air.

8.2.2 The term VOC (Volatile Organic Compound) is loosely applied to a wide range of organic compounds but in this context has been defined in the UNECE VOC Protocol (UNECE 1991) as 'organic compounds of anthropogenic nature, other than methane, that are capable of producing chemical oxidants by reactions with nitrogen oxides in the presence of sunlight'. There is a large variation in the importance of different VOCs in the production of ozone depending on their structure and reactivity. In order to assess the relative effect of different hydrocarbons in the episodic production of ozone and provide a basis for their control the UNECE VOC convention (UNECE 1991) has proposed the concept of the Photochemical Ozone Creation Potential (POCP). The POCP is defined as the ratio of the change in photochemical ozone production due to an emission of a particular VOC to the ozone created by the same additional emission of ethylene, ie:

$$POCP_i = \frac{Ozone\ increment\ for\ ith\ hydrocarbon}{Ozone\ increment\ with\ ehtylene} * 100$$

(Source: Derwent *et al* (1996))

The POCP may be determined by photochemical model calculations or by laboratory experiments.

8.2.3 In its strategy for reducing VOCs (DoE 1993) the Department of the Environment signalled its intention to meet its obligations under the UNECE protocol, ie a reduction of at least 30% in national annual emissions of VOCs by 1999, compared with 1988 levels. Also, the UK agreed to seek to target its abatement efforts as far as possible on VOCs with a high POCP and on sources which contribute to the worst UK occurrences of ground level ozone.

8.2.4 POCP values have been proposed for a range of substances in the VOC protocol (UNECE 1991) and in the UK by Derwent and Jenkin (1991), Derwent (1993) and Derwent *et al* (1996). Values have been determined using a photochemical trajectory model to calculate ozone production in air parcels advected across north west Europe and over the UK. The calculated POCP will depend on a variety of factors including the pollutant emission inventory used, choice of parameters such as reaction rate coefficients or dry deposition velocities and the nature of the chosen trajectory. However, provided it is understood that POCP values are used to provide a relative assessment of those VOCs which contribute most significantly to ozone formation then the concept provides a useful means for guiding emission control strategies.

8.2.5 The POCP value for 95 VOCs and methane are shown in Table 8.1 based on the work by Derwent *et al* (1996). Given the dependence of the values on the modelling conditions it is important that apparently equivalent data from other studies or sources are not used to fill any gaps in the emission inventory. Where consideration needs to be given to substances not listed in Table 8.1, it i suggested that the operator should discuss the requirement with the site inspector who, if necessary, can obtain further advice.

8.2.6 The POCP values shown in Table 8.1 can be used either as a basis for identifying less damaging substitutes for substances used in a process or to assess the relative ozone generating potential of different process options. When seeking to identify substitute compounds for those of a relatively high POCP value it is important that the properties of the proposed alternative are carefully considered. For example, although both benzene and methyl chloroform have low POCP values, benzene is a known carcinogen and methyl chloroform is relatively long lived and may persist into the stratosphere where it contributes to stratospheric ozone depletion.

8.2.7 When considering the POCP of different process options the total POCP of a particular process can be represented by:

$$POCP_{(total)} = \sum_{i=1}^{n} POCP_i * Mass_i$$

Where:

$POCP_{(total)}$ = the weighted sum of all potential ozone generating substances released from the process concerned.

$POCP_i$ = the POCP for substance i of n substances released from the process.

$Mass_i$ = the mass of substance i released from the process (tonnes/annum).

Table 8.1:
POCP values calculated relative to ethylene

Hydrocarbon	Photochemical ozone creation potential
alkanes	
methane	3.4
ethane	14.0
propane	41.1
n-butane	59.9
i-butane	42.6
n-pentane	62.4
i-pentane	59.8
n-hexane	64.8
2-methylpentane	77.8
3-methylpentane	66.1
2,2-dimethylbutane	32.1
2,3-dimethylbutane	94.3
n-heptane	77.0
2-methylhexane	71.9
3-methylhexane	73.0
n-octane	68.2
2-methylheptane	69.4
n-nonane	69.3
2-methyloctane	70.6
n-decane	68.0
2-methylnonane	65.7
n-undecane	61.6
n-dodecane	57.7
cyclohexane	59.5
methyl cyclohexane	73.2
alkenes	
ethylene	100.0
propylene	107.9
1-butene	113.2
2-butene	99.3
2-pentene	95.3

Hydrocarbon	Photochemical ozone creation potential
1-pentene	104.1
2-methylbut-1-ene	83.0
3-methylbut-1-ene	118.4
2-methylbut-2-ene	77.1
butylene	70.3
isoprene	117.8
styrene	7.7
alkynes	
acetylene	28.0
aromatics	
benzene	33.4
toluene	77.1
o-xylene	83.1
m-xylene	108.8
p-xylene	94.8
ethylbenzene	80.8
n-propylbenzene	71.3
i-propylbenzene	74.4
1,2,3-trimethylbenzene	124.5
1,2,4-trimethylbenzene	132.4
1,3,5-trimethylbenzene	129.9
o-ethyltoluene	84.6
m-ethyltoluene	98.5
p-ethyltoluene	93.5
3,5-dimethylethylbenzene	124.2
3,5-diethyltoluene	119.5
aldehydes	
formaldehyde	55.4
acetaldehyde	65.0
propionaldehyde	75.5
butyraldehyde	77.0
i-butyraldehyde	85.5
valeraldehyde	88.7
benzaldehyde	-5.6

Hydrocarbon	Photochemical ozone creation potential
ketones	
acetone	18.2
methylethylketone	51.1
methyl-i-butylketone	84.3
cyclohexanone	52.9
alcohols	
methyl alcohol	20.5
ethyl alcohol	44.6
i-propanol	21.6
n-butanol	62.8
i-butanol	59.1
s-butanol	46.8
t-butanol	19.1
diacetone alcohol	61.7
cyclohexanol	62.2
esters	
methyl acetate	4.6
ethyl acetate	32.8
n-propyl acetate	48.1
i-propyl acetate	29.1
n-butyl acetate	51.1
s-butyl acetate	45.2
organic acids	
formic acids	0.3
acetic acid	15.6
propionic acid	0.0
ethers	
butyl glycol	62.9
propylene glycol methyl ether	51.8
dimethyl ether	26.3
methyl-t-butyl ether	26.8
halocarbons	
chloromethane	3.5
methylene chloride	3.1
methylchloroform	0.2
tetrachloroethylene	3.5

Hydrocarbon	Photochemical ozone creation potential
trichloroethylene	7.5
vinyl chloride	27.2
1,1-dichloroethane	23.2
cis 1,2-dichloroethylene	17.2
trans 1,2-dichloroethylene	10.1
other pollutants	
nitric oxide	-42.7
nitrogen dioxide	2.8
sulphur dioxide	4.8
carbon monoxide	2.7

9 Hazard assessment of wastes arising from prescribed processes

9.1 Introduction

9.1.1 This section describes a method for assessing the potential environmental hazards arising from wastes produced by a prescribed processes. The approach enables wastes from different process options to be compared and ranked, thereby enabling a judgement to be made as to their relative environmental acceptability. The requirement for an assessment of waste arisings of this type rather than a consideration of the impact of wastes disposed or treated at a specific site is discussed in Volume I of the guidance note.

9.1.2 It is recognised that the hazard assessment approach adopted for the purposes of the BPEO assessment does not take into account differences in the releases which may occur from different forms of waste treatment or disposal, for example solvent recovery or incineration. It is proposed that further research will be undertaken by the Agency to develop an approach which can take these differences into consideration, however, this is a complex issue and is unlikely to be easily resolved.

9.1.3 In the interim, the hazard assessment approach does enable process options which give rise to wastes with potentially greater environmental effects to be identified. Moreover, it could be used within a site as part of a waste minimisation programme to prioritise waste streams for prevention and control measures.

9.2 Approach

9.2.1 In general two different approaches to hazard assessment can be identified. One approach is based on a hierarchical decision tree type of structure. This approach requires parameters to be given an order of importance as some characteristics will be considered higher up the 'tree' than others. Moreover the hierarchical structure tends to identify those compounds of concern but does not distinguish between them.

9.2.2 The second approach adopts a scoring system where factors representing the degree of exposure and 'toxicity' of the substance are allocated scores. Parameters of concern attract higher scores and a final hazard assessment is obtained by combining the scores in some way. This approach enables the relative hazard represented by a wide range of chemicals to be assessed.

9.2.3 The proposed scheme is based on the second of these two approaches with a number of different factors representing the exposure and toxicity of the substance being allocated a score.

9.2.4 Two main routes of exposure have been identified, via air and water. It is considered that for some highly volatile substances the main exposure route will be via the air. However, for the majority of chemicals the aquatic route will be the most significant. In assessing exposure the solubility, adsorption, persistence in air and water, volatility, and bioaccumulation potential in water, of the substance have been taken into consideration.

9.2.5 The effects assessment considers the potential impact of the substance in terms of aquatic toxicity to the most sensitive of representatives of different groups of organisms and mammalian toxicity (via air or water). Consequently, in carrying out the assessment, the potential hazard posed by a particular chemical has been determined separately for air and water and then combined to give an overall hazard score.

9.2.6 This 'Unit Hazard Score' can then be modified by the site-specific quantity of the substance being considered to generate an overall score for the substance produced by the particular process option at that location. The manner in which the quantity of waste is incorporated needs to be given careful consideration. The direct use of mass, whether in tonnes or kilogrammes, may lead to situations in which the final score is dominated by the quantity for disposal. Alternative approaches, for example by using logarithms to scale the quantity released, may result in the final score being relatively insensitive to modest but significant changes in the quantity for disposal. The approach which has been devised takes into account both the quantity of waste produced and the relative reductions which may occur as a result of the application of different process options.

9.2.7 It should be stressed that the Hazard Scores calculated using this approach can only provide an approximation to the actual hazard that may arise from the disposal of these substances. The actual hazard will be determined by the physico-chemical and biological characteristics of the particular waste being considered and by the nature of the receiving environment. For example, the additive or synergistic toxicological effects exerted by the waste, the size, sensitivity, location, dilution capacity etc of the receiving environment may be important. Careful judgement will therefore need to be applied in interpreting the outcome of this waste assessment methodology.

9.3 Unit hazard scores

9.3.1 A media specific hazard score for air and water was obtained by summing and multiplying the appropriate exposure and toxicity factors together ie:

Unit Hazard Score$_{water}$ (UH$_w$) = (S + A + D$_w$ + B$_w$) * T$_w$

Where:

S = substance solubility;
A = substance adsorption potential;
D$_w$ = degradation in water;
B$_w$ = potential for bioaccumulation of substance from water;
T$_w$ = potential effect through exposure route of water.

Unit Hazard Score$_{air}$ (UH$_a$) = (V + D$_a$) * T$_a$

Where:

V = volatility;
D$_a$ = degradation in air;
T$_a$ = potential effect through exposure route of air.

9.3.2 The overall Unit Hazard Score for the substance concerned was obtained by summing the medium specific values, as follows:

Unit Hazard Score$_{Total}$ = UH$_w$ + UH$_a$

Where UH$_w$ and UH$_a$ represent the Unit Hazard Scores for water and air respectively.

9.3.3 The final site and option specific waste hazard score takes into account the quantity of each waste substance, and is given by:

$$FHS = \sum_{i=1}^{n}(log_{10}(MQD_i) * RQS_i * UHS_{Total\ i})$$

Where:

i = ith of n component substances in waste produced by the process option being considered;

MQD$_i$ = Maximum quantity disposed of for substance i for any of the process options currently under consideration (kg);

UHS$_{Total\ i}$ = the Unit Hazard Score$_{Total}$ for substance i; and

RQS$_i$ = Relative quantity score as derived from Table 9.1.

9.3.4 The 'Unit Hazard Score' for each of a range of inorganic substances are shown in Annex E Table E1 and similarly for organic substances in Annex E, Table E2. The following sections describe the methodology used to derive these values in more detail. This methodology can be used to derive Unit Hazard Scores for other substances. However it is suggested that the operator should discuss the requirement with the site inspector who, if necessary, can obtain appropriate advice.

9.4 Exposure assessment: water

Solubility (S)

9.4.1 The potential mobility of the pollutant into ground or surface water will in part be determined by its solubility. Substances with high solubility will be relatively more mobile than those of lower solubility. Where the substance occurs in more than one form, the score for the most soluble compound was used. For inorganic compounds this will usually be the chloride or nitrate. Table 9.2 presents the scoring system on the basis of solubility of a substance.

Table 9.1:
Relative quantity score

Ratio of quantity of substance disposed of from process option, compared to maximum across all options	Score
80-100%	5
<80%	4
<60%	3
<40%	2
<20%	1

Table 9.2:
Scoring system based on the solubility

Solubility in water of most soluble form (mg/l)	Score
>1000	5
>100 - 1000	4
>10 - 100	3
>1 - 10	2
<1	1

9.4.2 Where no solubility data for organic substances were available values were derived from Structure Activity Relationships calculated using Syracuse Research Corporation (SRC 1994a) computer programs. For substances where the solubility could not be estimated or derived from other sources, a default value of 4 was used.

Adsorption (A)

9.4.3 Adsorption can be considered as the binding of a substance to the surface of a particle. Substances which are readily adsorbed might be expected to be bound to sediment in the aqueous phase. The potential for adsorption onto organic matter for non-ionic compounds can be related to the organic carbon partition coefficient (K_{oc}) for the substance concerned. Table 9.3 presents the scoring system on the basis of adsorption.

9.4.4 However, for inorganic compounds the use of the organic carbon partition coefficient is inappropriate and suitable equivalents for ionic species do not exist. For inorganic compounds the degree of mobility will depend principally on the solubility of the substance, which in turn is determined to a great extent by the pH. If conditions are favourable, some substances such as heavy metals may be converted into an insoluble form (eg sulphide or carbonate) (Sumner 1978). For ionic compounds 'adsorption' was scored on the basis of the solubility of the most insoluble form using the scoring system in section 9.4.1 (see Table 9.2). Ionic substances were therefore scored twice, once on the basis of solubility (considering the most soluble form) and secondly as a measure of 'adsorption' (considering the insoluble form).

Table 9.3:
Scoring system based on adsorption for non-ionic compounds

$Log_{10} K_{oc}$	Score
<0.5	5
>0.5 - 1.0	4
>1.0 - 1.5	3
>1.5 - 2.0	2
>2.0	1

9.4.5   Where no data on partition coefficients exist for organic compounds these have been estimated using Structure Activity Relationships (SRC 1992a).

Degradation (D_w)

9.4.6   The persistence of a substance will affect the degree to which a receptor may be exposed to the pollutant. Persistence is scored on the potential for degradation within the soil/water compartment.

9.4.7   A variety of degradation data may be available, the following scoring system, based on BRE (1991) is used (see Table 9.4). The sources of data were used in descending order of preference. Where no data existed then for organic substances Structure Activity Relationships (SRC 1992b) have been used to predict appropriate values. For inorganic substances a default value of 4 has been used.

Bioaccumulation Potential (B_w)

9.4.8   Organisms may accumulate compounds in their body tissues which once above some critical level exert an adverse effect. In addition, even if no adverse effects occur the organism may be consumed by one at a higher trophic level giving rise to impacts through the food chain. The potential for bioaccumulation is usually assessed by considering the ratio of the substance in the organism compared with that in the medium concerned. Bioaccumulation may either be measured directly or inferred from K_{ow}, the octanol/water partition coefficient. Where possible measure values should be used. Table 9.5 presents the scoring system.

9.4.9   Bioaccumulation is considered only for the aquatic exposure route since it is considered unlikely that highly volatile substances will be readily accumulated. This is supported by a review of the data for 89 priority organic substances (CRC 1992) which indicated that where the vapour pressure was high (>100kPa at $25°C$) the potential for bioaccumulation was low ($\log_{10}K_{ow} < 2$).

Table 9.4:
Scoring system based on degradation potential

Source of data	Data value	Score
Ready biodegradability testing	>70% degraded in 28 days	1
	20 - 70% degraded in 28 days	2
	<20% degraded in 28 days	4
Inherent testing	>30% degraded	2
	<30% degraded	4
BOD_5/COD or ThOD ratio	>0.7	1
	0.2 - 0.7	2
	<0.2	4
Half-life	In the order of weeks	1
	In the order of months	2
	In the order of years	4

Table 9.5:
Scoring system based on bioaccumulation potential

Source of data	Data value	Score
Observed bioaccumulation potential (Conc. organism/Conc. in water)	<10	1
	10 - 100	1.5
	> 100	2
Estimated from Log_{10} K_{ow}.	<1	1
	1 - 2	1.2
	2 - 3	1.4
	3 - 4	1.6
	4 - 5	1.8
	>5	2

9.4.10 If no data of either type are available then for organics, values were estimated using Structure Activity Relationships (SRC 1992b). For inorganic substances or where no other data were available for organics a default value of 1.5 was used.

9.5 Exposure assessment: air

Volatility (V)

9.5.1 For some volatile substances, particularly solvents, evaporation may be quite high. For other substances with a relatively low volatility the potential exposure via this route will be small. Table 9.6 provides a means of taking this into account in the hazard assessment.

9.5.2 Where no information is available then for organic substances a value was estimated using Structure Activity Relationships (SRC 1992c). Where no other data were available a default value of 2.5 was used. Many of the inorganic substances of interest were however of low volatility and a default score of 1 was used.

Degradation in air (D_a)

9.5.3 The degradation rate of a substance in the atmosphere will to some extent determine the exposure of a particular target organism either directly or via deposition and subsequent uptake. It is recognised that other processes such as wet or dry deposition may reduce the residence time of a pollutant in the atmosphere but these are generally related to atmospheric conditions and cannot be taken into consideration in this scheme.

9.5.4 To deal with the wide variety of degradation data available it is proposed that scoring is based on the general order of magnitude of the degradation rate exhibited by the substance (see Table 9.7). If no data were available then a default score of 2 was used.

Table 9.6:
Scoring system based on volatility potential

Volatility at 25° C	Score
>= 100 kPa	4
10 - <100 kPa	3
1 - <10 kPa	2
<1 kPa	1

Table 9.7:
Scoring system based on atmospheric degradation rate

Atmospheric degradation rate	Score
In the order of weeks	1
In the order of months	2
In the order of years	4

9.6 Effects assessment: water

Aquatic toxicity (AQT)

9.6.1   The approach to scoring of aquatic toxicity is based on BRE (1991). The score can be based on two types of data, acute or chronic toxicity (see Table 9.8). Chronic toxicity is preferred as it is thought to be more relevant to the long term exposure of aquatic organisms to low levels of pollutants. In the absence of chronic data, acute data were used.

9.6.2   For each substance an optimum data set was sought from three groups of organisms - fish, daphnia and algae with exposure durations consistent with OECD toxicity test guidelines. Preference was given to temperate species unless non-temperate species (eg fat-head minnow, bluegill sunfish) were an order of magnitude or greater more sensitive. In which case data from the more sensitive species were used.

Mammalian toxicity

9.6.3   The mammalian toxicity score was modified from that proposed by Shillaker (1991) to consider exposure by dermal or oral routes only. The consideration of mammalian toxicity needs to take into account direct effects such as acute or repeated toxicity, irritation and sensitisation and secondly, carcinogenic or reproductive effects. These two types of effect were scored separately and then combined to give an overall aquatic mammalian toxicity score.

9.6.4   The toxicity scores (see Table 9.9) are based on the R-phrases (Risk phrases) as defined under the Classification, Packaging and Labelling of Dangerous Substances Directive. Carcinogenic and reproductive scores are related to the classification of the substance by the International Agency for Research on Cancer (IARC).

Table 9.8:
Scoring system based on aquatic toxicity data

Source of data	Concentration at which an effect is shown (mg/l)	Score
Chronic toxicity test	>10	1
	1 - 10	2
	0.1 - 1	3
	0.01 - 0.1	4
	0.001 - 0.01	5
	< 0.001	6
Acute toxicity test (LC_{50}, EC_{50}, IC_{50})	>100	1
	10 - 100	2
	1 - 10	3
	0.1 - 1	4
	0.01 - 0.1	5
	< 0.01	6

Table 9.9:
Scoring system based on Risk Phrases

Mode of action	Severity of effect	R-Phrase	Score
Acute toxicity	Very toxic	27/28	6
	Toxic	24/25	4
	Harmful	21/22	2
	No R Phrase required		1
Irritation /corrosion	Any irritation or corrosive effects	34/35/36/ 38/39/41	2
	No R Phrase required		1
Sensitisation	Skin sensitiser	43	4
	No R Phrase required		1
Repeated exposure effects	Serious damage to health	48	6
	Cumulative effects	33	4
	No R phrase required		1

Direct mammalian effects (DME$_w$)

9.6.5 The pollutant may lead to a number of different effects on the target organism. The magnitude of each effect was identified from the appropriate R-Phrase and scored accordingly. The maximum value was selected to represent the direct aquatic mammalian toxicity of the substance.

9.6.6 Where there was no information on the direct effects of the substance to mammals a default value of 4 was used.

Mammalian reproductive or mutagenic effects (MRM$_w$)

9.6.7 Substances may lead to mutagenic or effects on reproduction and were scored according to the scheme outlined in Table 9.10. In developing the scheme it was considered important to differentiate between the different routes of exposure as substances which, for example, are carcinogenic by inhalation may not be so by ingestion.

9.6.8 Where the substance had not been examined by IARC a default score of 4 was applied. However, some substances, such as sodium chloride, are generally accepted as being 'safe' and no investigation of their carcinogenicity has been undertaken. A default score of 4 would be too high for substances of this type and therefore on the basis of judgement a value of 1 has been used.

Table 9.10:
Scoring system based on mammalian reproductive or mutagenic effects

Score criteria	Score
Substance is classified as IARC Group 1 or 2A and the supporting information indicates it is carcinogenic for the exposure route being examined.	9
Substance is classified as IARC Group 1 or 2A but no data is available on the route of exposure. or Substance is classified as IARC Group 2B and the supporting information indicates that it is carcinogenic for the exposure route being examined.	6
Substance is classified as IARC Group 2B but no data is available on the route of exposure. or Substance is classified as IARC Group 3 ie it is not classifiable as to its carcinogenicity.	4
Substance is classified as IARC Group 1 or 2A but there is evidence that it is not carcinogenic for the exposure route being examined. or Substance is classified as IARC Group 2B but there is evidence that it is not carcinogenic for the exposure route being examined.	1

Air toxicity

Direct Mammalian toxicity (DME$_a$)

9.6.9 An organism exposed to a substance in air may exhibit a number of different effects. The magnitude of each effect was identified from the appropriate R-Phrase and scored accordingly (see Table 9.11). The maximum value was then selected to represent the direct mammalian toxicity for exposure to air for the substance.

9.6.10 Where there was no information on the direct effects of the substance to mammals a default value of 4 has been used.

Table 9.11:
Scoring system based on Direct Mammalian Toxicity

Mode of action	Severity of effect	R-Phrase	Score
Acute toxicity	Very toxic	26	6
	Toxic	23	4
	Harmful	20	2
	No R-Phrase required		1
Irritation /corrosion	Any irritation or corrosive effects	34/35/36/37/ 38/39/41	2
	No R-Phrase required		1
Sensitisation	Respiratory sensitizer	42	9
	Skin sensitiser	43	4
	No R-Phrase required		1
Repeated exposure effects	Serious damage to health	48	6
	Cumulative effects	33	4
	No R-phrase required		1

Reproductive or mutagenic effects from exposure to air (MRM$_a$)

9.6.11 As discussed for releases to water, substances discharged to air may lead to mutagenic or effects on reproduction and were similarly scored according to the scheme developed for aquatic releases (see Table 9.12).

9.6.12 Where the substance had not been examined by IARC a default score of 4 was applied. However, some substances, such as sodium chloride, are generally accepted as being 'safe' and no investigation of their carcinogenicity has been undertaken. A default score of 4 would be too high for substances of this type and therefore on the basis of judgement a value of 1 has been used.

9.7 Calculation of toxicity score (T)

9.7.1 To take account of the difference in exposure routes the toxicity scores for air and water were determined separately. For each medium the maximum score for the mammalian direct effects (DME) was identified and added to that for the mutagenic/reproductive effects and non-mammalian toxicity (AQT) ie:

Aquatic Toxicity Score $(T_w) = AQT + Max(DME_w) + MRM_w$

Air Toxicity Score $(T_a) = Max(DME_a) + MRM_a$

Where:

AQT = aquatic toxicity;

DME$_{w/a}$ = direct mammalian effect $_{water/air}$;

MRM$_{w/a}$ = mammalian reproductive or mutagenic effect $_{water/air}$

Table 9.12:
Scoring system based on reproductive or mutagenic effects

Score criteria	Score
Substance is classified as IARC Group 1 or 2A and the supporting information indicates it is carcinogenic for the exposure route being examined.	9
Substance is classified as IARC Group 1 or 2A but no data is available on the route of exposure. or Substance is classified as IARC Group 2B and the supporting information indicates that it is carcinogenic for the exposure route being examined.	6
Substance is classified as IARC Group 2B but no data is available on the route of exposure. or Substance is classified as IARC Group 3 ie it is not classifiable as to its carcinogenicity.	4
Substance is classified as IARC Group 1 or 2A but there is evidence that it is not carcinogenic for the exposure route being examined. or Substance is classified as IARC Group 2B but there is evidence that it is not carcinogenic for the exposure route being examined.	1

10 Assessment of odours

10.1 Quantification of odours

10.1.1 The assessment of odours is a complex issue and beyond the scope of this guidance note to cover in its entirety. The purpose of this section is therefore to provide a brief overview of the topic and to direct the reader to work which provides more detailed discussion of particular aspects.

10.1.2 Odorous emissions may arise from a number of different sources within a process, as a result of discharges from chimneys or vents, fugitive emissions or as the result of handling of raw or waste materials. Emissions giving rise to odour problems are often a complex mix of chemicals and by implication it is their olfactory rather than chemical characteristics which are of concern. Therefore, any means of quantification should be related to the human olfactory sense.

10.1.3 Although the exact details of different methods of quantification may vary, in general a sample of odorous gas is diluted with odour free air and the dilution required for the odour to be just perceptible by 50% of the population is determined. This is known as the odour detection threshold, on occasion some studies have used other criteria such as the recognition threshold or different percentages of the population responding to the stimulus. Therefore, care should be exercised in interpreting reported values from field or literature studies.

10.1.4 Odours are often expressed in terms of odour units or dilutions to threshold. If an odour was attributable to just one compound present in the air, then the odour unit would reflect the threshold concentration for that compound. For example, the odour threshold for formaldehyde is approximately 1 part per million (ppm). Air with formaldehyde at a concentration of 10 ppm would contain 10 odour units.

10.1.5 This concept of odour units is useful for situations where the surrounding air is likely to contain a number of odorous compounds and their relative contribution is uncertain. In such cases, the threshold of detection or recognition can be defined for the odorous air as a whole. Further information on the quantification of odours can be found in Valentin and North (1980) and Woodfield and Hall (1994).

10.2 Prediction of atmospheric odour concentrations

10.2.1 There are many dispersion models available that can be used to predict the dispersion of compounds in the atmosphere. However, most of the these models can only predict ambient concentrations averaged over about an hour or longer periods. For an odour to be detected by the human nose the ambient concentration may need to be above the detection threshold for as little as one second. Moreover, the frequency with which the threshold concentration is exceeded will be important in influencing the way an individual responds to the exposure and therefore the manner in which it is assessed.

10.2.2 Currently, there is no completely satisfactory way of predicting the effective ambient concentration of odorous compounds as a result of a release. However, a number of pragmatic approaches to the problem have been developed particularly with regard to the determination of stack heights for odour control (Valentin and North 1980, Hall and Kukadia 1993 and Woodfield and Hall 1994) and reference should be made to these reports if further detail is required.

10.3 Odour detection thresholds

10.3.1 There are several published sources of odour detection and recognition thresholds, some more reliable than others. The reliability of the published data varies considerably and it is preferable to refer to several sources if available and compare the variability. Most of the variability in the published data derives from the measurement techniques but some also comes from the different sensitivities of the human nose.

10.3.2 Sources of information on odour thresholds are listed in Table 10.1 below. It should be noted that the inclusion of a particular document in the list below does not imply a particular endorsement of the values given and it is open to the operator to select values from these or other sources as appropriate. However, the source and derivation of any values used in an assessment should be clearly stated in any assessment. Data from the first listed reference are reproduced in Annex A, Table A2 (only data which are reported to have relatively high data quality are reproduced).

Table 10.1:
Sources of information on odour thresholds

1) AEA Technology, National Environmental Centre (1994) *Odour Measurement and Control - An Update* ed Woodfield M and Hall D, ISBN 0 85624 8258

2) Valentin and North (1980), *Odour Control - A Concise Guide*, prepared for the UK DOE

3) Leonardos G, Kendall D and Barnard N J (1969), *Air Pollution Control Association*, Volume 19 (2) pp 91-95

4) Health and Safety Handbook (1988) Volume 1, Section 7 (Air), Professional Publishing Limited, South Quay Plaza, 183 Marsh Wall, London E14

5) Hellman T M and Small F H (1974) *Characterisation of the Odour Properties of 101 Petrochemicals Using Sensory Methods*, Journal of the Air Pollution Control Association (JAPCA), Volume 24 (10), pp 979-982

6) World Health Organisation (1987) Air Quality Guidelines for Europe, European Series No. 23, Geneva

10.3.3 Information relating to toxic chemicals, including odour information is also available via the Internet; the quality of this information is, however, unknown.

ANNEX A Environmental Quality Standards and Environmental Assessment Levels for releases to air

Table A1:
EC Mandatory Environmental Quality Standards for Air Pollutants

Substance	Reference Period	Calculated from:	Limit value (µg/m³)	Associated Value for Suspended Particulates [1] (µg/m³)	Source
Sulphur Dioxide	Year	Median of daily means	80 120	> 40 ≤40	Statutory Instrument 1989 No. 317 (Directive 80/779/EEC)
	Winter 1 Oct – 31 Mar	Median of daily means	130 180	> 60 ≤60	
	Year	98th percentile of daily (24hr) means	250 350	> 150 ≤150	Statutory Instrument 1989 No. 317 (Directive 80/779/EEC)
Suspended Particulates [1]	Year	Median of daily means	80		
	Winter 1 Oct – 31 Mar	Median of daily means	130		
	Year	98th percentile of daily (24hr) means	250[2]		
Nitrogen Dioxide	Calendar Year	98th percentile from mean values per hour or lesser period	200		Statutory Instrument 1989 No. 317 (Directive 85/203/EEC)
Ozone [3]	24 hours[5] 8 hours[4] 1 hour[5] 1 hour[6] 1 hour[7]		65 110 200 180 360		Statutory Instrument 1994 No. 440 (Directive 92/72/EEC)
Lead	Year	Annual mean	2		Statutory Instrument 1989 No. 317 (Directive 82/884/EEC)

(1) Measured by black smoke method
(2) Not to be exceeded for more than three consecutive days
(3) The maximum, median and the 98th percentile of the mean values over one hour and eight hours recorded during the year in each measuring station are to be reported to the European Commission. Exceedances of thresholds to be detailed to the European Commission.
(4) Health protection threshold
(5) Vegetation protection thresholds
(6) Population information threshold; public to be informed in event of exceedance
(7) Population warning threshold; public to be informed in event of exceedance

Table A2:
Long and short term Environmental Assessment Levels for releases to air

Substance	Long term EAL[a], $\mu g/m^3$	Short term EAL[b], $\mu g/m^3$	Odour threshold[q], $\mu g/m^3$.
Acetic acid	250	3700	43
Acetic anhydride	–	2000	1.3
Acetone	17800	356000	13900
Acetonitrile	700	10500	–
o-Acetylsalicylic acid	50	1500	–
Acrylaldehyde	2.5	80	–
Acrylamide	0.6	18	–
Acrylic acid	300	6000	1.3
Acrylonitrile	8	240	–
Aldrin (ISO)	2.5	75	–
Allyl alcohol	50	1000	–
Allyl-2,3-epoxypropyl ether	220	4400	–
Aluminium alkyl compounds	20	600	–
Aluminium and compounds (as Al)	20	600	–
2-Aminoethanol	80	1500	–
Ammonia	170	2400	–
Ammonium sulphamidate	100	2000	–
Anisidines, o- and p- isomers	5	150	–
Antimony and compounds (as Sb) except antimony trisulphide and antimony trioxide	5	150	–
Arsenic and compounds (as As)	0.2	6	–
Arsine	2	60	–
Azinphos-methyl (ISO)	2	850	–
gamma-BHC (ISO)	5	150	–
Barium compounds, soluble (as Ba)	5	150	–
Benomyl (ISO)	100	1500	–
Benzene	3.24[c,d]	960	32500
Benzenethiol	20	600	–
Benzene-1,2,4-tricarboxylic acid, 1,2-anhydride	0.4	12	–
p-Benzoquinone	4	120	–
Benzyl butyl phthalate	50	1500	–
Beryllium and compounds (as Be)	0.004	0.12	–
Biphenyl	15	400	–
Bis(chloromethyl)ether	0.01	0.3	–
Bis(2,3-epoxypropyl)ether	6	180	–
Bis(2-ethylhexyl)phthalate	50	1000	–
Bornan-2-one	120	1800	–
Boron tribromide	–	1000	–
Boron trifluoride	–	300	–

Table A2 continued . . .

Substance	Long term EAL[a], $\mu g/m^3$	Short term EAL[b], $\mu g/m^3$	Odour threshold[q], $\mu g/m^3$.
Bromacil (ISO)	100	2000	–
Bromine	7	200	–
Bromine pentafluoride	7	200	–
Bromochloromethane	10500	130000	–
Bromoethane	8900	111000	–
Bromoform	50	1500	–
Bromomethane	200	6000	–
Bromotrifluoromethane	61000	730000	–
Buta-1,3-diene	2.21[c,d]	1320	1100
Butane	14300	178000	–
Butan-1-ol	–	15000	90
Butan-2-ol	3000	45000	3300
Butan-2-one	6000	90000	870
2-Butoxyethanol	240	7200	5.1
Butyl acetate	7100	95000	47
sec-Butyl acetate	9500	119000	–
tert-Butyl acetate	9500	119000	–
Butyl acrylate	550	16500	–
n-Butylamine	–	1500	–
n-Butyl chloroformate	56	1680	–
n-Butyl glycidyl ether	1350	40500	–
Butyl lactate	250	7500	–
2-sec-Butylphenol	300	9000	–
Cadmium and its compounds (as Cd)	0.005[e]	1.5	–
Caesium hydroxide	20	600	–
Calcium cyanamide	5	100	–
Calcium hydroxide	50	1500	–
Calcium oxide	20	600	–
Captafol (ISO)	1	30	–
Captan (ISO)	50	1500	–
Carbaryl (ISO)	50	1000	–
Carbofuran (ISO)	1	30	–
Carbon black	35	700	–
Carbon disulphide	60	100[e,h]	20[e,j,t]
Carbon monoxide	550	2900[c,l]	–
Carbon tetrabromide	14	400	–
Carbon tetrachloride	126	3780	280000
Chlorine	15	300	–
Chlorine dioxide	3	90	–

Table A2 continued . . .

Substance	Long term EAL[a], $\mu g/m^3$	Short term EAL[b], $\mu g/m^3$	Odour threshold[q], $\mu g/m^3$.
Chlorine trifluoride	–	40	–
Chloroacetaldehyde	–	300	–
2-Chloroacetophenone	3	90	–
Chlorobenzene	2300	69000	–
2-Chlorobuta-1,3-diene	360	10800	–
Chlorodifluoromethane	35000	1050000	–
1-Chloro-2,3-epoxypropane	4	120	–
Chloroethane	26000	325000	–
2-Chloroethanol	–	300	–
Chloroform	98	2940	–
Chloromethane	1050	21000	–
1-Chloro-4-nitrobenzene	10	200	–
Chloropentafluoroethane	63200	1896000	–
Chlorosulphonic acid	10	300	–
2-Chlorotoluene	2500	75000	–
2-Chloro-6-(trichloromethyl)pyridine	100	2000	–
Chlorpyrifos (ISO)	2	60	–
Chromium, chromium (II) compounds and chromium (III) compounds (as Cr)	5	150	–
Chromium (VI) compounds (as Cr)	0.1	3	–
Cobalt and compounds (as Co)	0.2	6	–
Copper	10	200	–
Cresols, all isomers	220	6600	See footnote[r]
Cryofluorane (INN)	70000	875000	–
Cumene	1200	37000	–
Cyanamide	20	600	–
Cyanides, except HCN, cyanogen and cyanogen chloride, (as CN)	50	1500	–
Cyanogen chloride	–	60	–
Cyclohexane	3400	103000	315000
Cyclohexanol	2000	60000	–
Cyclohexanone	1000	40000	83
Cyclohexene	10150	304500	–
Cyclohexylamine	400	12000	–
Cyhexatin (ISO)	50	1000	–
2,4-D (ISO)	100	2000	–
Dialkyl 79 phthalate	50	1500	–
Diallyl phthalate	50	1500	–
1,2-Diaminoethane	250	7500	–
Diammonium peroxodisulphate (measured as [S_2O_8])	10	300	–

Table A2 continued . . .

Substance	Long term EAL[a], $\mu g/m^3$	Short term EAL[b], $\mu g/m^3$	Odour threshold[q], $\mu g/m^3$.
Diazinon (ISO)	1	30	–
Dibenzoyl peroxide	50	1500	–
Dibismuth tritelluride	100	2000	–
Dibismuth tritelluride, selenium doped	50	1000	–
Diborane	1	30	–
Diboron trioxide	100	2000	–
Dibromodifluoromethane	8600	129000	–
1,2-Dibromoethane	8	240	–
2,6-Di-tert-butyl-p-cresol	100	3000	–
Dibutyl hydrogen phosphate	50	1000	–
Dibutyl phthalate	50	1000	–
6,6'-Di-tert-butyl-4,4'-thiodi-m-cresol	100	2000	–
6,6-Di-tert-butyl-4,4-thiodi-m-cresol	100	2000	–
Dichloroacetylene	–	40	–
1,2-Dichlorobenzene	–	30000	–
1,4-Dichlorobenzene	1500	30000	–
Dichlorodifluoromethane	49500	620000	–
1,3-Dichloro-5,5-dimethyl-hydantoin	2	40	–
1,1-Dichloroethane	8100	162000	–
1,2-Dichloroethane	40	700[e,h]	–
1,2-Dichloroethylene, cis:trans isomers 60:40	7900	100000	–
Dichlorofluoromethane	400	12000	–
Dichloromethane	700	3000[e,h]	3420
2,2'-Dichloro-4,4'-methylene dianiline	0.01	0.3	–
Dichlorvos (ISO)	10	300	–
Dicyclohexyl phthalate	50	1500	–
Dicyclopentadiene	300	9000	–
Dieldrin (ISO)	2.5	75	–
Diethylamine	300	7500	–
2-Diethylaminoethanol	500	15000	–
Diethyl ether	12000	150000	–
Diethyl phthalate	50	1000	–
Diisobutyl phthalate	50	1500	–
Diisodecyl phthalate	50	1500	–
Diisononyl phthalate	50	1500	–
Diisooctyl phthalate	50	1500	–
Diisopropylamine	200	6000	–
Diisopropyl ether	10500	132000	–
Di-linear 79 phthalate	50	1500	–

Table A2 continued . . .

Substance	Long term EAL[(a)], $\mu g/m^3$	Short term EAL[(b)], $\mu g/m^3$	Odour threshold[(q)], $\mu g/m^3$.
Dimethoxymethane	31000	388000	–
NN-Dimethylacetamide	360	7100	–
Dimethylamine	180	5400	–
NN-Dimethylaniline	250	5000	–
1,3-Dimethylbutyl acetate	3000	60000	–
NN-Dimethylethylamine	300	4500	–
Dimethylformamide	300	6000	–
2,6-Dimethylheptan-4-one	1500	45000	–
Dimethyl phthalate	50	1000	–
Dinitrobenzene, all isomers	10	300	–
Dinonyl phthalate	50	1500	–
1,4-Dioxane	900	36000	30600
Dioxathion (ISO)	2	60	–
Diphenylamine	100	2000	–
Diphenyl ether	70	2100	–
Diphosphorus pentasulphide	10	300	–
Diphosphorus pentoxide	–	200	–
Dipotassium peroxodisulphate (measured as [S_2O_8])	10	300	–
Diquat dibromide (ISO)	5	100	–
Disodium disulphite	50	1500	–
Disodium peroxodisulphate (measured as [S_2O_8])	10	300	–
Disodium tetraborate	10	300	–
Disulfoton (ISO)	1	30	–
Disulphur dichloride	–	600	–
Disulphur decafluoride	2.5	75	–
Diuron (ISO)	100	3000	–
Divanadium pentaoxide (as V)	0.5	15	–
Divinylbenzene	500	15000	–
Endosulfan (ISO)	1	30	–
Endrin (ISO)	1	30	–
2,3-Epoxypropyl isopropyl ether	2400	36000	–
Ethane-1,2-diol	100	3000	–
Ethanethiol	10	300	–
Ethanol	19000	570000	280
2-Ethoxyethanol	74	2220	–
2-Ethoxyethyl acetate	108	3240	–
Ethyl acetate	14000	420000	2410
Ethyl acrylate	200	6000	–
Ethylamine	180	5400	–

Table A2 continued . . .

Substance	Long term EAL[a], $\mu g/m^3$	Short term EAL[b], $\mu g/m^3$	Odour threshold[q], $\mu g/m^3$.
Ethylbenzene	4350	54500	–
Ethyl chloroformate	44	1320	–
Ethylene dinitrate	12	120	–
Ethylene oxide	20	600	–
Ethyl formate	3000	45000	–
2-Ethylhexyl chloroformate	79	2370	–
4-Ethylmorpholine	230	9500	–
Fenchlorphos (ISO)	100	3000	–
Ferbam (ISO)	100	2000	–
Ferrocene	100	2000	–
Fluoride (as F)	1[i]	2.8[h,i]	–
Fluorine	–	150	–
Formaldehyde	5	100[e,j]	–
Formamide	300	4500	–
Formic acid	90	2700	–
2-Furaldehyde	80	4000	250
Furfuryl alcohol	200	6000	–
Germane	6	180	–
Glutaraldehyde	–	70	–
Glycerol	100	3000	–
Hafnium	5	150	–
n-Heptane	16000	200000	–
Heptan-2-one	2400	48000	–
Heptan-3-one	2400	48000	–
Hexachloroethane	50	1500	–
Hexahydro-1,3,5-trinitro-1,3,5-triazine	15	300	–
Hexane, all isomers except n-Hexane	18000	360000	–
n-Hexane	700	21000	–
1,6-Hexanolactam	10	300	–
Hexan-2-one	200	6000	–
Hydrogen bromide	–	1000	–
Hydrogen chloride	7[f]	700	–
Hydrogen cyanide	–	200	–
Hydrogen fluoride (as F)	–	250	–
Hydrogen peroxide	15	300	–
Hydrogen selenide (as Se)	2	60	–
Hydrogen sulphide	140	150[e,h]	0.76
Hydroquinone	20	400	–
4-Hydroxy-4-methyl-pentan-2-one	2400	36000	–

Table A2 continued . . .

Substance	Long term EAL[a], $\mu g/m^3$	Short term EAL[b], $\mu g/m^3$	Odour threshold[q], $\mu g/m^3$.
2-Hydroxypropyl acrylate	30	900	–
2,2'-Iminodiethanol	150	4500	–
2,2'-Iminodi(ethylamine)	40	1200	–
Indene	450	7000	–
Indium and compounds (as In)	1	30	–
Iodine	–	100	–
Iodoform	100	2000	–
Iron salts (as Fe)	10	200	–
Isobutyl acetate	7000	87500	–
Isocyanates (as CNO)	0.04	1.4	–
Isooctyl alcohol (mixed isomers)	2700	81000	–
Isopentyl acetate	5250	65500	–
Isopropyl acetate	–	84000	–
Isopropyl chloroformate	50	1500	–
Ketene	9	300	–
Lead	Refer to Table A1	–	–
Lithium hydride	0.25	7.5	–
Lithium hydroxide	–	100	–
Malathion (ISO)	100	3000	–
Manganese and compounds (as Mn)	1[d,e]	1500	–
Mequinol (INN)	50	1500	–
Mercaptoacetic acid	50	1500	–
Mercury alkyls (as Hg)	0.1	3	–
Mercury and compounds, except mercury alkyls, (as Hg)	1[d,e]	15	–
Methacrylic acid	700	14000	–
Methacrylonitrile	30	900	–
Methanethiol	10	300	–
Methanol	2600	31000	–
Methomyl (ISO)	25	750	–
Methoxychlor (ISO)	100	3000	–
2-Methoxyethanol	32	960	–
2-Methoxyethyl acetate	48	1440	–
1-Methoxypropan-2-ol	3600	108000	12.2
Methyl acetate	6100	76000	–
Methyl acrylate	350	10500	–
Methylamine	120	3600	–
N-Methylaniline	20	600	–
3-Methylbutan-1-ol	3600	45000	–

Table A2 continued . . .

Substance	Long term EAL[a], $\mu g/m^3$	Short term EAL[b], $\mu g/m^3$	Odour threshold[q], $\mu g/m^3$.
1-Methylbutyl acetate	–	80000	–
Methyl 2-cyanoacrylate	80	1600	–
Methylcyclohexane	16000	200000	–
Methylcyclohexanol	2350	35000	–
2-Methylcyclohexanone	2300	34500	–
2-Methyl-4,6-dinitrophenol	2	60	–
4,4'-Methylenedianiline	0.16	4.8	–
Methyl ethyl ketone peroxides	–	150	–
Methyl formate	2500	37500	–
5-Methylheptan-3-one	1300	39000	–
5-Methylhexan-2-one	2400	48000	–
Methyl methacrylate	4100	51000	380
2-Methylpentane-2,4-diol	1250	12500	–
4-Methylpentan-2-ol	1000	16000	–
4-Methylpentan-2-one	2050	41000	540
4-Methylpent-3-en-2-one	600	10000	–
2-Methylpropan-1-ol	1500	22500	–
2-Methylpropan-2-ol	3000	45000	71000
1-Methyl-2-pyrrolidone	4000	120000	–
Methylstyrenes, all isomers except α-methylstyrene	4800	72000	–
N-Methyl-N, 2,4,6-tetranitroaniline	15	300	–
Mevinphos (ISO)	1	30	–
Molybdenum compounds (as Mo)	50	1000	–
Monochloroacetic acid	10	300	–
Morpholine	700	10500	–
Naled (ISO)	30	600	–
Napthalene	500	7500	–
Nickel and inorganic compounds (as Ni)	0.2	6	–
Nickel, organic compounds (as Ni)	10	300	–
Nicotine	5	150	–
Nitric acid	50	1000	–
4-Nitroaniline	60	1800	–
Nitrobenzene	50	1000	–
Nitroethane	3100	93000	–
Nitrogen dioxide	40[d,k]	286[c,l]	–
Nitrogen monoxide	300	4500	–
Nitrogen trifluoride	300	4500	–
Nitromethane	2500	37500	–
1-Nitropropane	900	27000	28200

Table A2 continued . . .

Substance	Long term EAL[(a)], $\mu g/m^3$	Short term EAL[(b)], $\mu g/m^3$	Odour threshold[(q)], $\mu g/m^3$.
2-Nitropropane	36	1080	–
Nitrotoluene, all isomers	300	6000	–
Octachloronaphthalene	1	30	–
n-Octane	14500	180000	–
Orthophosphoric acid	–	200	–
Osmium tetraoxide (as Os)	0.02	0.6	–
Oxalic acid	10	200	–
Oxalonitrile	200	6000	–
2,2′-Oxydiethanol	1000	30000	–
Ozone	2	100[(c,m)]	–
Parathion (ISO)	1	30	–
Parathion-methyl (ISO)	2	60	–
Particulates	Refer to Table A1	50[(c,h,n)]	–
Pentacarbonyliron (as Fe)	0.8	24	–
Pentachlorophenol	5	150	–
Pentane, all isomers	18000	225000	–
Pentan-2-one	7000	87500	–
Pentan-3-one	7000	87500	–
Pentyl acetate	5300	80000	–
Perchloryl fluoride	140	2800	–
Phenol	190	3800	–
p-Phenylenediamine	1	30	–
Phenyl-2,3-epoxypropyl ether	60	1800	–
2-Phenylpropene	–	48000	–
Phorate (ISO)	0.5	20	–
Phosgene	0.8	25	–
Phosphine	–	40	–
Phosphorus, yellow	1	30	–
Phosphorus pentachloride	10	300	–
Phosphorus trichloride	15	300	–
Phosphoryl trichloride	12	360	–
Picloram (ISO)	100	2000	–
Picric acid	1	30	–
Piperazine dihydrochloride	50	1500	–
Piperidine	35	1050	–
Platinum metal	50	1500	–
Platinum salts, soluble (as Pt)	0.02	0.6	–
Potassium hydroxide	–	200	–
Propane-1,2-diol	100	3000	–

Table A2 continued . . .

Substance	Long term EAL[a], $\mu g/m^3$	Short term EAL[b], $\mu g/m^3$	Odour threshold[q], $\mu g/m^3$.
Propan-1-ol	5000	62500	–
Propan-2-ol	9800	122500	1185
Propionic acid	300	4500	–
Propoxur (ISO)	5	200	–
n-Propyl acetate	8400	105000	–
Propylene dinitrate	12	120	–
Prop-2-yn-1-ol	20	600	–
Pyrethrins (ISO)	50	1000	–
Pyridine	150	3000	–
2-Pyridylamine	20	800	–
Rhodium and compounds (as Rh)	0.01	0.3	–
Rotenone (ISO)	50	1000	–
Selenium and compounds, except hydrogen selenide (as Se)	1	30	–
Silane	7	150	–
Silver compounds (as Ag)	0.1	3	–
Sodium azide (as NaN_3)	–	30	–
Sodium 2-(2,4-dichlorophenoxy)ethyl sulphate	100	2000	–
Sodium fluoroacetate	0.5	15	–
Sodium hydrogensulphite	50	1500	–
Sodium hydroxide	–	200	–
Stibine	5	150	–
Strychnine	1.5	45	–
Styrene	840	800[e,h]	160
Sulfotep (ISO)	2	60	–
Sulphur dioxide	Refer to Table A1	267[c,o]	–
Sulphur hexafluoride	60000	750000	–
Sulphuric acid	10	300	–
Sulphur tetrafluoride	4	100	–
Sulphuryl difluoride	200	4000	–
2,4,5-T (ISO)	100	2000	–
TEPP (ISO)	0.5	20	–
Tantalum	50	1000	–
Tellurium and compounds, except hydrogen telluride, (as Te)	1	30	–
Terphenyls, all isomers	–	500	–
1,1,2,2-Tetrabromoethane	70	2100	–
Tetracarbonylnickel (as Ni)	–	24	–
1,1,1,2-Tetrachloro-2,2-difluoroethane	8340	83400	–
1,1,2,2-Tetrachloro-1,2-difluoroethane	8340	83400	–

Table A2 continued . . .

Substance	Long term EAL[a], $\mu g/m^3$	Short term EAL[b], $\mu g/m^3$	Odour threshold[q], $\mu g/m^3$.
Tetrachloroethylene	3350	5000[e,h]	8000[e,j]
Tetrachloronaphthalenes, all isomers	20	400	–
Tetraethyl orthosilicate	850	25500	–
Tetrahydrofuran	2950	59000	–
Tetramethyl orthosilicate	60	3000	–
Tetramethyl succinonitrile	30	900	–
Tetrasodium pyrophosphate	50	1500	–
Thallium, soluble compounds (as Tl)	1	30	–
Thionyl chloride	–	500	–
Thiram (ISO)	50	1000	–
Tin compounds, inorganic, except SnH$_4$, (as Sn)	20	400	–
Tin compounds, organic, except cyhexatin (ISO), (as Sn)	1	20	–
Titanium dioxide	50	1500	–
Toluene	1880	8000[e,h]	644
p-Toluenesulphonyl chloride	–	500	–
Tributyl phosphate, all isomers	50	500	–
Tricarbonyl(eta-cyclopentadienyl) manganese (as Mn)	1	30	–
Tricarbonyl(methylcyclopentadienyl) manganese (as Mn)	2	60	–
1,2,4-Trichlorobenzene	400	4000	–
1,1,1-Trichlorobis(chlorophenyl)ethane	10	300	–
1,1,1-Trichloroethane	3800	49000	–
Trichloroethylene	1070	1000[e,h]	8000
Trichlorofluoromethane	56000	700000	–
Trichloronitromethane	7	200	–
1,2,3-Trichloropropane	3000	45000	–
1,1,2-Trichlorotrifluoroethane	76000	950000	–
Triethylamine	400	6000	–
Trimanganese tetraoxide	10	300	–
Trimethylamine	240	3600	2.6
Trimethylbenzenes, all isomers or mixtures	1230	36900	–
3,5,5-Trimethylcyclohex-2-enone	–	2500	–
Trimethyl phosphite	100	3000	–
2,4,6-Trinitrotoluene	5	150	–
Triphenyl phosphate	30	600	–
Tri-o-tolyl phosphate	1	30	–
Tungsten and compounds (as W)	10	300	–
Turpentine	5600	84000	–
Uranium compounds, natural, soluble, (as U)	2	60	–

Table A2 continued . . .

Substance	Long term EAL[a], $\mu g/m^3$	Short term EAL[b], $\mu g/m^3$	Odour threshold[q], $\mu g/m^3$.
Vanadium	–	1[e,h]	–
Vinyl acetate	300	6000	–
Vinyl chloride	155[p]	1087	–
Vinylidene chloride	80	2400	–
Warfarin (ISO)	1	30	–
White spirit	5750	72000	–
Xylene, o-, m-, p- or mixed isomers	4350	65000	78[s]
Xylidine, all isomers	100	5000	–
Yttrium	10	300	–
Zirconium compounds (as Zr)	50	1000	–

(a) *Unless otherwise stated, derived from Health & Safety Executive, EH40/95, Occupational Exposure Limits 1995; 8 hour reference period*

(b) *Unless otherwise stated, derived from Health & Safety Executive, EH40/95, Occupational Exposure Limits 1995; 15 minute reference period*

(c) *Source: Expert Panel on Air Quality Standards*

(d) *Annual reference period*

(e) *Source: World Health Organisation, Air Quality Guidelines for Europe. WHO Regional Publications, European Series No. 23, 1987*

(f) *Source: US Environmental Protection Agency, Integrated Risk Information System*

(g) *Based on values for indoor pollution*

(h) *24 hour reference period*

(i) *Source: R.H. Schulze, Trinity Consultants Inc. Practical Guide to Atmospheric Dispersion Modelling 1993 Ambient air quality standards set in Germany (annual average) and the Netherlands (24 hour average)*

(j) *30 minute reference period*

(k) *Source: World Health Organisation WHO Air Quality Guidelines for Europe – Update and Revision. EUR/IGP/EHAZ94.05/PB01, 1995 This new guideline is an interim document which has been put out by WHO in advance of the next edition of the WHO Guidelines book, which is not due for publication until 1997*

(l) *1 hour reference period*

(m) *8 hour reference period*

(n) PM_{10}

(o) *15 minute reference period*

(p) *Overriding annual average MEL of 3 ppm. As it is an annual MEL instead of an 8 hour, a safety factor of 50 has been applied*

(q) *Source: AEA Technology. Odour Measurement and Control - An Update Report AEA/CS/REMA-038 (M. Woodfield & D. Hall, eds.) 1994*

(r) *Odour thresholds are: m-cresol: 1.3 $\mu g/m^3$; o-cresol: 2.8 $\mu g/m^3$; p-cresol: 2.9 $\mu g/m^3$*

(s) *Mixed isomers*

(t) *In viscose emissions*

Table A3 *Critical levels for the assessment of sensitive vegetation*

Substance	Vegetation type	Averaging period	Value (μg/m^3)
Sulphur dioxide	Lichens	Annual mean	10
	Forest ecosystems	Annual and winter mean (October – March)	20[1]
	Natural vegetation	Annual and winter mean (October – March)	20[1]
	Agricultural crops	Annual and winter mean (October – March)	30
Nitrogen oxides (as NO$_x$)	All vegetation types	Annual mean	30
Ammonia	All vegetation types	Annual mean	8

(1) A critical level of 15 μg/m^3 should be used where the effective temperature sum (ETS) above 5°C is below 1000 degree centigrade days. ie:

$$ETS = \sum_{i=1}^{n} d_i(T_i - 5^o\,C)$$

Where: $d_i = 1$ if $T_i > 5^o$ C
$d_i = 0$ if $T_i \leq 5^o$ C
T_i = mean daily temperature (°C) on day i.
n = number of days in the year.

ANNEX B Environmental Quality Standards and Assessment Levels for releases to water

Table B1:
Environmental Quality Standards for Water

Substance	Inland Waters (μg/l as annual mean)	Estuary and Coastal Waters (μg/l as annual mean)
Aldrin[1]	0.01	0.01
Dieldrin[1]	0.01	0.01
Endrin[1]	0.005	0.005
Isodrin[1]	0.005	0.005
Cadmium and its compounds[1]	5 (total soluble & insoluble Cd)	2.5 (coastal) 5 (estuarine) (dissolved Cd)
Carbon tetrachloride[1]	12	12
Chloroform[1]	12	12
DDT (all isomers)[1]	0.025	0.025
para-para-DDT[1]	0.01	0.01
1,2 Dichloroethane[2]	10	10
Hexachlorobenzene[1]	0.03	0.03
Hexachlorobutadiene[1]	0.1	0.1
Hexachlorocyclo-hexane[1]	0.1	0.02
Mercury and its compounds[1]	1 (total soluble & insoluble Hg)	0.3 (coastal) 0.5 (estuarine) (dissolved Hg)
Pentachlorophenol and its compounds[1]	2	2
Perchloroethylene[2]	10	10
Trichlorobenzene[2]	0.4	0.4
Trichloroethylene[2]	10	10

(1) Surface Waters (Dangerous Substances) (Classification) Regulations 1989, Statutory Instrument 1989 No.2286

(2) Surface Waters (Dangerous Substances) (Classification) Regulations 1992, Statutory Instrument 1992 No.337

Table B2:

Environmental Assessment Levels for Water (values as 'total' annual average unless otherwise stated)
Short term EALs are shown in dark shaded boxes.

Substance	Inland Waters					Estuary and coastal waters (µg/l)	Comments/Source
	Designated[1] fisheries		Aquatic life				
	Salmonid (µg/l)	Cyprinid (µg/l)	Hardness (mg/l CaCO$_3$)	Salmonid (µg/l)	Cyprinid (µg/l)		
Aldrin	See EQS Table						
Ammonia (unionised) (as N)	4 (G) 95%ile 21 (M) 95%ile	4 (G) 95%ile 21 (M) 95%ile		15 (Proposed)	15 (Proposed)	21 (Proposed)	Seager et al (1988)
Ammonium (total) (as N)	31 (G) 95%ile 778 (M) 95%ile	156 (G) 95%ile 778 (M) 95%ile					
Arsenic[4][3]				50	50	25	Dissolved. Circular 7/89[2]
Atrazine (+ simazine)				2 / 10 MAC	2 / 10 MAC	2 / 10 MAC	Dissolved conc[ns] & combined with simazine. Proposed. DoE (1991)
Azinphos methyl				0.01 / 0.04 MAC	0.01 / 0.04 MAC	0.01 / 0.04 MAC	Dissolved conc[ns]. Proposed. DoE (1991)
Biphenyl				25	25	25 (G)	Proposed. Barry et al (1994)
BOD$_5$	3000 (G) 95%ile	6000 (G) 95%ile					
Boron				2000	2000	7000	Circular 7/89[2]
Bromoxynil				100 / 1000 MAC	100 / 1000 MAC	100 (G) / 1000 MAC	Proposed. Murgatroyd et al (1995)
Cadmium	See EQS Table						
Carbon tetra-chloride	See EQS Table						

Table B2 continued . . .

Substance	Inland Waters Designated[1] fisheries Salmonid (μg/l)	Cyprinid (μg/l)	Aquatic life Hardness (mg/l CaCO₃)	Salmonid (μg/l)	Cyprinid (μg/l)	Estuary and coastal waters (μg/l)	Comments/Source
Chlorine (as HOCl)	5 (M) 95%ile at pH 6	5 (M) 95%ile at pH 6					6.8 if measured as Cl₂. Higher conc[n] allowed if pH >6.
Chloroform	See EQS Table						
Chloronitro-toluenes				10	10	10 (G)	As total of isomers 2,4-, 2,5-, 2,6-, 4,2-, 4,3-). Proposed Jerman et al (1992)
				100 MAC	100 MAC	100 (G) MAC	
Chromium[(4)(3)]			0-50 50-100 100-200 >200	5 10 20 50	150 175 200 250	15	Dissolved conc[ns]. Circular 7/89[(2)]
Copper[(4)(3)]	5 (G) 95%ile 22 (G) 95%ile 40 (G) 95%ile 112 (G) 95%ile	5 (G) 95%ile 22 (G) 95%ile 40 (G) 95%ile 112 (G) 95%ile	10 50 100 500				Dissolved conc[ns]
			0 - 50 50 - 100 100 - 250 >250	1 6 10 28	1 6 10 28	5	Dissolved conc[ns]. (95%ile values also proposed.) Circular 7/89[(2)]
Cyfluthrin	0.001 95%ile	0.001 95%ile		0.001 95%ile	0.001 95%ile	0.001 95%ile	Circular 7/89[(2)]
DDT (all isomers)	See EQS Table						
1,2-Di-chloroethane	See EQS Table						
Dichlorvos				0.001	0.001	0.04	Proposed. DoE (1991) (Also MAC values specific to marine fish farm use.)

Table B2 continued . . .

Substance	Inland Waters Designated[1] fisheries Salmonid (µg/l)	Cyprinid (µg/l)	Aquatic life Hardness (mg/l CaCO₃)	Salmonid (µg/l)	Cyprinid (µg/l)	Estuary and coastal waters (µg/l)	Comments/ Source
Dieldrin	See EQS Table						
Dissolved oxygen	>9000 (M) 50%ile >9000 (G) 50%ile >7000 (G) 100%ile	>7000 (M) 50%ile >8000 (G) 50%ile >5000 (G) 100%ile					
Dimethoate				1 (Proposed)	1 (Proposed)	1 (Proposed)	Murgatroyd et al (1994)
Endosulfan				0.003 0.3 MAC	0.003 0.3 MAC	0.003	Dissolved conc[ns]. Proposed. DoE (1991)
Endrin	See EQS Table						
Fenitrothion				0.01 0.25 MAC	0.01 0.25 MAC	0.01 0.25 MAC	Proposed. DoE (1991)
Flucofuron				1 95%ile	1 95%ile	1 95%ile	Circular 7/89[2]
Formaldehyde				5 50 MAC	5 50 MAC		Proposed. Jerman et al (1993)
Hexachloro-benzene	See EQS Table						
Hexachloro-butadiene	See EQS Table						
Hexachloro-cyclohexane (all isomers)	See EQS Table						
Ioxynil				10 100 MAC	10 100 MAC	10 (G) 100 (G) MAC	Proposed. Murgatroyd et al (1995)

Table B2 continued ...

Substance	Inland Waters Designated[1] fisheries		Aquatic life			Estuary and coastal waters (µg/l)	Comments/ Source
	Salmonid (µg/l)	Cyprinid (µg/l)	Hardness (mg/l CaCO$_3$)	Salmonid (µg/l)	Cyprinid (µg/l)		
Ioxynil				10	10	10 G	Murgatroyd et al (1995)
				100 MAC	100 MAC	100 (G) MAC	Proposed
Iron				1000	1000	1000	Dissolved conc[ns]. Circular 7/89[2]
Isodrin	See EQS Table						
Lead[3]			0-50 50-150 >150	4 10 20	50 125 250	25	Dissolved conc[ns]. Standards halved if breeding trout present. Circular 7/89[2]
Malachite green				0.5	0.5		Proposed. Burchmore et al (1993)
				100 MAC	100 MAC		
Malathion				0.01	0.01	0.02	DoE (1991)
				0.5 MAC	0.5 MAC	0.5 MAC	Proposed
Mercury	See EQS Table						
Nickel[3]			0-50 50-100 100-200 >200	50 100 150 200	50 100 150 200	30	Dissolved conc[ns]. Circular 7/89[2]
Nitrite (as N)	3 (G) 95%ile	9 (G) 95%ile					
p-p-DDT	See EQS Table						
PCSDs				0.05 95%ile	0.05 95%ile	0.05 95%ile	Circular 7/89[2]
Pentachloro-phenol & compounds	See EQS Table						
Perchloro-ethylene	See EQS Table						
Permethrin				0.01 95%ile	0.01 95%ile	0.01 95%ile	Circular 7/89[2]

Technical Guidance Notes

CUSTOMER FEEDBACK

The structure and content of Technical Guidance Notes (TGNs) have been evolving in response to internal and external consultation. It is now timely to seek feedback from users of TGNs.

Please complete the following questionnaire adding any further comments as necessary, either on a particular TGN or TGNs in general.

Completed forms should be returned to:
The Environment Agency, Government Buildings, Burghill Road, Westbury-on-Trym, Bristol BS10 6EZ.

1. Which TGN are you commenting on? _____

tick box

2. Which is your user group?

Environment Agency Inspector

Process operator or representative

Other (specify):

In answering the remaining questions please circle the appropriate letter:

a – very well, b – well, c – not very well, d – inadequately

3. Content of this TGN – how well does it:

(a) provide valid and relevant technical information

a	b	c	d

(b) assist you with understanding and applying the concepts/practices

a	b	c	d

4. Presentation of this TGN – how well is the text presented in terms of:

(a) coverage of relevant subject matter

a	b	c	d

(b) clarity of message

a	b	c	d

(c) structure and organisation

a	b	c	d

(d) balance between sections

a	b	c	d

Thank you for taking the time to complete this questionnaire. If you have any further comments to make on the subject of Technical Guidance Notes, please append them.

Table B2 continued . . .

Substance	Inland Waters					Estuary and coastal waters (µg/l)	Comments/ Source
	Designated[1] fisheries		Aquatic life				
	Salmonid (µg/l)	Cyprinid (µg/l)	Hardness (mg/l CaCO$_3$)	Salmonid (µg/l)	Cyprinid (µg/l)		
pH	>6.0 (M) 95%ile <9.0 (M) 95%ile	>6.0 (M) 95%ile <9.0 (M) 95%ile		>6.0 95%ile <9.0 95%ile	>6.0- 95%ile <9.0 95%ile	>6.0 95%ile (>7.0 for shellfish) <8.5 95%ile	Also artificial variations should not exceed 0.5 pH units. Circular 7/89[2]
Phosphorus (as P)	65 (G) MAC	130 (G) MAC					Limit values to reduce eutrophication
Simazine (+ atrazine)				2 10 MAC	2 10 MAC	2 10 MAC	Dissolved conc[ns] and combined with atrazine. Proposed. DoE (1991)
Sulcofuron				25 95%ile	25 95%ile	2.5 95%ile	Circular 7/89[2]
Suspended solids	25 000 (G)	25 000 (G)					
Temperature	δT < 1.5°C (M) 98%ile T < 21.5°C (M) 98%ile	δT < 3.0°C (M) 98%ile T < 28.0°C (M) 98%ile					Also T < 10.0°C during breeding season of fish species needing cold water for reproduction (98%ile).
Tecnazene				1 10 MAC	1 10 MAC	1 10 MAC	Proposed. Murgatroyd et al (1993)
Tin (inorganic)				25	25	10	Proposed. Mance et al (1988)
Toluene				50 500 MAC	50 500 MAC	40 400 MAC	Proposed. Jones et al (1992)
Tributyl tin				0.02 MAC	0.02 MAC	0.002 MAC	Circular 7/89[2]
Trichloro-benzenes (all isomers)	See EQS Table						

Table B2 continued . . .

Substance	Inland Waters Designated[1] fisheries Salmonid (μg/l)	Cyprinid (μg/l)	Aquatic life Hardness (mg/l CaCO₃)	Salmonid (μg/l)	Cyprinid (μg/l)	Estuary and coastal waters (μg/l)	Comments/ Source
1,1,1-Tri-chloroethane				100 / 1000 MAC	100 / 1000 MAC	100 (G) / 1000 (G) MAC	Proposed. Rees et al (1992)
Trichloroethylene	See EQS Table						
Trifluralin				0.1 dissolved / 1 MAC dissolved 20 MAC	0.1 dissolved / 1 MAC dissolved 20 MAC	0.1 dissolved / 20 MAC	Proposed. DoE (1991)
Triphenyl tin				0.02 MAC	0.02 MAC	0.008 MAC	Circular 7/89[2]
Vanadium			0-200 / >200	20 / 60	20 / 60	100	Circular 7/89[2]
Zinc[3]	30 (M) 95%ile / 200 (M) 95%ile / 300 (M) 95%ile / 500 (M) 95%ile	300 (M) 95%ile / 700 (M) 95%ile / 1000 (M) 95%ile / 2000 (M) 95%ile	0 - 50 / 50 - 100 / 100 - 250 / >250	8 / 50 / 75 / 125	75 / 175 / 250 / 500	40 dissolved	(95%ile values also proposed.) Circular 7/89[2]

Notes:

(1) Directive on the quality of freshwaters needing protection or improvement in order to support freshwater fish life. 18th July 1978 (78/659/EEC). Official Journal **L222**, 14th August, 1978)

(2) Department of the Environment and Welsh Office. Water and the Environment Circular 7/89 (Circular 16/89 Welsh Office), 30th March 1989

(3) EQS values for these substances are currently under review by the DoE. The EALs presented here are based on EQS values laid down in Circular 7/89[2]

MAC   Maximum Allowable Concentration

(G)   Guideline value (for those figures in 'Designated Fisheries' columns, applies only to those waters designated under the Directive[1])

(M)   Mandatory value (for those figures in 'Designated Fisheries' columns, applies only to those waters designated under the Directive[1])

ANNEX C Environmental Assessment Levels for releases to land (via deposition)

Table C1:
Maximum deposition rates for pollutants released to land (via deposition)

Substance	Soil Quality Criteria	Median soil conc. (mg/kg)	Assumed half-life (days)	Max Rate Deposition (mg/m²/d)
Arsenic	50 [2]	–	–	0.02 [9]
Atrazine	3 [3a]	–	358 [5]	0.44
Barium	413 [3a]	121 [4]	–	1.2
Benzene	0.53 [3a]	–	11 [5]	2.5
Cadmium	3 [1]	0.7 [4]	–	0.009
Carbaryl	2.5 [3b]	–	13 [6]	10
Carbofuran	1 [3b]	–	45 [7]	1.2
Chlorobenzenes (total mono, di, tri, tetra, penta & hexa)	15 [3b]	–	570 [5]	1.4
Chloronaphthalene	5 [3b]	–	63 [8]	4.1
Chlorophenols (total mono, di, tri, tetra and penta)	5 [3b]	–	38 [5] [6] nominal	6.8
Chromium	400 [2]	39.3 [4]	–	1.5
Cobalt	130 [3a]	9.8 [4]	–	0.49
Copper	80 [1]	18.1 [4]	–	0.25
Cresols (total)	2.5 [3b]	–	200 [6]	0.66
Cyanide (free)	11 [3a]	–	–	0.045
Cyanide (complex) pH≥5	28 [3a]	–	–	0.12
pH<5	328 [3a]	–	–	1.3
Thiocyanates	10 [3b]	–	–	0.041
DDD/DDE/DDT (total)	2 [3a]	–	365 nominal	0.28
Dichloromethane	10 [3b]	–	97 [6]	5.4
Drins (total aldrin, dieldrin, endrin, isodrin)	2 [3b]	–	2237 [5]	0.046
Ethyl benzene	25 [3a]	–	7 [5]	186
Fluoride	500 [2]	–	–	2.1
HCH compounds (alpha, beta, delta & gamma isomers)	1 [3b]	–	365 [6] nominal	0.14
Lead	300 [1]	40 [4]	–	1.1
Maneb	18 [3b]	–	25 [7]	37
Mercury	1 [1]	–	–	0.004
Molybdenum	4 [2]	–	–	0.016
Nickel	50 [1]	22.6 [4]	–	0.11
PAHs (total anthracene, benzo(a)anthracene, benzo(k)fluoranthene, benzo(a)pyrene, chrysene, phenanthrene, fluoranthene, indeno(1,2,3-cd)pyrene, naphthalene, benzo(ghi)perylene)	21 [3a]	–	280 [5]	3.9
PCBs (total PCBs 28, 52, 101, 118, 138, 153, 180)	0.51 [3a]	–	3650 nominal	0.007

Table C1 continued . . .

Substance	Soil Quality Criteria	Median soil conc. (mg/kg)	Assumed half-life (days)	Max Rate Deposition (mg/m²/d)
Phenol	20 [3a]	–	4 [5] [6]	260
Phthalates (total)	30 [3a]	–	100 [6] nominal	16
Pyridine	0.55 [3a]	–	42 [5]	0.68
Selenium	3 [2]	–	–	0.012
Styrene	50 [3a]	–	56 [5]	46
Toluene	65 [3a]	–	13 [5]	260
Trichloroethylene	30 [3a]	–	100 [5] [8] nominal	16
Xylene	13 [3a]	–	18 [5]	38
Zinc	200 [1]	82 [4]	–	0.48

Notes:

[1] The Sludge (Use in Agriculture) Regulations. Statutory Instrument No.1263 HMSO London, 1989

[2] Code of Practice for Agricultural Use of Sewage Sludge, Department of the Environment HMSO, London, 1989

[3] Circular on Intervention Values for Soil Remediation. Ministry of Housing, Spatial Planning and Environment, The Hague, NL, ref. DBO/07494013, 9 May 1994
   a Soil quality criteria derived from: 0.5x(intervention value + target value)
   b Soil quality criteria derived from: 0.5x(intervention value)

[4] McGrath SP and Loveland PJ (1992) The Soil Geochemical Atlas of England and Wales. Blackie Academic & Professional, London

[5] Thanigasalam P, Loveland PJ and Thompson TRE (1994) Soil Chemical Quality Database and Classification Soil Survey and Land Research Centre report to Her Majesty's Inspectorate of Pollution
   Report No. DoE/HMIP/RR/94/018

[6] World Health Organization, International Programme on Chemical Safety, Environmental Health Criteria numbers: 71 Pentachlorophenol; 93 Chlorophenols other than pentachlorophenol; 131 Diethylhexyl phthalate; 153 Carbaryl; 161 Phenol; 168 Cresols; Di-n-butyl phthalate (draft); Lindane (draft); Methylene chloride (draft).

[7] The Pesticide Manual. Incorporating the Agrochemicals Handbook. 10th Edition, British Crop Protection Council and Royal Society of Chemistry

[8] Department of the Environment (Toxic Substances Division, Directorate for Air, Climate and Toxic Substances), Environmental Hazard Assessment: Di-(2-ethylhexyl)phthalate; Halogenated naphthalenes; Trichloroethylene

[9] Value proposed by MAFF (pers. comm. 1996) to protect consumers against accumulation in agricultural foodstuffs

[10] Mean half-lives based on data from cited sources. Nominal half-lives used where data are inadequate

ANNEX D 'Significant' release rates for pollutant releases to air, water and land (via deposition) from prescribed processes

Table D1:
Significant release rates for pollutants released to air and land (via deposition)

Substance	Test	Release Rate[a] (g/s) for Stack Height (m)								
		0	10	20	30	50	70	100	150	200
Acetic acid	Air	1.82e-3	1.64e-2	3.70e-2	9.14e-2	2.74e-1	5.48e-1	1.19	2.64	4.93
	Land	–	–	–	–	–	–	–	–	–
Acetic anhydride	Air	9.83e-4	8.89e-3	2.00e-2	4.94e-2	1.48e-1	2.96e-1	6.45e-1	1.43	2.67
	Land	–	–	–	–	–	–	–	–	–
Acetone	Air	1.75e-1	1.58	3.56	8.79	2.64e+1	5.27e+1	1.15e+2	2.54e+2	4.75e+2
	Land	–	–	–	–	–	–	–	–	–
Acetonitrile	Air	5.16e-3	4.67e-2	1.05e-1	2.59e-1	7.78e-1	1.56	3.39	7.50	1.40e+1
	Land	–	–	–	–	–	–	–	–	–
o-Acetylsalicylic acid	Air	7.37e-4	6.67e-3	1.50e-2	3.70e-2	1.11e-1	2.22e-1	4.84e-1	1.07	2.00
	Land	–	–	–	–	–	–	–	–	–
Acrylaldehyde	Air	8.33e-5	3.33e-4	1.85e-3	5.56e-3	1.85e-2	4.55e-2	1.14e-1	3.33e-1	7.69e-1
	Land	–	–	–	–	–	–	–	–	–
Acrylamide	Air	8.85e-6	8.00e-5	1.80e-4	4.44e-4	1.33e-3	2.67e-3	5.81e-3	1.29e-2	2.40e-2
	Land	–	–	–	–	–	–	–	–	–
Acrylic acid	Air	2.95e-3	2.67e-2	6.00e-2	1.48e-1	4.44e-1	8.89e-1	1.94	4.29	8.00
	Land	–	–	–	–	–	–	–	–	–
Acrylonitrile	Air	1.18e-4	1.07e-3	2.40e-3	5.93e-3	1.78e-2	3.56e-2	7.74e-2	1.71e-1	3.20e-1
	Land	–	–	–	–	–	–	–	–	–

Table D1 continued . . .

Substance	Test	Release Rate[a] (g/s) for Stack Height (m)								
		0	10	20	30	50	70	100	150	200
Aldrin (ISO)	Air	3.69e-5	3.33e-4	7.50e-4	1.85e-3	5.56e-3	1.11e-2	2.42e-2	5.36e-2	1.00e-1
	Land	–	–	–	–	–	–	–	–	–
Allyl alcohol	Air	4.91e-4	4.44e-3	1.00e-2	2.47e-2	7.41e-2	1.48e-1	3.23e-1	7.14e-1	1.33
	Land	–	–	–	–	–	–	–	–	–
Allyl-2,3-epoxypropyl ether	Air	2.16e-3	1.96e-2	4.40e-2	1.09e-1	3.26e-1	6.52e-1	1.42	3.14	5.87
	Land	–	–	–	–	–	–	–	–	–
Aluminium alkyl compounds	Air	2.95e-4	2.67e-3	6.00e-3	1.48e-2	4.44e-2	8.89e-2	1.94e-1	4.29e-1	8.00e-1
	Land	–	–	–	–	–	–	–	–	–
Aluminium and compounds (as Al)	Air	2.95e-4	2.67e-3	6.00e-3	1.48e-2	4.44e-2	8.89e-2	1.94e-1	4.29e-1	8.00e-1
	Land	–	–	–	–	–	–	–	–	–
2-Aminoethanol	Air	7.37e-4	6.67e-3	1.50e-2	3.70e-2	1.11e-1	2.22e-1	4.84e-1	1.07	2.00
	Land	–	–	–	–	–	–	–	–	–
Ammonia	Air	1.18e-3	1.07e-2	2.40e-2	5.93e-2	1.78e-1	3.56e-1	7.74e-1	1.71	3.20
	Land	–	–	–	–	–	–	–	–	–
Ammonium sulphamidate	Air	9.83e-4	8.89e-3	2.00e-2	4.94e-2	1.48e-1	2.96e-1	6.45e-1	1.43	2.67
	Land	–	–	–	–	–	–	–	–	–
Anisidines, o- and p- isomers	Air	7.37e-5	6.67e-4	1.50e-3	3.70e-3	1.11e-2	2.22e-2	4.84e-2	1.07e-1	2.00e-1
	Land	–	–	–	–	–	–	–	–	–
Antimony and compounds (as Sb) except antimony trisulphide and antimony trioxide	Air	7.37e-5	6.67e-4	1.50e-3	3.70e-3	1.11e-2	2.22e-2	4.84e-2	1.07e-1	2.00e-1
	Land	–	–	–	–	–	–	–	–	–

Table D1 continued . . .

Substance	Test	Release Rate[a] (g/s) for Stack Height (m)								
		0	10	20	30	50	70	100	150	200
Arsenic and compounds (as As)	Air	2.95e-6	2.67e-5	6.00e-5	1.48e-4	4.44e-4	8.89e-4	1.94e-3	4.29e-3	8.00e-3
	Land	2.57e-7	1.03e-6	5.72e-6	1.71e-5	5.72e-5	1.40e-4	3.51e-4	1.03e-3	2.37e-3
Arsine	Air	2.95e-5	2.67e-4	6.00e-4	1.48e-3	4.44e-3	8.89e-3	1.94e-2	4.29e-2	8.00e-2
	Land	–	–	–	–	–	–	–	–	–
Atrazine	Air	–	–	–	–	–	–	–	–	–
	Land	5.66e-6	2.26e-5	1.26e-4	3.77e-4	1.26e-3	3.09e-3	7.72e-3	2.26e-2	5.22e-2
Azinphos-methyl (ISO)	Air	6.67e-5	2.67e-4	1.48e-3	4.44e-3	1.48e-2	3.64e-2	9.09e-2	2.67e-1	6.15e-1
	Land	–	–	–	–	–	–	–	–	–
γ-BHC (ISO)	Air	7.37e-5	6.67e-4	1.50e-3	3.70e-3	1.11e-2	2.22e-2	4.84e-2	1.07e-1	2.00e-1
	Land	–	–	–	–	–	–	–	–	–
Barium and its compounds, soluble (as Ba)	Air	7.37e-5	6.67e-4	1.50e-3	3.70e-3	1.11e-2	2.22e-2	4.84e-2	1.07e-1	2.00e-1
	Land	1.54e-5	6.17e-5	3.43e-4	1.03e-3	3.43e-3	8.42e-3	2.10e-2	6.17e-2	1.42e-1
Benomyl (ISO)	Air	7.37e-4	6.67e-3	1.50e-2	3.70e-2	1.11e-1	2.22e-1	4.84e-1	1.07	2.00
	Land	–	–	–	–	–	–	–	–	–
Benzene	Air	4.72e-4	4.27e-3	9.60e-3	2.37e-2	7.11e-2	1.42e-1	3.10e-1	6.86e-1	1.28
	Land	3.22e-5	1.29e-4	7.14e-4	2.14e-3	7.14e-3	1.75e-2	4.38e-2	1.29e-1	2.97e-1
Benzenethiol	Air	2.95e-4	2.67e-3	6.00e-3	1.48e-2	4.44e-2	8.89e-2	1.94e-1	4.29e-1	8.00e-1
	Land	–	–	–	–	–	–	–	–	–
Benzene-1,2,4-tricarboxylic acid, 1,2-anhydride	Air	5.90e-6	5.33e-5	1.20e-4	2.96e-4	8.89e-4	1.78e-3	3.87e-3	8.57e-3	1.60e-2
	Land	–	–	–	–	–	–	–	–	–
p-Benzoquinone	Air	5.90e-5	5.33e-4	1.20e-3	2.96e-3	8.89e-3	1.78e-2	3.87e-2	8.57e-2	1.60e-1
	Land	–	–	–	–	–	–	–	–	–

Table D1 continued . . .

Substance	Test	Release Rate[a] (g/s) for Stack Height (m)								
		0	10	20	30	50	70	100	150	200
Benzyl butyl phthalate	Air	7.37e-4	6.67e-3	1.50e-2	3.70e-2	1.11e-1	2.22e-1	4.84e-1	1.07	2.00
	Land	–	–	–	–	–	–	–	–	–
Beryllium and compounds (as Be)	Air	5.90e-8	5.33e-7	1.20e-6	2.96e-6	8.89e-6	1.78e-5	3.87e-5	8.57e-5	1.60e-4
	Land	–	–	–	–	–	–	–	–	–
Biphenyl	Air	1.97e-4	1.78e-3	4.00e-3	9.88e-3	2.96e-2	5.93e-2	1.29e-1	2.86e-1	5.33e-1
	Land	–	–	–	–	–	–	–	–	–
Bis(chloromethyl) ether	Air	1.47e-7	1.33e-6	3.00e-6	7.41e-6	2.22e-5	4.44e-5	9.68e-5	2.14e-4	4.00e-4
	Land	–	–	–	–	–	–	–	–	–
Bis(2,3-epoxypropyl) ether	Air	8.85e-5	8.00e-4	1.80e-3	4.44e-3	1.33e-2	2.67e-2	5.81e-2	1.29e-1	2.40e-1
	Land	–	–	–	–	–	–	–	–	–
Bis(2-ethylhexyl) phthalate	Air	4.91e-4	4.44e-3	1.00e-2	2.47e-2	7.41e-2	1.48e-1	3.23e-1	7.14e-1	1.33
	Land	–	–	–	–	–	–	–	–	–
Bornan-2-one	Air	8.85e-4	8.00e-3	1.80e-2	4.44e-2	1.33e-1	2.67e-1	5.81e-1	1.29	2.40
	Land	–	–	–	–	–	–	–	–	–
Boron tribromide	Air	4.91e-4	4.44e-3	1.00e-2	2.47e-2	7.41e-2	1.48e-1	3.23e-1	7.14e-1	1.33
	Land	–	–	–	–	–	–	–	–	–
Boron trifluoride	Air	1.47e-4	1.33e-3	3.00e-3	7.41e-3	2.22e-2	4.44e-2	9.68e-2	2.14e-1	4.00e-1
	Land	–	–	–	–	–	–	–	–	–
Bromacil (ISO)	Air	9.83e-4	8.89e-3	2.00e-2	4.94e-2	1.48e-1	2.96e-1	6.45e-1	1.43	2.67
	Land	–	–	–	–	–	–	–	–	–
Bromine	Air	9.83e-5	8.89e-4	2.00e-3	4.94e-3	1.48e-2	2.96e-2	6.45e-2	1.43e-1	2.67e-1
	Land	–	–	–	–	–	–	–	–	–

Table D1 continued . . . .

Substance	Test	Release Rate[a] (g/s) for Stack Height (m)								
		0	10	20	30	50	70	100	150	200
Bromine pentafluoride	Air	9.83e-5	8.89e-4	2.00e-3	4.94e-3	1.48e-2	2.96e-2	6.45e-2	1.43e-1	2.67e-1
	Land	–	–	–	–	–	–	–	–	–
Bromochloromethane	Air	6.39e-2	5.78e-1	1.30	3.21	9.63	1.93e+1	4.19e+1	9.29e+1	1.73e+2
	Land	–	–	–	–	–	–	–	–	–
Bromoethane	Air	5.45e-2	4.93e-1	1.11	2.74	8.22	1.64e+1	3.58e+1	7.93e+1	1.48e+2
	Land	–	–	–	–	–	–	–	–	–
Bromoform	Air	7.37e-4	6.67e-3	1.50e-2	3.70e-2	1.11e-1	2.22e-1	4.84e-1	1.07	2.00
	Land	–	–	–	–	–	–	–	–	–
Bromomethane	Air	2.95e-3	2.67e-2	6.00e-2	1.48e-1	4.44e-1	8.89e-1	1.94	4.29	8.00
	Land	–	–	–	–	–	–	–	–	–
Bromotrifluoro-methane	Air	3.59e-1	3.24	7.30	1.80e+1	5.41e+1	1.08e+2	2.35e+2	5.21e+2	9.73e+2
	Land	–	–	–	–	–	–	–	–	–
Buta-1,3-diene	Air	6.49e-4	5.87e-3	1.32e-2	3.26e-2	9.78e-2	1.96e-1	4.26e-1	9.43e-1	1.76
	Land	–	–	–	–	–	–	–	–	–
Butane	Air	8.75e-2	7.91e-1	1.78	4.40	1.32e+1	2.64e+1	5.74e+1	1.27e+2	2.37e+2
	Land	–	–	–	–	–	–	–	–	–
Butan-1-ol	Air	7.37e-3	6.67e-2	1.50e-1	3.70e-1	1.11	2.22	4.84	1.07e+1	2.00e+1
	Land	–	–	–	–	–	–	–	–	–
Butan-2-ol	Air	2.21e-2	2.00e-1	4.50e-1	1.11	3.33	6.67	1.45e+1	3.21e+1	6.00e+1
	Land	–	–	–	–	–	–	–	–	–
Butan-2-one	Air	4.42e-2	4.00e-1	9.00e-1	2.22	6.67	1.33e+1	2.90e+1	6.43e+1	1.20e+2
	Land	–	–	–	–	–	–	–	–	–

Technical Guidance Note (Environmental) E1 Volume II

Table D1 continued . . .

Substance	Test	Release Rate[a] (g/s) for Stack Height (m)								
		0	10	20	30	50	70	100	150	200
2-Butoxyethanol	Air	3.54e-3	3.20e-2	7.20e-2	1.78e-1	5.33e-1	1.07	2.32	5.14	9.60
	Land	–	–	–	–	–	–	–	–	–
Butyl acetate	Air	4.67e-2	4.22e-1	9.50e-1	2.35	7.04	1.41e+1	3.06e+1	6.79e+1	1.27e+2
	Land	–	–	–	–	–	–	–	–	–
sec-Butyl acetate	Air	5.85e-2	5.29e-1	1.19	2.94	8.81	1.76e+1	3.84e+1	8.50e+1	1.59e+2
	Land	–	–	–	–	–	–	–	–	–
tert-Butyl acetate	Air	5.85e-2	5.29e-1	1.19	2.94	8.81	1.76e+1	3.84e+1	8.50e+1	1.59e+2
	Land	–	–	–	–	–	–	–	–	–
Butyl acrylate	Air	8.11e-3	7.33e-2	1.65e-1	4.07e-1	1.22	2.44	5.32	1.18e+1	2.20e+1
	Land	–	–	–	–	–	–	–	–	–
n-Butylamine	Air	7.37e-4	6.67e-3	1.50e-2	3.70e-2	1.11e-1	2.22e-1	4.84e-1	1.07	2.00
	Land	–	–	–	–	–	–	–	–	–
n-Butyl chloroformate	Air	8.26e-4	7.47e-3	1.68e-2	4.15e-2	1.24e-1	2.49e-1	5.42e-1	1.20	2.24
	Land	–	–	–	–	–	–	–	–	–
n-Butyl glycidyl ether	Air	1.99e-2	1.80e-1	4.05e-1	1.00	3.00	6.00	1.31e+1	2.89e+1	5.40e+1
	Land	–	–	–	–	–	–	–	–	–
Butyl lactate	Air	3.69e-3	3.33e-2	7.50e-2	1.85e-1	5.56e-1	1.11	2.42	5.36	1.00e+1
	Land	–	–	–	–	–	–	–	–	–
2-sec-Butylphenol	Air	4.42e-3	4.00e-2	9.00e-2	2.22e-1	6.67e-1	1.33	2.90	6.43	1.20e+1
	Land	–	–	–	–	–	–	–	–	–
Cadmium and compounds (except CdO fume, CdS, CdS pigments) (as Cd)	Air	7.37e-7	6.67e-6	1.50e-5	3.70e-5	1.11e-4	2.22e-4	4.84e-4	1.07e-3	2.00e-3
	Land	1.16e-7	4.63e-7	2.57e-6	7.72e-6	2.57e-5	6.31e-5	1.58e-4	4.63e-4	1.07e-3

Table D1 continued . . .

Substance	Test	Release Rate[a] (g/s) for Stack Height (m)								
		0	10	20	30	50	70	100	150	200
Caesium hydroxide	Air	2.95e-4	2.67e-3	6.00e-3	1.48e-2	4.44e-2	8.89e-2	1.94e-1	4.29e-1	8.00e-1
	Land	–	–	–	–	–	–	–	–	–
Calcium cyanamide	Air	4.91e-5	4.44e-4	1.00e-3	2.47e-3	7.41e-3	1.48e-2	3.23e-2	7.14e-2	1.33e-1
	Land	–	–	–	–	–	–	–	–	–
Calcium hydroxide	Air	7.37e-4	6.67e-3	1.50e-2	3.70e-2	1.11e-1	2.22e-1	4.84e-1	1.07	2.00
	Land	–	–	–	–	–	–	–	–	–
Calcium oxide	Air	2.95e-4	2.67e-3	6.00e-3	1.48e-2	4.44e-2	8.89e-2	1.94e-1	4.29e-1	8.00e-1
	Land	–	–	–	–	–	–	–	–	–
Captafol (ISO)	Air	1.47e-5	1.33e-4	3.00e-4	7.41e-4	2.22e-3	4.44e-3	9.68e-3	2.14e-2	4.00e-2
	Land	–	–	–	–	–	–	–	–	–
Captan (ISO)	Air	7.37e-4	6.67e-3	1.50e-2	3.70e-2	1.11e-1	2.22e-1	4.84e-1	1.07	2.00
	Land	–	–	–	–	–	–	–	–	–
Carbaryl (ISO)	Air	4.91e-4	4.44e-3	1.00e-2	2.47e-2	7.41e-2	1.48e-1	3.23e-1	7.14e-1	1.33
	Land	1.29e-4	5.14e-4	2.86e-3	8.57e-3	2.86e-2	7.01e-2	1.75e-1	5.14e-1	1.19
Carbofuran (ISO)	Air	1.47e-5	1.33e-4	3.00e-4	7.41e-4	2.22e-3	4.44e-3	9.68e-3	2.14e-2	4.00e-2
	Land	1.54e-5	6.17e-5	3.43e-4	1.03e-3	3.43e-3	8.42e-3	2.10e-2	6.17e-2	1.42e-1
Carbon black	Air	3.44e-4	3.11e-3	7.00e-3	1.73e-2	5.19e-2	1.04e-1	2.26e-1	5.00e-1	9.33e-1
	Land	–	–	–	–	–	–	–	–	–
Carbon disulphide	Air	4.91e-5	4.44e-4	1.00e-3	2.47e-3	7.41e-3	1.48e-2	3.23e-2	7.14e-2	1.33e-1
	Land	–	–	–	–	–	–	–	–	–
Carbon monoxide	Air	1.42e-2	1.23e-2	2.9e-1	7.16e-1	2.15	4.30	9.35	2.07e+1	4.83e+1
	Land	–	–	–	–	–	–	–	–	–

Table D1 continued . . .

Substance	Test	Release Rate[a] (g/s) for Stack Height (m)								
		0	10	20	30	50	70	100	150	200
Carbon tetrabromide	Air	1.97e-4	1.78e-3	4.00e-3	9.88e-3	2.96e-2	5.93e-2	1.29e-1	2.86e-1	5.33e-1
	Land	–	–	–	–	–	–	–	–	–
Carbon tetrachloride	Air	1.86e-3	1.68e-2	3.78e-2	9.33e-2	2.80e-1	5.60e-1	1.22	2.70	5.04
	Land	–	–	–	–	–	–	–	–	–
Chlorine	Air	1.47e-4	1.33e-3	3.00e-3	7.41e-3	2.22e-2	4.44e-2	9.68e-2	2.14e-1	4.00e-1
	Land	–	–	–	–	–	–	–	–	–
Chlorine dioxide	Air	4.42e-5	4.00e-4	9.00e-4	2.22e-3	6.67e-3	1.33e-2	2.90e-2	6.43e-2	1.20e-1
	Land	–	–	–	–	–	–	–	–	–
Chlorine trifluoride	Air	1.97e-5	1.78e-4	4.00e-4	9.88e-4	2.96e-3	5.93e-3	1.29e-2	2.86e-2	5.33e-2
	Land	–	–	–	–	–	–	–	–	–
Chloroacetaldehyde	Air	1.47e-4	1.33e-3	3.00e-3	7.41e-3	2.22e-2	4.44e-2	9.68e-2	2.14e-1	4.00e-1
	Land	–	–	–	–	–	–	–	–	–
2-Chloroacetophenone	Air	4.42e-5	4.00e-4	9.00e-4	2.22e-3	6.67e-3	1.33e-2	2.90e-2	6.43e-2	1.20e-1
	Land	–	–	–	–	–	–	–	–	–
Chlorobenzene	Air	3.39e-2	3.07e-1	6.90e-1	1.70	5.11	1.02e+1	2.23e+1	4.93e+1	9.20e+1
	Land	–	–	–	–	–	–	–	–	–
Chlorobenzenes (total mono, di, tri, tetra, penta and hexa)	Air	–	–	–	–	–	–	–	–	–
	Land	1.80e-5	7.20e-5	4.00e-4	1.20e-3	4.00e-3	9.82e-3	2.46e-2	7.20e-2	1.66e-1
2-Chlorobuta-1,3-diene	Air	5.31e-3	4.80e-2	1.08e-1	2.67e-1	8.00e-1	1.60	3.48	7.71	1.44e+1
	Land	–	–	–	–	–	–	–	–	–
Chlorodifluoromethane	Air	5.16e-1	4.67	1.05e+1	2.59e+1	7.78e+1	1.56e+2	3.39e+2	7.50e+2	1.40e+3
	Land	–	–	–	–	–	–	–	–	–

Table D1 continued . . .

Substance	Test	Release Rate[a] (g/s) for Stack Height (m)								
		0	10	20	30	50	70	100	150	200
1-Chloro-2,3-epoxy-propane	Air	5.90e-5	5.33e-4	1.20e-3	2.96e-3	8.89e-3	1.78e-2	3.87e-2	8.57e-2	1.60e-1
	Land	–	–	–	–	–	–	–	–	–
Chloroethane	Air	1.60e-1	1.44	3.25	8.02	2.41e+1	4.81e+1	1.05e+2	2.32e+2	4.33e+2
	Land	–	–	–	–	–	–	–	–	–
2-Chloroethanol	Air	1.47e-4	1.33e-3	3.00e-3	7.41e-3	2.22e-2	4.44e-2	9.68e-2	2.14e-1	4.00e-1
	Land	–	–	–	–	–	–	–	–	–
Chloroform	Air	1.44e-3	1.31e-2	2.94e-2	7.26e-2	2.18e-1	4.36e-1	9.48e-1	2.10	3.92
	Land	–	–	–	–	–	–	–	–	–
Chloromethane	Air	1.03e-2	9.33e-2	2.10e-1	5.19e-1	1.56	3.11	6.77	1.50e+1	2.80e+1
	Land	–	–	–	–	–	–	–	–	–
Chloronaphthalene	Air	–	–	–	–	–	–	–	–	–
	Land	5.27e-5	2.11e-4	1.17e-3	3.52e-3	1.17e-2	2.88e-2	7.19e-2	2.11e-1	4.87e-1
1-Chloro-4-nitro-benzene	Air	9.83e-5	8.89e-4	2.00e-3	4.94e-3	1.48e-2	2.96e-2	6.45e-2	1.43e-1	2.67e-1
	Land	–	–	–	–	–	–	–	–	–
Chloropentafluoro-ethane	Air	9.32e-1	8.43	1.90e+1	4.68e+1	1.40e+2	2.81e+2	6.12e+2	1.35e+3	2.53e+3
	Land	–	–	–	–	–	–	–	–	–
Chlorophenols (total mono, di, tri, tetra, penta and hexa)	Air	–	–	–	–	–	–	–	–	–
	Land	8.74e-5	3.50e-4	1.94e-3	5.83e-3	1.94e-2	4.77e-2	1.19e-1	3.50e-1	8.07e-1
Chlorosulphonic acid	Air	1.47e-4	1.33e-3	3.00e-3	7.41e-3	2.22e-2	4.44e-2	9.68e-2	2.14e-1	4.00e-1
	Land	–	–	–	–	–	–	–	–	–
2-Chlorotoluene	Air	3.69e-2	3.33e-1	7.50e-1	1.85	5.56	1.11e+1	2.42e+1	5.36e+1	1.00e+2
	Land	–	–	–	–	–	–	–	–	–

Table D1 continued . . . .

Substance	Test	Release Rate[a] (g/s) for Stack Height (m)								
		0	10	20	30	50	70	100	150	200
2-Chloro-6-(trichloromethyl)pyridine	Air	9.83e-4	8.89e-3	2.00e-2	4.94e-2	1.48e-1	2.96e-1	6.45e-1	1.43	2.67
	Land	–	–	–	–	–	–	–	–	–
Chlorpyrifos (ISO)	Air	2.95e-5	2.67e-4	6.00e-4	1.48e-3	4.44e-3	8.89e-3	1.94e-2	4.29e-2	8.00e-2
	Land	–	–	–	–	–	–	–	–	–
Chromium, chromium (II) compounds and chromium (III) compounds (as Cr)	Air	7.37e-5	6.67e-4	1.50e-3	3.70e-3	1.11e-2	2.22e-2	4.84e-2	1.07e-1	2.00e-1
	Land	1.93e-5	7.72e-5	4.29e-4	1.29e-3	4.29e-3	1.05e-2	2.63e-2	7.72e-2	1.78e-1
Chromium (VI) compounds (as Cr)	Air	1.47e-6	1.33e-5	3.00e-5	7.41e-5	2.22e-4	4.44e-4	9.68e-4	2.14e-3	4.00e-3
	Land	–	–	–	–	–	–	–	–	–
Cobalt and compounds (as Co)	Air	2.95e-6	2.67e-5	6.00e-5	1.48e-4	4.44e-4	8.89e-4	1.94e-3	4.29e-3	8.00e-3
	Land	6.30e-6	2.52e-5	1.40e-4	4.20e-4	1.40e-3	3.44e-3	8.59e-3	2.52e-2	5.82e-2
Copper	Air	9.83e-5	8.89e-4	2.00e-3	4.94e-3	1.48e-2	2.96e-2	6.45e-2	1.43e-1	2.67e-1
	Land	3.22e-6	1.29e-5	7.14e-5	2.14e-4	7.14e-4	1.75e-3	4.38e-3	1.29e-2	2.97e-2
Cresols, all isomers[b]	Air	3.24e-3	2.93e-2	6.60e-2	1.63e-1	4.89e-1	9.78e-1	2.13	4.71	8.80
	Land	8.49e-6	3.40e-5	1.89e-4	5.66e-4	1.89e-3	4.63e-3	1.16e-2	3.40e-2	7.83e-2
Cryofluorane (INN)	Air	4.30e-1	3.89	8.75	2.16e+1	6.48e+1	1.30e+2	2.82e+2	6.25e+2	1.17e+3
	Land	–	–	–	–	–	–	–	–	–
Cumene	Air	4.00e-2	1.60e-1	8.89e-1	2.67	8.89	2.18e+1	5.45e+1	1.60e+2	3.69e+2
	Land	–	–	–	–	–	–	–	–	–
Cyanamide	Air	2.95e-4	2.67e-3	6.00e-3	1.48e-2	4.44e-2	8.89e-2	1.94e-1	4.29e-1	8.00e-1
	Land	–	–	–	–	–	–	–	–	–
Cyanide (free)	Air	–	–	–	–	–	–	–	–	–
	Land	5.79e-7	2.31e-6	1.29e-5	3.86e-5	1.29e-4	3.16e-4	7.89e-4	2.31e-3	5.34e-3

Table D1 continued . . .

Substance	Test	Release Rate[a] (g/s) for Stack Height (m)								
		0	10	20	30	50	70	100	150	200
Cyanide (complex) pH≥5	Air	–	–	–	–	–	–	–	–	–
	Land	1.54e-6	6.17e-6	3.43e-5	1.03e-4	3.43e-4	8.42e-4	2.10e-3	6.17e-3	1.42e-2
Cyanide (complex) pH<5	Air	–	–	–	–	–	–	–	–	–
	Land	1.67e-5	6.69e-5	3.72e-4	1.11e-3	3.72e-3	9.12e-3	2.28e-2	6.69e-2	1.54e-1
Cyanides, except HCN, cyanogen and cyanogen chloride (as CN)	Air	7.37e-4	6.67e-3	1.50e-2	3.70e-2	1.11e-1	2.22e-1	4.84e-1	1.07	2.00
	Land	–	–	–	–	–	–	–	–	–
Cyanogen chloride	Air	2.95e-5	2.67e-4	6.00e-4	1.48e-3	4.44e-3	8.89e-3	1.94e-2	4.29e-2	8.00e-2
	Land	–	–	–	–	–	–	–	–	–
Cyclohexane	Air	1.13e-1	4.53e-1	2.52	7.56	2.52e+1	6.18e+1	1.55e+2	4.53e+2	1.05e+3
	Land	–	–	–	–	–	–	–	–	–
Cyclohexanol	Air	2.95e-2	2.67e-1	6.00e-1	1.48	4.44	8.89	1.94e+1	4.29e+1	8.00e+1
	Land	–	–	–	–	–	–	–	–	–
Cyclohexanone	Air	3.33e-2	1.33e-1	7.41e-1	2.22	7.41	1.82e+1	4.55e+1	1.33e+2	3.08e+2
	Land	–	–	–	–	–	–	–	–	–
Cyclohexene	Air	1.50e-1	1.35	3.05	7.52	2.26e+1	4.51e+1	9.82e+1	2.18e+2	4.06e+2
	Land	–	–	–	–	–	–	–	–	–
Cyclohexylamine	Air	5.90e-3	5.33e-2	1.20e-1	2.96e-1	8.89e-1	1.78	3.87	8.57	1.60e+1
	Land	–	–	–	–	–	–	–	–	–
Cyhexatin (ISO)	Air	4.91e-4	4.44e-3	1.00e-2	2.47e-2	7.41e-2	1.48e-1	3.23e-1	7.14e-1	1.33
	Land	–	–	–	–	–	–	–	–	–
2,4-D (ISO)	Air	9.83e-4	8.89e-3	2.00e-2	4.94e-2	1.48e-1	2.96e-1	6.45e-1	1.43	2.67
	Land	–	–	–	–	–	–	–	–	–

Table D1 continued . . .

Substance	Test	Release Rate[a] (g/s) for Stack Height (m)								
		0	10	20	30	50	70	100	150	200
DDD/DDE/DDT (total)	Air	–	–	–	–	–	–	–	–	–
	Land	3.60e-6	1.44e-5	8.00e-5	2.40e-4	8.00e-4	1.96e-3	4.91e-3	1.44e-2	3.32e-2
Dialkyl 79 phthalate	Air	7.37e-4	6.67e-3	1.50e-2	3.70e-2	1.11e-1	2.22e-1	4.84e-1	1.07	2.00
	Land	–	–	–	–	–	–	–	–	–
Diallyl phthalate	Air	7.37e-4	6.67e-3	1.50e-2	3.70e-2	1.11e-1	2.22e-1	4.84e-1	1.07	2.00
	Land	–	–	–	–	–	–	–	–	–
1,2-Diaminoethane	Air	3.69e-3	3.33e-2	7.50e-2	1.85e-1	5.56e-1	1.11	2.42	5.36	1.00e+1
	Land	–	–	–	–	–	–	–	–	–
Diammonium peroxodisulphate (measured as [S$_2$O$_8$])	Air	1.47e-4	1.33e-3	3.00e-3	7.41e-3	2.22e-2	4.44e-2	9.68e-2	2.14e-1	4.00e-1
	Land	–	–	–	–	–	–	–	–	–
Diazinon (ISO)	Air	1.47e-5	1.33e-4	3.00e-4	7.41e-4	2.22e-3	4.44e-3	9.68e-3	2.14e-2	4.00e-2
	Land	–	–	–	–	–	–	–	–	–
Dibenzoyl peroxide	Air	7.37e-4	6.67e-3	1.50e-2	3.70e-2	1.11e-1	2.22e-1	4.84e-1	1.07	2.00
	Land	–	–	–	–	–	–	–	–	–
Dibismuth tritelluride	Air	9.83e-4	8.89e-3	2.00e-2	4.94e-2	1.48e-1	2.96e-1	6.45e-1	1.43	2.67
	Land	–	–	–	–	–	–	–	–	–
Dibismuth tritelluride, selenium doped	Air	4.91e-4	4.44e-3	1.00e-2	2.47e-2	7.41e-2	1.48e-1	3.23e-1	7.14e-1	1.33
	Land	–	–	–	–	–	–	–	–	–
Diborane	Air	1.47e-5	1.33e-4	3.00e-4	7.41e-4	2.22e-3	4.44e-3	9.68e-3	2.14e-2	4.00e-2
	Land	–	–	–	–	–	–	–	–	–
Diboron trioxide	Air	9.83e-4	8.89e-3	2.00e-2	4.94e-2	1.48e-1	2.96e-1	6.45e-1	1.43	2.67
	Land	–	–	–	–	–	–	–	–	–

Table D1 continued . . .

Substance	Test	Release Rate[a] (g/s) for Stack Height (m)								
		0	10	20	30	50	70	100	150	200
Dibromodifluoro-methane	Air	6.34e-2	5.73e-1	1.29	3.19	9.56	1.91e+1	4.16e+1	9.21e+1	1.72e+2
	Land	–	–	–	–	–	–	–	–	–
1,2-Dibromoethane	Air	1.18e-4	1.07e-3	2.40e-3	5.93e-3	1.78e-2	3.56e-2	7.74e-2	1.71e-1	3.20e-1
	Land	–	–	–	–	–	–	–	–	–
2,6-Di-tert-butyl-p-cresol	Air	4.91e-4	4.44e-3	1.00e-2	2.47e-2	7.41e-2	1.48e-1	3.23e-1	7.14e-1	1.33
	Land	–	–	–	–	–	–	–	–	–
Dibutyl hydrogen phosphate	Air	4.91e-4	4.44e-3	1.00e-2	2.47e-2	7.41e-2	1.48e-1	3.23e-1	7.14e-1	1.33
	Land	–	–	–	–	–	–	–	–	–
Dibutyl phthalate	Air	9.83e-4	8.89e-3	2.00e-2	4.94e-2	1.48e-1	2.96e-1	6.45e-1	1.43	2.67
	Land	–	–	–	–	–	–	–	–	–
6,6'-Di-tert-butyl-4,4'-thiodi-m-cresol	Air	1.97e-5	1.78e-4	4.00e-4	9.88e-4	2.96e-3	5.93e-3	1.29e-2	2.86e-2	5.33e-2
	Land	–	–	–	–	–	–	–	–	–
6,6-Di-tert-butyl-4,4-thiodi-m-cresol	Air	1.47e-2	1.33e-1	3.00e-1	7.41e-1	2.22	4.44	9.68	2.14e+1	4.00e+1
	Land	–	–	–	–	–	–	–	–	–
Dichloroacetylene	Air	1.47e-2	1.33e-1	3.00e-1	7.41e-1	2.22	4.44	9.68	2.14e+1	4.00e+1
	Land	–	–	–	–	–	–	–	–	–
1,2-Dichlorobenzene	Air	3.05e-1	2.76	6.20	1.53e+1	4.59e+1	9.19e+1	2.00e+2	4.43e+2	8.27e+2
	Land	–	–	–	–	–	–	–	–	–
1,4-Dichlorobenzene	Air	1.97e-5	1.78e-4	4.00e-4	9.88e-4	2.96e-3	5.93e-3	1.29e-2	2.86e-2	5.33e-2
	Land	–	–	–	–	–	–	–	–	–
Dichlorodifluoro-methane	Air	7.96e-2	7.20e-1	1.62	4.00	1.20e+1	2.40e+1	5.23e+1	1.16e+2	2.16e+2
	Land	–	–	–	–	–	–	–	–	–

Technical Guidance Note (Environmental) E1 Volume II

Table D1 continued . . . .

Substance	Test	Release Rate[a] (g/s) for Stack Height (m)								
		0	10	20	30	50	70	100	150	200
1,3-Dichloro-5,5-dimethyl-hydantoin	Air	3.44e-4	3.11e-3	7.00e-3	1.73e-2	5.19e-2	1.04e-1	2.26e-1	5.00e-1	9.33e-1
	Land	–	–	–	–	–	–	–	–	–
1,1-Dichloroethane	Air	4.91e-2	4.44e-1	1.00	2.47	7.41	1.48e+1	3.23e+1	7.14e+1	1.33e+2
	Land	–	–	–	–	–	–	–	–	–
1,2-Dichloroethane	Air	5.90e-3	5.33e-2	1.20e-1	2.96e-1	8.89e-1	1.78	3.87	8.57	1.60e+1
	Land	–	–	–	–	–	–	–	–	–
1,2-Dichloroethylene, *cis:trans* isomers 60:40	Air	1.47e-3	1.33e-2	3.00e-2	7.41e-2	2.22e-1	4.44e-1	9.68e-1	2.14	4.00
	Land	6.94e-5	2.78e-4	1.54e-3	4.63e-3	1.54e-2	3.79e-2	9.47e-2	2.78e-1	6.41e-1
Dichlorofluoro-methane	Air	1.47e-7	1.33e-6	3.00e-6	7.41e-6	2.22e-5	4.44e-5	9.68e-5	2.14e-4	4.00e-4
	Land	–	–	–	–	–	–	–	–	–
Dichloromethane	Air	1.47e-4	1.33e-3	3.00e-3	7.41e-3	2.22e-2	4.44e-2	9.68e-2	2.14e-1	4.00e-1
	Land	–	–	–	–	–	–	–	–	–
2,2'-Dichloro-4,4'-methylene dianiline	Air	7.37e-4	6.67e-3	1.50e-2	3.70e-2	1.11e-1	2.22e-1	4.84e-1	1.07	2.00
	Land	–	–	–	–	–	–	–	–	–
Dichlorvos (ISO)	Air	4.42e-3	4.00e-2	9.00e-2	2.22e-1	6.67e-1	1.33	2.90	6.43	1.20e+1
	Land	–	–	–	–	–	–	–	–	–
Dicyclohexyl phthalate	Air	3.69e-5	3.33e-4	7.50e-4	1.85e-3	5.56e-3	1.11e-2	2.42e-2	5.36e-2	1.00e-1
	Land	–	–	–	–	–	–	–	–	–
Dicyclopentadiene	Air	3.69e-3	3.33e-2	7.50e-2	1.85e-1	5.56e-1	1.11	2.42	5.36	1.00e+1
	Land	–	–	–	–	–	–	–	–	–
Dieldrin (ISO)	Air	7.37e-3	6.67e-2	1.50e-1	3.70e-1	1.11	2.22	4.84	1.07e+1	2.00e+1
	Land	–	–	–	–	–	–	–	–	–

Table D1 continued . . .

Substance	Test	Release Rate[a] (g/s) for Stack Height (m)								
		0	10	20	30	50	70	100	150	200
Diethylamine	Air	7.37e-2	6.67e-1	1.50	3.70	1.11e+1	2.22e+1	4.84e+1	1.07e+2	2.00e+2
	Land	–	–	–	–	–	–	–	–	–
2-Diethylamino ethanol	Air	4.91e-4	4.44e-3	1.00e-2	2.47e-2	7.41e-2	1.48e-1	3.23e-1	7.14e-1	1.33
	Land	–	–	–	–	–	–	–	–	–
Diethyl ether	Air	7.37e-4	6.67e-3	1.50e-2	3.70e-2	1.11e-1	2.22e-1	4.84e-1	1.07	2.00
	Land	–	–	–	–	–	–	–	–	–
Diethyl phthalate	Air	7.37e-4	6.67e-3	1.50e-2	3.70e-2	1.11e-1	2.22e-1	4.84e-1	1.07	2.00
	Land	–	–	–	–	–	–	–	–	–
Diisobutyl phthalate	Air	7.37e-4	6.67e-3	1.50e-2	3.70e-2	1.11e-1	2.22e-1	4.84e-1	1.07	2.00
	Land	–	–	–	–	–	–	–	–	–
Diisodecyl phthalate	Air	7.37e-4	6.67e-3	1.50e-2	3.70e-2	1.11e-1	2.22e-1	4.84e-1	1.07	2.00
	Land	–	–	–	–	–	–	–	–	–
Diisononyl phthalate	Air	2.95e-3	2.67e-2	6.00e-2	1.48e-1	4.44e-1	8.89e-1	1.94	4.29	8.00
	Land	–	–	–	–	–	–	–	–	–
Diisooctyl phthalate	Air	6.49e-2	5.87e-1	1.32	3.26	9.78	1.96e+1	4.26e+1	9.43e+1	1.76e+2
	Land	–	–	–	–	–	–	–	–	–
Diisopropylamine	Air	7.37e-4	6.67e-3	1.50e-2	3.70e-2	1.11e-1	2.22e-1	4.84e-1	1.07	2.00
	Land	–	–	–	–	–	–	–	–	–
Diisopropyl ether	Air	1.91e-1	1.72	3.88	9.58	2.87e+1	5.75e+1	1.25e+2	2.77e+2	5.17e+2
	Land	–	–	–	–	–	–	–	–	–
Di-linear 79 phthalate	Air	3.49e-3	3.16e-2	7.10e-2	1.75e-1	5.26e-1	1.05	2.29	5.07	9.47
	Land	–	–	–	–	–	–	–	–	–

Table D1 continued . . . .

Substance	Test	Release Rate[a] (g/s) for Stack Height (m)								
		0	10	20	30	50	70	100	150	200
Dimethoxymethane	Air	2.65e-3	2.40e-2	5.40e-2	1.33e-1	4.00e-1	8.00e-1	1.74	3.86	7.20
	Land	–	–	–	–	–	–	–	–	–
NN-Dimethyl acetamide	Air	2.46e-3	2.22e-2	5.00e-2	1.23e-1	3.70e-1	7.41e-1	1.61	3.57	6.67
	Land	–	–	–	–	–	–	–	–	–
Dimethylamine	Air	2.95e-2	2.67e-1	6.00e-1	1.48	4.44	8.89	1.94e+1	4.29e+1	8.00e+1
	Land	–	–	–	–	–	–	–	–	–
NN-Dimethylaniline	Air	2.21e-3	2.00e-2	4.50e-2	1.11e-1	3.33e-1	6.67e-1	1.45	3.21	6.00
	Land	–	–	–	–	–	–	–	–	–
1,3-Dimethylbutyl acetate	Air	2.95e-3	2.67e-2	6.00e-2	1.48e-1	4.44e-1	8.89e-1	1.94	4.29	8.00
	Land	–	–	–	–	–	–	–	–	–
NN-Dimethylethyl amine	Air	2.21e-2	2.00e-1	4.50e-1	1.11	3.33	6.67	1.45e+1	3.21e+1	6.00e+1
	Land	–	–	–	–	–	–	–	–	–
Dimethylformamide	Air	4.91e-4	4.44e-3	1.00e-2	2.47e-2	7.41e-2	1.48e-1	3.23e-1	7.14e-1	1.33
	Land	–	–	–	–	–	–	–	–	–
2,6-Dimethylheptan-4-one	Air	1.47e-4	1.33e-3	3.00e-3	7.41e-3	2.22e-2	4.44e-2	9.68e-2	2.14e-1	4.00e-1
	Land	–	–	–	–	–	–	–	–	–
Dimethyl phthalate	Air	7.37e-4	6.67e-3	1.50e-2	3.70e-2	1.11e-1	2.22e-1	4.84e-1	1.07	2.00
	Land	–	–	–	–	–	–	–	–	–
Dinitrobenzene, all isomers	Air	3.00e-2	1.20e-1	6.67e-1	2.00	6.67	1.64e+1	4.09e+1	1.20e+2	2.77e+2
	Land	–	–	–	–	–	–	–	–	–
Dinonyl phthalate	Air	2.95e-5	2.67e-4	6.00e-4	1.48e-3	4.44e-3	8.89e-3	1.94e-2	4.29e-2	8.00e-2
	Land	–	–	–	–	–	–	–	–	–

Table D1 continued . . .

Substance	Test	Release Rate[a] (g/s) for Stack Height (m)								
		0	10	20	30	50	70	100	150	200
1,4-Dioxane	Air	9.83e-4	8.89e-3	2.00e-2	4.94e-2	1.48e-1	2.96e-1	6.45e-1	1.43	2.67
	Land	–	–	–	–	–	–	–	–	–
Dioxathion (ISO)	Air	1.03e-3	9.33e-3	2.10e-2	5.19e-2	1.56e-1	3.11e-1	6.77e-1	1.50	2.80
	Land	–	–	–	–	–	–	–	–	–
Diphenylamine	Air	1.47e-4	1.33e-3	3.00e-3	7.41e-3	2.22e-2	4.44e-2	9.68e-2	2.14e-1	4.00e-1
	Land	–	–	–	–	–	–	–	–	–
Diphenyl ether (vapour)	Air	9.83e-5	8.89e-4	2.00e-3	4.94e-3	1.48e-2	2.96e-2	6.45e-2	1.43e-1	2.67e-1
	Land	–	–	–	–	–	–	–	–	–
Diphosphorus pentasulphide	Air	1.47e-4	1.33e-3	3.00e-3	7.41e-3	2.22e-2	4.44e-2	9.68e-2	2.14e-1	4.00e-1
	Land	–	–	–	–	–	–	–	–	–
Diphosphorus pentoxide	Air	4.91e-5	4.44e-4	1.00e-3	2.47e-3	7.41e-3	1.48e-2	3.23e-2	7.14e-2	1.33e-1
	Land	–	–	–	–	–	–	–	–	–
Dipotassium peroxodisulphate (measured as [S_2O_8])	Air	7.37e-4	6.67e-3	1.50e-2	3.70e-2	1.11e-1	2.22e-1	4.84e-1	1.07	2.00
	Land	–	–	–	–	–	–	–	–	–
Diquat dibromide (ISO)	Air	1.47e-4	1.33e-3	3.00e-3	7.41e-3	2.22e-2	4.44e-2	9.68e-2	2.14e-1	4.00e-1
	Land	–	–	–	–	–	–	–	–	–
Disodium disulphite	Air	1.47e-4	1.33e-3	3.00e-3	7.41e-3	2.22e-2	4.44e-2	9.68e-2	2.14e-1	4.00e-1
	Land	–	–	–	–	–	–	–	–	–
Disodium peroxodisulphate (measured as [S_2O_8])	Air	1.47e-5	1.33e-4	3.00e-4	7.41e-4	2.22e-3	4.44e-3	9.68e-3	2.14e-2	4.00e-2
	Land	–	–	–	–	–	–	–	–	–
Disodium tetraborate	Air	2.95e-4	2.67e-3	6.00e-3	1.48e-2	4.44e-2	8.89e-2	1.94e-1	4.29e-1	8.00e-1
	Land	–	–	–	–	–	–	–	–	–

Table D1 continued . . .

Substance	Test	Release Rate[a] (g/s) for Stack Height (m)								
		0	10	20	30	50	70	100	150	200
Disulfoton (ISO)	Air	3.69e-5	3.33e-4	7.50e-4	1.85e-3	5.56e-3	1.11e-2	2.42e-2	5.36e-2	1.00e-1
	Land	-	-	-	-	-	-	-	-	-
Disulphur dichloride	Air	1.47e-3	1.33e-2	3.00e-2	7.41e-2	2.22e-1	4.44e-1	9.68e-1	2.14	4.00
	Land	-	-	-	-	-	-	-	-	-
Disulphur decafluoride	Air	9.83e-4	8.89e-3	2.00e-2	4.94e-2	1.48e-1	2.96e-1	6.45e-1	1.43	2.67
	Land	-	-	-	-	-	-	-	-	-
Diuron (ISO)	Air	1.47e-3	1.33e-2	3.00e-2	7.41e-2	2.22e-1	4.44e-1	9.68e-1	2.14	4.00
	Land	-	-	-	-	-	-	-	-	-
Divanadium pentaoxide (as V)	Air	7.37e-6	6.67e-5	1.50e-4	3.70e-4	1.11e-3	2.22e-3	4.84e-3	1.07e-2	2.00e-2
	Land	-	-	-	-	-	-	-	-	-
Divinylbenzene	Air	7.37e-3	6.67e-2	1.50e-1	3.70e-1	1.11	2.22	4.84	1.07e+1	2.00e+1
	Land	-	-	-	-	-	-	-	-	-
Drins (total aldrin, dieldrin, endrin, isodrin)	Air	-	-	-	-	-	-	-	-	-
	Land	5.92e-7	2.37e-6	1.31e-5	3.94e-5	1.31e-4	3.23e-4	8.07e-4	2.37e-3	5.46e-3
Endosulfan (ISO)	Air	1.47e-5	1.33e-4	3.00e-4	7.41e-4	2.22e-3	4.44e-3	9.68e-3	2.14e-2	4.00e-2
	Land	-	-	-	-	-	-	-	-	-
Endrin (ISO)	Air	1.47e-5	1.33e-4	3.00e-4	7.41e-4	2.22e-3	4.44e-3	9.68e-3	2.14e-2	4.00e-2
	Land	-	-	-	-	-	-	-	-	-
2,3-Epoxypropyl isopropyl ether	Air	1.77e-2	1.60e-1	3.60e-1	8.89e-1	2.67	5.33	1.16e+1	2.57e+1	4.80e+1
	Land	-	-	-	-	-	-	-	-	-
Ethane-1,2-diol	Air	1.47e-3	1.33e-2	3.00e-2	7.41e-2	2.22e-1	4.44e-1	9.68e-1	2.14	4.00
	Land	-	-	-	-	-	-	-	-	-

Table D1 continued . . .

Substance	Test	Release Rate[a] (g/s) for Stack Height (m)								
		0	10	20	30	50	70	100	150	200
Ethanethiol	Air	1.47e-4	1.33e-3	3.00e-3	7.41e-3	2.22e-2	4.44e-2	9.68e-2	2.14e-1	4.00e-1
	Land	-	-	-	-	-	-	-	-	-
Ethanol	Air	2.80e-1	2.53	5.70	1.41e+1	4.22e+1	8.44e+1	1.84e+2	4.07e+2	7.60e+2
	Land	-	-	-	-	-	-	-	-	-
2-Ethoxyethanol	Air	1.09e-3	9.87e-3	2.22e-2	5.48e-2	1.64e-1	3.29e-1	7.16e-1	1.59	2.96
	Land	-	-	-	-	-	-	-	-	-
2-Ethoxyethyl acetate	Air	1.59e-3	1.44e-2	3.24e-2	8.00e-2	2.40e-1	4.80e-1	1.05	2.31	4.32
	Land	-	-	-	-	-	-	-	-	-
Ethyl acetate	Air	2.06e-1	1.87	4.20	1.04e+1	3.11e+1	6.22e+1	1.35e+2	3.00e+2	5.60e+2
	Land	-	-	-	-	-	-	-	-	-
Ethyl acrylate	Air	2.95e-3	2.67e-2	6.00e-2	1.48e-1	4.44e-1	8.89e-1	1.94	4.29	8.00
	Land	-	-	-	-	-	-	-	-	-
Ethylamine	Air	2.65e-3	2.40e-2	5.40e-2	1.33e-1	4.00e-1	8.00e-1	1.74	3.86	7.20
	Land	-	-	-	-	-	-	-	-	-
Ethylbenzene	Air	2.68e-2	2.42e-1	5.45e-1	1.35	4.04	8.07	1.76e+1	3.89e+1	7.27e+1
	Land	2.39e-3	9.57e-3	5.32e-2	1.59e-1	5.32e-1	1.30	3.26	9.57	2.21e+1
Ethyl chloroformate	Air	6.49e-4	5.87e-3	1.32e-2	3.26e-2	9.78e-2	1.96e-1	4.26e-1	9.43e-1	1.76
	Land	-	-	-	-	-	-	-	-	-
Ethylene dinitrate	Air	5.90e-5	5.33e-4	1.20e-3	2.96e-3	8.89e-3	1.78e-2	3.87e-2	8.57e-2	1.60e-1
	Land	-	-	-	-	-	-	-	-	-
Ethylene oxide	Air	2.95e-4	2.67e-3	6.00e-3	1.48e-2	4.44e-2	8.89e-2	1.94e-1	4.29e-1	8.00e-1
	Land	-	-	-	-	-	-	-	-	-

Table D1 continued . . .

Substance	Test	Release Rate[a] (g/s) for Stack Height (m)								
		0	10	20	30	50	70	100	150	200
Ethyl formate	Air	2.21e-2	2.00e-1	4.50e-1	1.11	3.33	6.67	1.45e+1	3.21e+1	6.00e+1
	Land	–	–	–	–	–	–	–	–	–
2-Ethylhexyl chloroformate	Air	1.16e-3	1.05e-2	2.37e-2	5.85e-2	1.76e-1	3.51e-1	7.65e-1	1.69	3.16
	Land	–	–	–	–	–	–	–	–	–
4-Ethylmorpholine	Air	7.67e-3	3.07e-2	1.70e-1	5.11e-1	1.70	4.18	1.05e+1	3.07e+1	7.08e+1
	Land	–	–	–	–	–	–	–	–	–
Fenchlorphos (ISO)	Air	1.47e-3	1.33e-2	3.00e-2	7.41e-2	2.22e-1	4.44e-1	9.68e-1	2.14	4.00
	Land	–	–	–	–	–	–	–	–	–
Ferbam (ISO)	Air	9.83e-4	8.89e-3	2.00e-2	4.94e-2	1.48e-1	2.96e-1	6.45e-1	1.43	2.67
	Land	–	–	–	–	–	–	–	–	–
Ferrocene	Air	9.83e-4	8.89e-3	2.00e-2	4.94e-2	1.48e-1	2.96e-1	6.45e-1	1.43	2.67
	Land	–	–	–	–	–	–	–	–	–
Fluoride (as F)	Air	1.38e-6	1.24e-5	2.80e-5	6.91e-5	2.07e-4	4.15e-4	9.03e-4	2.00e-3	3.73e-3
	Land	2.70e-5	1.08e-4	6.00e-4	1.80e-3	6.00e-3	1.47e-2	3.68e-2	1.08e-1	2.49e-1
Formaldehyde	Air	4.91e-5	4.44e-4	1.00e-3	2.47e-3	7.41e-3	1.48e-2	3.23e-2	7.14e-2	1.33e-1
	Land	–	–	–	–	–	–	–	–	–
Formamide	Air	2.21e-3	2.00e-2	4.50e-2	1.11e-1	3.33e-1	6.67e-1	1.45	3.21	6.00
	Land	–	–	–	–	–	–	–	–	–
Formic acid	Air	1.33e-3	1.20e-2	2.70e-2	6.67e-2	2.00e-1	4.00e-1	8.71e-1	1.93	3.60
	Land	–	–	–	–	–	–	–	–	–

Table D1 continued . . .

Substance	Test	Release Rate[a] (g/s) for Stack Height (m)								
		0	10	20	30	50	70	100	150	200
2-Furaldehyde	Air	2.67e-3	1.07e-2	5.93e-2	1.78e-1	5.93e-1	1.45	3.64	1.07e+1	2.46e+1
	Land	–	–	–	–	–	–	–	–	–
Furfuryl alcohol	Air	2.95e-3	2.67e-2	6.00e-2	1.48e-1	4.44e-1	8.89e-1	1.94	4.29	8.00
	Land	–	–	–	–	–	–	–	–	–
Germane	Air	8.85e-5	8.00e-4	1.80e-3	4.44e-3	1.33e-2	2.67e-2	5.81e-2	1.29e-1	2.40e-1
	Land	–	–	–	–	–	–	–	–	–
Glutaraldehyde	Air	3.44e-5	3.11e-4	7.00e-4	1.73e-3	5.19e-3	1.04e-2	2.26e-2	5.00e-2	9.33e-2
	Land	–	–	–	–	–	–	–	–	–
Glycerol	Air	1.47e-3	1.33e-2	3.00e-2	7.41e-2	2.22e-1	4.44e-1	9.68e-1	2.14	4.00
	Land	–	–	–	–	–	–	–	–	–
Hafnium	Air	7.37e-5	6.67e-4	1.50e-3	3.70e-3	1.11e-2	2.22e-2	4.84e-2	1.07e-1	2.00e-1
	Land	–	–	–	–	–	–	–	–	–
HCH compounds (α, β, d and γ isomers)	Air	–	–	–	–	–	–	–	–	–
	Land	1.80e-6	7.20e-6	4.00e-5	1.20e-4	4.00e-4	9.82e-4	2.46e-3	7.20e-3	1.66e-2
n-Heptane	Air	9.83e-2	8.89e-1	2.00	4.94	1.48e+1	2.96e+1	6.45e+1	1.43e+2	2.67e+2
	Land	–	–	–	–	–	–	–	–	–
Heptan-2-one	Air	2.36e-2	2.13e-1	4.80e-1	1.19	3.56	7.11	1.55e+1	3.43e+1	6.40e+1
	Land	–	–	–	–	–	–	–	–	–
Heptan-3-one	Air	2.36e-2	2.13e-1	4.80e-1	1.19	3.56	7.11	1.55e+1	3.43e+1	6.40e+1
	Land	–	–	–	–	–	–	–	–	–
Hexachloroethane	Air	7.37e-4	6.67e-3	1.50e-2	3.70e-2	1.11e-1	2.22e-1	4.84e-1	1.07	2.00
	Land	–	–	–	–	–	–	–	–	–

Table D1 continued . . .

Substance	Test	Release Rate[a] (g/s) for Stack Height (m)								
		0	10	20	30	50	70	100	150	200
Hexahydro-1,3,5-trinitro-1,3,5-triazine	Air	1.47e-4	1.33e-3	3.00e-3	7.41e-3	2.22e-2	4.44e-2	9.68e-2	2.14e-1	4.00e-1
	Land	—	—	—	—	—	—	—	—	—
Hexane, all isomers except n-Hexane	Air	1.77e-1	1.60	3.60	8.89	2.67e+1	5.33e+1	1.16e+2	2.57e+2	4.80e+2
	Land	—	—	—	—	—	—	—	—	—
n-Hexane	Air	1.03e-2	9.33e-2	2.10e-1	5.19e-1	1.56	3.11	6.77	1.50e+1	2.80e+1
	Land	—	—	—	—	—	—	—	—	—
1,6-Hexanolactam	Air	1.47e-4	1.33e-3	3.00e-3	7.41e-3	2.22e-2	4.44e-2	9.68e-2	2.14e-1	4.00e-1
	Land	—	—	—	—	—	—	—	—	—
Hexan-2-one	Air	2.95e-3	2.67e-2	6.00e-2	1.48e-1	4.44e-1	8.89e-1	1.94	4.29	8.00
	Land	—	—	—	—	—	—	—	—	—
Hydrogen bromide	Air	4.91e-4	4.44e-3	1.00e-2	2.47e-2	7.41e-2	1.48e-1	3.23e-1	7.14e-1	1.33
	Land	—	—	—	—	—	—	—	—	—
Hydrogen chloride	Air	3.44e-4	3.11e-3	7.00e-3	1.73e-2	5.19e-2	1.04e-1	2.26e-1	5.00e-1	9.33e-1
	Land	—	—	—	—	—	—	—	—	—
Hydrogen cyanide	Air	9.83e-5	8.89e-4	2.00e-3	4.94e-3	1.48e-2	2.96e-2	6.45e-2	1.43e-1	2.67e-1
	Land	—	—	—	—	—	—	—	—	—
Hydrogen fluoride (as F)	Air	1.23e-4	1.11e-3	2.50e-3	6.17e-3	1.85e-2	3.70e-2	8.06e-2	1.79e-1	3.33e-1
	Land	—	—	—	—	—	—	—	—	—
Hydrogen peroxide	Air	1.47e-4	1.33e-3	3.00e-3	7.41e-3	2.22e-2	4.44e-2	9.68e-2	2.14e-1	4.00e-1
	Land	—	—	—	—	—	—	—	—	—
Hydrogen selenide (as Se)	Air	2.95e-5	2.67e-4	6.00e-4	1.48e-3	4.44e-3	8.89e-3	1.94e-2	4.29e-2	8.00e-2
	Land	—	—	—	—	—	—	—	—	—

Table D1 continued . . . .

Substance	Test	Release Rate[a] (g/s) for Stack Height (m)								
		0	10	20	30	50	70	100	150	200
Hydrogen sulphide	Air	7.37e-5	6.67e-4	1.50e-3	3.70e-3	1.11e-2	2.22e-2	4.84e-2	1.07e-1	2.00e-1
	Land	–	–	–	–	–	–	–	–	–
Hydroquinone	Air	1.97e-4	1.78e-3	4.00e-3	9.88e-3	2.96e-2	5.93e-2	1.29e-1	2.86e-1	5.33e-1
	Land	–	–	–	–	–	–	–	–	–
4-Hydroxy-4-methyl-pentan-2-one	Air	1.77e-2	1.60e-1	3.60e-1	8.89e-1	2.67	5.33	1.16e+1	2.57e+1	4.80e+1
	Land	–	–	–	–	–	–	–	–	–
2-Hydroxypropyl acrylate	Air	4.42e-4	4.00e-3	9.00e-3	2.22e-2	6.67e-2	1.33e-1	2.90e-1	6.43e-1	1.20
	Land	–	–	–	–	–	–	–	–	–
2,2'-Iminodiethanol	Air	2.21e-3	2.00e-2	4.50e-2	1.11e-1	3.33e-1	6.67e-1	1.45	3.21	6.00
	Land	–	–	–	–	–	–	–	–	–
2,2'-Iminodi(ethyl amine)	Air	5.90e-4	5.33e-3	1.20e-2	2.96e-2	8.89e-2	1.78e-1	3.87e-1	8.57e-1	1.60
	Land	–	–	–	–	–	–	–	–	–
Indene	Air	3.44e-3	3.11e-2	7.00e-2	1.73e-1	5.19e-1	1.04	2.26	5.00	9.33
	Land	–	–	–	–	–	–	–	–	–
Indium and compounds (as In)	Air	1.47e-5	1.33e-4	3.00e-4	7.41e-4	2.22e-3	4.44e-3	9.68e-3	2.14e-2	4.00e-2
	Land	–	–	–	–	–	–	–	–	–
Iodine	Air	4.91e-5	4.44e-4	1.00e-3	2.47e-3	7.41e-3	1.48e-2	3.23e-2	7.14e-2	1.33e-1
	Land	–	–	–	–	–	–	–	–	–
Iodoform	Air	9.83e-4	8.89e-3	2.00e-2	4.94e-2	1.48e-1	2.96e-1	6.45e-1	1.43	2.67
	Land	–	–	–	–	–	–	–	–	–
Iron salts (as Fe)	Air	9.83e-5	8.89e-4	2.00e-3	4.94e-3	1.48e-2	2.96e-2	6.45e-2	1.43e-1	2.67e-1
	Land	–	–	–	–	–	–	–	–	–

Table D1 continued . . .

Substance	Test	Release Rate[a] (g/s) for Stack Height (m)								
		0	10	20	30	50	70	100	150	200
Isobutyl acetate	Air	4.30e-2	3.89e-1	8.75e-1	2.16	6.48	1.30e+1	2.82e+1	6.25e+1	1.17e+2
	Land	–	–	–	–	–	–	–	–	–
Isocyanates	Air	6.88e-7	6.22e-6	1.40e-5	3.46e-5	1.04e-4	2.07e-4	4.52e-4	1.00e-3	1.87e-3
	Land	–	–	–	–	–	–	–	–	–
Isooctyl alcohol (mixed isomers)	Air	3.98e-2	3.60e-1	8.10e-1	2.00	6.00	1.20e+1	2.61e+1	5.79e+1	1.08e+2
	Land	–	–	–	–	–	–	–	–	–
Isopentyl acetate	Air	3.22e-2	2.91e-1	6.55e-1	1.62	4.85	9.70	2.11e+1	4.68e+1	8.73e+1
	Land	–	–	–	–	–	–	–	–	–
Isopropyl acetate	Air	4.13e-2	3.73e-1	8.40e-1	2.07	6.22	1.24e+1	2.71e+1	6.00e+1	1.12e+2
	Land	–	–	–	–	–	–	–	–	–
Isopropyl chloroformate	Air	7.37e-4	6.67e-3	1.50e-2	3.70e-2	1.11e-1	2.22e-1	4.84e-1	1.07	2.00
	Land	–	–	–	–	–	–	–	–	–
Ketene	Air	3.00e-4	1.20e-3	6.67e-3	2.00e-2	6.67e-2	1.64e-1	4.09e-1	1.20	2.77
	Land	–	–	–	–	–	–	–	–	–
Lead	Air	6.67e-5	2.67e-4	1.48e-3	4.44e-3	1.48e-2	3.64e-2	9.09e-2	2.67e-1	6.15e-1
	Land	1.41e-5	5.66e-5	3.14e-4	9.43e-4	3.14e-3	7.72e-3	1.93e-2	5.66e-2	1.31e-1
Lithium hydride	Air	3.69e-6	3.33e-5	7.50e-5	1.85e-4	5.56e-4	1.11e-3	2.42e-3	5.36e-3	1.00e-2
	Land	–	–	–	–	–	–	–	–	–
Lithium hydroxide	Air	4.91e-5	4.44e-4	1.00e-3	2.47e-3	7.41e-3	1.48e-2	3.23e-2	7.14e-2	1.33e-1
	Land	–	–	–	–	–	–	–	–	–
Malathion (ISO)	Air	1.47e-3	1.33e-2	3.00e-2	7.41e-2	2.22e-1	4.44e-1	9.68e-1	2.14	4.00
	Land	–	–	–	–	–	–	–	–	–

Table D1 continued . . . .

Substance	Test	Release Rate[a] (g/s) for Stack Height (m)								
		0	10	20	30	50	70	100	150	200
Maneb	Air	–	–	–	–	–	–	–	–	–
	Land	4.76e-4	1.90e-3	1.06e-2	3.17e-2	1.06e-1	2.60e-1	6.49e-1	1.90	4.39
Manganese and compounds (as Mn)	Air	7.37e-4	6.67e-3	1.50e-2	3.70e-2	1.11e-1	2.22e-1	4.84e-1	1.07	2.00
	Land	–	–	–	–	–	–	–	–	–
Mequinol (INN)	Air	7.37e-4	6.67e-3	1.50e-2	3.70e-2	1.11e-1	2.22e-1	4.84e-1	1.07	2.00
	Land	–	–	–	–	–	–	–	–	–
Mercaptoacetic acid	Air	7.37e-4	6.67e-3	1.50e-2	3.70e-2	1.11e-1	2.22e-1	4.84e-1	1.07	2.00
	Land	–	–	–	–	–	–	–	–	–
Mercury alkyls (as Hg)	Air	1.47e-6	1.33e-5	3.00e-5	7.41e-5	2.22e-4	4.44e-4	9.68e-4	2.14e-3	4.00e-3
	Land	–	–	–	–	–	–	–	–	–
Mercury and compounds, except mercury alkyls, (as Hg)	Air	7.37e-6	6.67e-5	1.50e-4	3.70e-4	1.11e-3	2.22e-3	4.84e-3	1.07e-2	2.00e-2
	Land	5.14e-8	2.06e-7	1.14e-6	3.43e-6	1.14e-5	2.81e-5	7.01e-5	2.06e-4	4.75e-4
Methacrylic acid	Air	6.88e-3	6.22e-2	1.40e-1	3.46e-1	1.04	2.07	4.52	1.00e+1	1.87e+1
	Land	–	–	–	–	–	–	–	–	–
Methacrylonitrile	Air	4.42e-4	4.00e-3	9.00e-3	2.22e-2	6.67e-2	1.33e-1	2.90e-1	6.43e-1	1.20
	Land	–	–	–	–	–	–	–	–	–
Methanethiol	Air	1.47e-4	1.33e-3	3.00e-3	7.41e-3	2.22e-2	4.44e-2	9.68e-2	2.14e-1	4.00e-1
	Land	–	–	–	–	–	–	–	–	–
Methanol	Air	1.52e-2	1.38e-1	3.10e-1	7.65e-1	2.30	4.59	1.00e+1	2.21e+1	4.13e+1
	Land	–	–	–	–	–	–	–	–	–
Methomyl (ISO)	Air	3.69e-4	3.33e-3	7.50e-3	1.85e-2	5.56e-2	1.11e-1	2.42e-1	5.36e-1	1.00
	Land	–	–	–	–	–	–	–	–	–

Table D1 continued . . .

Substance	Test	Release Rate[a] (g/s) for Stack Height (m)								
		0	10	20	30	50	70	100	150	200
Methoxychlor (ISO)	Air	1.47e-3	1.33e-2	3.00e-2	7.41e-2	2.22e-1	4.44e-1	9.68e-1	2.14	4.00
	Land	–	–	–	–	–	–	–	–	–
2-Methoxyethanol	Air	4.72e-4	4.27e-3	9.60e-3	2.37e-2	7.11e-2	1.42e-1	3.10e-1	6.86e-1	1.28
	Land	–	–	–	–	–	–	–	–	–
2-Methoxyethyl acetate	Air	7.08e-4	6.40e-3	1.44e-2	3.56e-2	1.07e-1	2.13e-1	4.65e-1	1.03	1.92
	Land	–	–	–	–	–	–	–	–	–
1-Methoxypropan-2-ol	Air	5.31e-2	4.80e-1	1.08	2.67	8.00	1.60e+1	3.48e+1	7.71e+1	1.44e+2
	Land	–	–	–	–	–	–	–	–	–
Methyl acetate	Air	3.73e-2	3.38e-1	7.60e-1	1.88	5.63	1.13e+1	2.45e+1	5.43e+1	1.01e+2
	Land	–	–	–	–	–	–	–	–	–
Methyl acrylate	Air	5.16e-3	4.67e-2	1.05e-1	2.59e-1	7.78e-1	1.56	3.39	7.50	1.40e+1
	Land	–	–	–	–	–	–	–	–	–
Methylamine	Air	1.77e-3	1.60e-2	3.60e-2	8.89e-2	2.67e-1	5.33e-1	1.16	2.57	4.80
	Land	–	–	–	–	–	–	–	–	–
N-Methylaniline	Air	2.95e-4	2.67e-3	6.00e-3	1.48e-2	4.44e-2	8.89e-2	1.94e-1	4.29e-1	8.00e-1
	Land	–	–	–	–	–	–	–	–	–
3-Methylbutan-1-ol	Air	2.21e-2	2.00e-1	4.50e-1	1.11	3.33	6.67	1.45e+1	3.21e+1	6.00e+1
	Land	–	–	–	–	–	–	–	–	–
1-Methylbutyl acetate	Air	3.93e-2	3.56e-1	8.00e-1	1.98	5.93	1.19e+1	2.58e+1	5.71e+1	1.07e+2
	Land	–	–	–	–	–	–	–	–	–
Methyl 2-cyanoacrylate	Air	7.86e-4	7.11e-3	1.60e-2	3.95e-2	1.19e-1	2.37e-1	5.16e-1	1.14	2.13
	Land	–	–	–	–	–	–	–	–	–

Table D1 continued . . .

Substance	Test	Release Rate[a] (g/s) for Stack Height (m)								
		0	10	20	30	50	70	100	150	200
Methylcyclohexane	Air	9.83e-2	8.89e-1	2.00	4.94	1.48e+1	2.96e+1	6.45e+1	1.43e+2	2.67e+2
	Land	—	—	—	—	—	—	—	—	—
Methylcyclohexanol	Air	1.72e-2	1.56e-1	3.50e-1	8.64e-1	2.59	5.19	1.13e+1	2.50e+1	4.67e+1
	Land	—	—	—	—	—	—	—	—	—
2-Methylcyclohexanone	Air	1.70e-2	1.53e-1	3.45e-1	8.52e-1	2.56	5.11	1.11e+1	2.46e+1	4.60e+1
	Land	—	—	—	—	—	—	—	—	—
2-Methyl-4,6-dinitrophenol	Air	2.95e-5	2.67e-4	6.00e-4	1.48e-3	4.44e-3	8.89e-3	1.94e-2	4.29e-2	8.00e-2
	Land	—	—	—	—	—	—	—	—	—
4,4'-Methylenedianiline	Air	2.36e-6	2.13e-5	4.80e-5	1.19e-4	3.56e-4	7.11e-4	1.55e-3	3.43e-3	6.40e-3
	Land	—	—	—	—	—	—	—	—	—
Methyl ethyl ketone peroxides	Air	7.37e-5	6.67e-4	1.50e-3	3.70e-3	1.11e-2	2.22e-2	4.84e-2	1.07e-1	2.00e-1
	Land	—	—	—	—	—	—	—	—	—
Methyl formate	Air	1.84e-2	1.67e-1	3.75e-1	9.26e-1	2.78	5.56	1.21e+1	2.68e+1	5.00e+1
	Land	—	—	—	—	—	—	—	—	—
5-Methylheptan-3-one	Air	1.92e-2	1.73e-1	3.90e-1	9.63e-1	2.89	5.78	1.26e+1	2.79e+1	5.20e+1
	Land	—	—	—	—	—	—	—	—	—
5-Methylhexan-2-one	Air	2.36e-2	2.13e-1	4.80e-1	1.19	3.56	7.11	1.55e+1	3.43e+1	6.40e+1
	Land	—	—	—	—	—	—	—	—	—
Methyl methacrylate	Air	2.51e-2	2.27e-1	5.10e-1	1.26	3.78	7.56	1.65e+1	3.64e+1	6.80e+1
	Land	—	—	—	—	—	—	—	—	—
2-Methylpentane-2,4-diol	Air	6.14e-3	5.56e-2	1.25e-1	3.09e-1	9.26e-1	1.85	4.03	8.93	1.67e+1
	Land	—	—	—	—	—	—	—	—	—

Table D1 continued . . . .

Substance	Test	Release Rate[a] (g/s) for Stack Height (m)								
		0	10	20	30	50	70	100	150	200
4-Methylpentan-2-ol	Air	7.86e-3	7.11e-2	1.60e-1	3.95e-1	1.19	2.37	5.16	1.14e+1	2.13e+1
	Land	–	–	–	–	–	–	–	–	–
4-Methylpentan-2-one	Air	2.01e-2	1.82e-1	4.10e-1	1.01	3.04	6.07	1.32e+1	2.93e+1	5.47e+1
	Land	–	–	–	–	–	–	–	–	–
4-Methylpent-3-en-2-one	Air	4.91e-3	4.44e-2	1.00e-1	2.47e-1	7.41e-1	1.48	3.23	7.14	1.33e+1
	Land	–	–	–	–	–	–	–	–	–
2-Methylpropan-1-ol	Air	1.11e-2	1.00e-1	2.25e-1	5.56e-1	1.67	3.33	7.26	1.61e+1	3.00e+1
	Land	–	–	–	–	–	–	–	–	–
2-Methylpropan-2-ol	Air	2.21e-2	2.00e-1	4.50e-1	1.11	3.33	6.67	1.45e+1	3.21e+1	6.00e+1
	Land	–	–	–	–	–	–	–	–	–
1-Methyl-2-pyrrolidone	Air	5.90e-2	5.33e-1	1.20	2.96	8.89	1.78e+1	3.87e+1	8.57e+1	1.60e+2
	Land	–	–	–	–	–	–	–	–	–
Methylstyrenes, all isomers except α-methylstyrene	Air	3.54e-2	3.20e-1	7.20e-1	1.78	5.33	1.07e+1	2.32e+1	5.14e+1	9.60e+1
	Land	–	–	–	–	–	–	–	–	–
N-Methyl-N, 2,4,6-tetranitroaniline	Air	1.47e-4	1.33e-3	3.00e-3	7.41e-3	2.22e-2	4.44e-2	9.68e-2	2.14e-1	4.00e-1
	Land	–	–	–	–	–	–	–	–	–
Mevinphos (ISO)	Air	1.47e-5	1.33e-4	3.00e-4	7.41e-4	2.22e-3	4.44e-3	9.68e-3	2.14e-2	4.00e-2
	Land	–	–	–	–	–	–	–	–	–
Molybdenum compounds (as Mo)	Air	4.91e-4	4.44e-3	1.00e-2	2.47e-2	7.41e-2	1.48e-1	3.23e-1	7.14e-1	1.33
	Land	2.06e-7	8.23e-7	4.57e-6	1.37e-5	4.57e-5	1.12e-4	2.81e-4	8.23e-4	1.90e-3
Monochloroacetic acid	Air	1.47e-4	1.33e-3	3.00e-3	7.41e-3	2.22e-2	4.44e-2	9.68e-2	2.14e-1	4.00e-1
	Land	–	–	–	–	–	–	–	–	–

Table D1 continued . . .

Substance	Test	Release Rate[a] (g/s) for Stack Height (m)								
		0	10	20	30	50	70	100	150	200
Morpholine	Air	5.16e-3	4.67e-2	1.05e-1	2.59e-1	7.78e-1	1.56	3.39	7.50	1.40e+1
	Land	-	-	-	-	-	-	-	-	-
Naled (ISO)	Air	2.95e-4	2.67e-3	6.00e-3	1.48e-2	4.44e-2	8.89e-2	1.94e-1	4.29e-1	8.00e-1
	Land	-	-	-	-	-	-	-	-	-
Napthalene	Air	3.69e-3	3.33e-2	7.50e-2	1.85e-1	5.56e-1	1.11	2.42	5.36	1.00e+1
	Land	-	-	-	-	-	-	-	-	-
Nickel and inorganic compounds (as Ni)	Air	2.95e-6	2.67e-5	6.00e-5	1.48e-4	4.44e-4	8.89e-4	1.94e-3	4.29e-3	8.00e-3
	Land	1.41e-6	5.66e-6	3.14e-5	9.43e-5	3.14e-4	7.72e-4	1.93e-3	5.66e-3	1.31e-2
Nickel, organic compounds (as Ni)	Air	1.47e-4	1.33e-3	3.00e-3	7.41e-3	2.22e-2	4.44e-2	9.68e-2	2.14e-1	4.00e-1
	Land	-	-	-	-	-	-	-	-	-
Nicotine	Air	7.37e-5	6.67e-4	1.50e-3	3.70e-3	1.11e-2	2.22e-2	4.84e-2	1.07e-1	2.00e-1
	Land	-	-	-	-	-	-	-	-	-
Nitric acid	Air	4.91e-4	4.44e-3	1.00e-2	2.47e-2	7.41e-2	1.48e-1	3.23e-1	7.14e-1	1.33
	Land	-	-	-	-	-	-	-	-	-
4-Nitroaniline	Air	8.85e-4	8.00e-3	1.80e-2	4.44e-2	1.33e-1	2.67e-1	5.81e-1	1.29	2.40
	Land	-	-	-	-	-	-	-	-	-
Nitrobenzene	Air	4.91e-4	4.44e-3	1.00e-2	2.47e-2	7.41e-2	1.48e-1	3.23e-1	7.14e-1	1.33
	Land	-	-	-	-	-	-	-	-	-
Nitroethane	Air	4.57e-2	4.13e-1	9.30e-1	2.30	6.89	1.38e+1	3.00e+1	6.64e+1	1.24e+2
	Land	-	-	-	-	-	-	-	-	-
Nitrogen dioxide	Air	1.41e-3	1.27e-3	2.86e-3	7.07e-3	2.12e-2	4.24e-2	9.24e-2	2.05e-1	3.82e-1
	Land	-	-	-	-	-	-	-	-	-

Table D1 continued . . .

Substance	Test	Release Rate[a] (g/s) for Stack Height (m)								
		0	10	20	30	50	70	100	150	200
Nitrogen monoxide	Air	2.21e-3	2.00e-2	4.50e-2	1.11e-1	3.33e-1	6.67e-1	1.45	3.21	6.00
	Land	–	–	–	–	–	–	–	–	–
Nitrogen trifluoride	Air	2.21e-3	2.00e-2	4.50e-2	1.11e-1	3.33e-1	6.67e-1	1.45	3.21	6.00
	Land	–	–	–	–	–	–	–	–	–
Nitromethane	Air	1.84e-2	1.67e-1	3.75e-1	9.26e-1	2.78	5.56	1.21e+1	2.68e+1	5.00e+1
	Land	–	–	–	–	–	–	–	–	–
1-Nitropropane	Air	1.33e-2	1.20e-1	2.70e-1	6.67e-1	2.00	4.00	8.71	1.93e+1	3.60e+1
	Land	–	–	–	–	–	–	–	–	–
2-Nitropropane	Air	5.31e-4	4.80e-3	1.08e-2	2.67e-2	8.00e-2	1.60e-1	3.48e-1	7.71e-1	1.44
	Land	–	–	–	–	–	–	–	–	–
Nitrotoluene, all isomers	Air	2.95e-3	2.67e-2	6.00e-2	1.48e-1	4.44e-1	8.89e-1	1.94	4.29	8.00
	Land	–	–	–	–	–	–	–	–	–
Octachloro-naphthalene	Air	1.47e-5	1.33e-4	3.00e-4	7.41e-4	2.22e-3	4.44e-3	9.68e-3	2.14e-2	4.00e-2
	Land	–	–	–	–	–	–	–	–	–
n-Octane	Air	8.85e-2	8.00e-1	1.80	4.44	1.33e+1	2.67e+1	5.81e+1	1.29e+2	2.40e+2
	Land	–	–	–	–	–	–	–	–	–
Orthophosphoric acid	Air	9.83e-5	8.89e-4	2.00e-3	4.94e-3	1.48e-2	2.96e-2	6.45e-2	1.43e-1	2.67e-1
	Land	–	–	–	–	–	–	–	–	–
Osmium tetraoxide (as Os)	Air	2.95e-7	2.67e-6	6.00e-6	1.48e-5	4.44e-5	8.89e-5	1.94e-4	4.29e-4	8.00e-4
	Land	–	–	–	–	–	–	–	–	–
Oxalic acid	Air	9.83e-5	8.89e-4	2.00e-3	4.94e-3	1.48e-2	2.96e-2	6.45e-2	1.43e-1	2.67e-1
	Land	–	–	–	–	–	–	–	–	–

Table D1 continued . . .

Substance	Test	Release Rate[a] (g/s) for Stack Height (m)								
		0	10	20	30	50	70	100	150	200
Oxalonitrile	Air	2.95e-3	2.67e-2	6.00e-2	1.48e-1	4.44e-1	8.89e-1	1.94	4.29	8.00
	Land	–	–	–	–	–	–	–	–	–
2,2'-Oxydiethanol	Air	1.47e-2	1.33e-1	3.00e-1	7.41e-1	2.22	4.44	9.68	2.14e+1	4.00e+1
	Land	–	–	–	–	–	–	–	–	–
Ozone	Air	6.67e-5	2.67e-4	1.48e-3	4.44e-3	1.48e-2	3.64e-2	9.09e-2	2.67e-1	6.15e-1
	Land	–	–	–	–	–	–	–	–	–
PAHs[c]	Air	–	–	–	–	–	–	–	–	–
	Land	5.02e-5	2.01e-4	1.11e-3	3.34e-3	1.11e-2	2.74e-2	6.84e-2	2.01e-1	4.63e-1
Parathion (ISO)	Air	1.47e-5	1.33e-4	3.00e-4	7.41e-4	2.22e-3	4.44e-3	9.68e-3	2.14e-2	4.00e-2
	Land	–	–	–	–	–	–	–	–	–
Parathion-methyl (ISO)	Air	2.95e-5	2.67e-4	6.00e-4	1.48e-3	4.44e-3	8.89e-3	1.94e-2	4.29e-2	8.00e-2
	Land	–	–	–	–	–	–	–	–	–
Particulates	Air	2.46e-5	2.22e-4	5.00e-4	1.23e-3	3.70e-3	7.41e-3	1.61e-2	3.57e-2	6.67e-2
	Land	–	–	–	–	–	–	–	–	–
PCBs[d]	Air	–	–	–	–	–	–	–	–	–
	Land	9.00e-8	3.60e-7	2.00e-6	6.00e-6	2.00e-5	4.91e-5	1.23e-4	3.60e-4	8.31e-4
Pentacarbonyliron (as Fe)	Air	1.18e-5	1.07e-4	2.40e-4	5.93e-4	1.78e-3	3.56e-3	7.74e-3	1.71e-2	3.20e-2
	Land	–	–	–	–	–	–	–	–	–
Pentachlorophenol	Air	7.37e-5	6.67e-4	1.50e-3	3.70e-3	1.11e-2	2.22e-2	4.84e-2	1.07e-1	2.00e-1
	Land	–	–	–	–	–	–	–	–	–
Pentane, all isomers	Air	1.11e-1	1.00	2.25	5.56	1.67e+1	3.33e+1	7.26e+1	1.61e+2	3.00e+2
	Land	–	–	–	–	–	–	–	–	–

Table D1 continued . . .

Substance	Test	Release Rate[a] (g/s) for Stack Height (m)								
		0	10	20	30	50	70	100	150	200
Pentan-2-one	Air	4.30e-2	3.89e-1	8.75e-1	2.16	6.48	1.30e+1	2.82e+1	6.25e+1	1.17e+2
	Land	–	–	–	–	–	–	–	–	–
Pentan-3-one	Air	4.30e-2	3.89e-1	8.75e-1	2.16	6.48	1.30e+1	2.82e+1	6.25e+1	1.17e+2
	Land	–	–	–	–	–	–	–	–	–
Pentyl acetate	Air	3.93e-2	3.56e-1	8.00e-1	1.98	5.93	1.19e+1	2.58e+1	5.71e+1	1.07e+2
	Land	–	–	–	–	–	–	–	–	–
Perchloryl fluoride	Air	1.38e-3	1.24e-2	2.80e-2	6.91e-2	2.07e-1	4.15e-1	9.03e-1	2.00	3.73
	Land	–	–	–	–	–	–	–	–	–
Phenol	Air	1.87e-3	1.69e-2	3.80e-2	9.38e-2	2.81e-1	5.63e-1	1.23	2.71	5.07
	Land	3.34e-3	1.34e-2	7.43e-2	2.23e-1	7.43e-1	1.82	4.56	1.34e+1	3.09e+1
p-Phenylenediamine	Air	1.47e-5	1.33e-4	3.00e-4	7.41e-4	2.22e-3	4.44e-3	9.68e-3	2.14e-2	4.00e-2
	Land	–	–	–	–	–	–	–	–	–
Phenyl-2,3-epoxy-propyl ether	Air	8.85e-4	8.00e-3	1.80e-2	4.44e-2	1.33e-1	2.67e-1	5.81e-1	1.29	2.40
	Land	–	–	–	–	–	–	–	–	–
2-Phenylpropene	Air	2.36e-2	2.13e-1	4.80e-1	1.19	3.56	7.11	1.55e+1	3.43e+1	6.40e+1
	Land	–	–	–	–	–	–	–	–	–
Phorate (ISO)	Air	1.67e-5	6.67e-5	3.70e-4	1.11e-3	3.70e-3	9.09e-3	2.27e-2	6.67e-2	1.54e-1
	Land	–	–	–	–	–	–	–	–	–
Phosgene	Air	2.67e-5	1.07e-4	5.93e-4	1.78e-3	5.93e-3	1.45e-2	3.64e-2	1.07e-1	2.46e-1
	Land	–	–	–	–	–	–	–	–	–
Phosphine	Air	1.97e-5	1.78e-4	4.00e-4	9.88e-4	2.96e-3	5.93e-3	1.29e-2	2.86e-2	5.33e-2
	Land	–	–	–	–	–	–	–	–	–

Table D1 continued . . .

Substance	Test	Release Rate[a] (g/s) for Stack Height (m)								
		0	10	20	30	50	70	100	150	200
Phosphorus, yellow	Air	1.47e-5	1.33e-4	3.00e-4	7.41e-4	2.22e-3	4.44e-3	9.68e-3	2.14e-2	4.00e-2
	Land	–	–	–	–	–	–	–	–	–
Phosphorus pentachloride	Air	1.47e-4	1.33e-3	3.00e-3	7.41e-3	2.22e-2	4.44e-2	9.68e-2	2.14e-1	4.00e-1
	Land	–	–	–	–	–	–	–	–	–
Phosphorus trichloride	Air	1.47e-4	1.33e-3	3.00e-3	7.41e-3	2.22e-2	4.44e-2	9.68e-2	2.14e-1	4.00e-1
	Land	–	–	–	–	–	–	–	–	–
Phosphoryl trichloride	Air	1.77e-4	1.60e-3	3.60e-3	8.89e-3	2.67e-2	5.33e-2	1.16e-1	2.57e-1	4.80e-1
	Land	–	–	–	–	–	–	–	–	–
Phthalates (total)	Air	–	–	–	–	–	–	–	–	–
	Land	2.06e-4	8.23e-4	4.57e-3	1.37e-2	4.57e-2	1.12e-1	2.81e-1	8.23e-1	1.90
Picloram (ISO)	Air	9.83e-4	8.89e-3	2.00e-2	4.94e-2	1.48e-1	2.96e-1	6.45e-1	1.43	2.67
	Land	–	–	–	–	–	–	–	–	–
Picric acid	Air	1.47e-5	1.33e-4	3.00e-4	7.41e-4	2.22e-3	4.44e-3	9.68e-3	2.14e-2	4.00e-2
	Land	–	–	–	–	–	–	–	–	–
Piperazine dihydrochloride	Air	7.37e-4	6.67e-3	1.50e-2	3.70e-2	1.11e-1	2.22e-1	4.84e-1	1.07	2.00
	Land	–	–	–	–	–	–	–	–	–
Piperidine	Air	5.16e-4	4.67e-3	1.05e-2	2.59e-2	7.78e-2	1.56e-1	3.39e-1	7.50e-1	1.40
	Land	–	–	–	–	–	–	–	–	–
Platinum metal	Air	7.37e-4	6.67e-3	1.50e-2	3.70e-2	1.11e-1	2.22e-1	4.84e-1	1.07	2.00
	Land	–	–	–	–	–	–	–	–	–
Platinum salts, soluble (as Pt)	Air	2.95e-7	2.67e-6	6.00e-6	1.48e-5	4.44e-5	8.89e-5	1.94e-4	4.29e-4	8.00e-4
	Land	–	–	–	–	–	–	–	–	–

Table D1 continued . . .

Substance	Test	Release Rate[a] (g/s) for Stack Height (m)								
		0	10	20	30	50	70	100	150	200
Potassium hydroxide	Air	9.83e-5	8.89e-4	2.00e-3	4.94e-3	1.48e-2	2.96e-2	6.45e-2	1.43e-1	2.67e-1
	Land	–	–	–	–	–	–	–	–	–
Propane-1,2-diol	Air	1.47e-3	1.33e-2	3.00e-2	7.41e-2	2.22e-1	4.44e-1	9.68e-1	2.14	4.00
	Land	–	–	–	–	–	–	–	–	–
Propan-1-ol	Air	3.07e-2	2.78e-1	6.25e-1	1.54	4.63	9.26	2.02e+1	4.46e+1	8.33e+1
	Land	–	–	–	–	–	–	–	–	–
Propan-2-ol	Air	6.02e-2	5.44e-1	1.23	3.02	9.07	1.81e+1	3.95e+1	8.75e+1	1.63e+2
	Land	–	–	–	–	–	–	–	–	–
Propionic acid	Air	2.21e-3	2.00e-2	4.50e-2	1.11e-1	3.33e-1	6.67e-1	1.45	3.21	6.00
	Land	–	–	–	–	–	–	–	–	–
Propoxur (ISO)	Air	1.67e-4	6.67e-4	3.70e-3	1.11e-2	3.70e-2	9.09e-2	2.27e-1	6.67e-1	1.54
	Land	–	–	–	–	–	–	–	–	–
n-Propyl acetate	Air	5.16e-2	4.67e-1	1.05	2.59	7.78	1.56e+1	3.39e+1	7.50e+1	1.40e+2
	Land	–	–	–	–	–	–	–	–	–
Propylene dinitrate	Air	5.90e-5	5.33e-4	1.20e-3	2.96e-3	8.89e-3	1.78e-2	3.87e-2	8.57e-2	1.60e-1
	Land	–	–	–	–	–	–	–	–	–
Prop-2-yn-1-ol	Air	2.95e-4	2.67e-3	6.00e-3	1.48e-2	4.44e-2	8.89e-2	1.94e-1	4.29e-1	8.00e-1
	Land	–	–	–	–	–	–	–	–	–
Pyrethrins (ISO)	Air	4.91e-4	4.44e-3	1.00e-2	2.47e-2	7.41e-2	1.48e-1	3.23e-1	7.14e-1	1.33
	Land	–	–	–	–	–	–	–	–	–
Pyridine	Air	1.47e-3	1.33e-2	3.00e-2	7.41e-2	2.22e-1	4.44e-1	9.68e-1	2.14	4.00
	Land	8.74e-6	3.50e-5	1.94e-4	5.83e-4	1.94e-3	4.77e-3	1.19e-2	3.50e-2	8.07e-2

Table D1 continued . . .

Substance	Test	Release Rate[a] (g/s) for Stack Height (m)								
		0	10	20	30	50	70	100	150	200
2-Pyridylamine	Air	6.67e-4	2.67e-3	1.48e-2	4.44e-2	1.48e-1	3.64e-1	9.09e-1	2.67	6.15
	Land	–	–	–	–	–	–	–	–	–
Rhodium and compounds (as Rh)	Air	1.47e-7	1.33e-6	3.00e-6	7.41e-6	2.22e-5	4.44e-5	9.68e-5	2.14e-4	4.00e-4
	Land	–	–	–	–	–	–	–	–	–
Rotenone (ISO)	Air	4.91e-4	4.44e-3	1.00e-2	2.47e-2	7.41e-2	1.48e-1	3.23e-1	7.14e-1	1.33
	Land	–	–	–	–	–	–	–	–	–
Selenium and compounds, except hydrogen selenide (as Se)	Air	1.47e-5	1.33e-4	3.00e-4	7.41e-4	2.22e-3	4.44e-3	9.68e-3	2.14e-2	4.00e-2
	Land	1.54e-7	6.17e-7	3.43e-6	1.03e-5	3.43e-5	8.42e-5	2.10e-4	6.17e-4	1.42e-3
Silane	Air	7.37e-5	6.67e-4	1.50e-3	3.70e-3	1.11e-2	2.22e-2	4.84e-2	1.07e-1	2.00e-1
	Land	–	–	–	–	–	–	–	–	–
Silver compounds (as Ag)	Air	1.47e-6	1.33e-5	3.00e-5	7.41e-5	2.22e-4	4.44e-4	9.68e-4	2.14e-3	4.00e-3
	Land	–	–	–	–	–	–	–	–	–
Sodium azide (as NaN$_3$)	Air	1.47e-5	1.33e-4	3.00e-4	7.41e-4	2.22e-3	4.44e-3	9.68e-3	2.14e-2	4.00e-2
	Land	–	–	–	–	–	–	–	–	–
Sodium 2-(2,4-dichlorophenoxy)ethyl sulphate	Air	9.83e-4	8.89e-3	2.00e-2	4.94e-2	1.48e-1	2.96e-1	6.45e-1	1.43	2.67
	Land	–	–	–	–	–	–	–	–	–
Sodium fluoroacetate	Air	7.37e-6	6.67e-5	1.50e-4	3.70e-4	1.11e-3	2.22e-3	4.84e-3	1.07e-2	2.00e-2
	Land	–	–	–	–	–	–	–	–	–
Sodium hydrogensulphite	Air	7.37e-4	6.67e-3	1.50e-2	3.70e-2	1.11e-1	2.22e-1	4.84e-1	1.07	2.00
	Land	–	–	–	–	–	–	–	–	–
Sodium hydroxide	Air	9.83e-5	8.89e-4	2.00e-3	4.94e-3	1.48e-2	2.96e-2	6.45e-2	1.43e-1	2.67e-1
	Land	–	–	–	–	–	–	–	–	–

Table D1 continued . . . .

Substance	Test	Release Rate[a] (g/s) for Stack Height (m)								
		0	10	20	30	50	70	100	150	200
Stibine	Air	7.37e-5	6.67e-4	1.50e-3	3.70e-3	1.11e-2	2.22e-2	4.84e-2	1.07e-1	2.00e-1
	Land	–	–	–	–	–	–	–	–	–
Strychnine	Air	2.21e-5	2.00e-4	4.50e-4	1.11e-3	3.33e-3	6.67e-3	1.45e-2	3.21e-2	6.00e-2
	Land	–	–	–	–	–	–	–	–	–
Styrene	Air	3.93e-4	3.56e-3	8.00e-3	1.98e-2	5.93e-2	1.19e-1	2.58e-1	5.71e-1	1.07
	Land	5.92e-4	2.37e-3	1.31e-2	3.94e-2	1.31e-1	3.23e-1	8.07e-1	2.37	5.46
Sulfotep (ISO)	Air	2.95e-5	2.67e-4	6.00e-4	1.48e-3	4.44e-3	8.89e-3	1.94e-2	4.29e-2	8.00e-2
	Land	–	–	–	–	–	–	–	–	–
Sulphur dioxide	Air	1.31e-4	1.19e-3	2.67e-3	6.59e-3	1.98e-2	3.96e-2	8.61e-2	1.91e-1	3.56e-1
	Land	–	–	–	–	–	–	–	–	–
Sulphur hexafluoride	Air	3.69e-1	3.33	7.50	1.85e+1	5.56e+1	1.11e+2	2.42e+2	5.36e+2	1.00e+3
	Land	–	–	–	–	–	–	–	–	–
Sulphuric acid	Air	1.47e-4	1.33e-3	3.00e-3	7.41e-3	2.22e-2	4.44e-2	9.68e-2	2.14e-1	4.00e-1
	Land	–	–	–	–	–	–	–	–	–
Sulphur tetrafluoride	Air	4.91e-5	4.44e-4	1.00e-3	2.47e-3	7.41e-3	1.48e-2	3.23e-2	7.14e-2	1.33e-1
	Land	–	–	–	–	–	–	–	–	–
Sulphuryl difluoride	Air	1.97e-3	1.78e-2	4.00e-2	9.88e-2	2.96e-1	5.93e-1	1.29	2.86	5.33
	Land	–	–	–	–	–	–	–	–	–
2,4,5-T (ISO)	Air	9.83e-4	8.89e-3	2.00e-2	4.94e-2	1.48e-1	2.96e-1	6.45e-1	1.43	2.67
	Land	–	–	–	–	–	–	–	–	–
TEPP (ISO)	Air	1.67e-5	6.67e-5	3.70e-4	1.11e-3	3.70e-3	9.09e-3	2.27e-2	6.67e-2	1.54e-1
	Land	–	–	–	–	–	–	–	–	–

Table D1 continued . . .

Substance	Test	Release Rate[a] (g/s) for Stack Height (m)								
		0	10	20	30	50	70	100	150	200
Tantalum	Air	4.91e-4	4.44e-3	1.00e-2	2.47e-2	7.41e-2	1.48e-1	3.23e-1	7.14e-1	1.33
	Land	–	–	–	–	–	–	–	–	–
Tellurium and compounds, except hydrogen telluride (as Te)	Air	1.47e-5	1.33e-4	3.00e-4	7.41e-4	2.22e-3	4.44e-3	9.68e-3	2.14e-2	4.00e-2
	Land	–	–	–	–	–	–	–	–	–
Terphenyls, all isomers	Air	2.46e-4	2.22e-3	5.00e-3	1.23e-2	3.70e-2	7.41e-2	1.61e-1	3.57e-1	6.67e-1
	Land	–	–	–	–	–	–	–	–	–
1,1,2,2-Tetrabromo-ethane	Air	1.03e-3	9.33e-3	2.10e-2	5.19e-2	1.56e-1	3.11e-1	6.77e-1	1.50	2.80
	Land	–	–	–	–	–	–	–	–	–
Tetracarbonylnickel (as Ni)	Air	1.18e-5	1.07e-4	2.40e-4	5.93e-4	1.78e-3	3.56e-3	7.74e-3	1.71e-2	3.20e-2
	Land	–	–	–	–	–	–	–	–	–
1,1,1,2-Tetrachloro-2,2-difluoroethane	Air	4.10e-2	3.71e-1	8.34e-1	2.06	6.18	1.24e+1	2.69e+1	5.96e+1	1.11e+2
	Land	–	–	–	–	–	–	–	–	–
1,1,2,2-Tetrachloro-1,2-difluoroethane	Air	4.10e-2	3.71e-1	8.34e-1	2.06	6.18	1.24e+1	2.69e+1	5.96e+1	1.11e+2
	Land	–	–	–	–	–	–	–	–	–
Tetrachloroethylene	Air	2.46e-3	2.22e-2	5.00e-2	1.23e-1	3.70e-1	7.41e-1	1.61	3.57	6.67
	Land	–	–	–	–	–	–	–	–	–
Tetrachloro-naphthalenes, all isomers	Air	1.97e-4	1.78e-3	4.00e-3	9.88e-3	2.96e-2	5.93e-2	1.29e-1	2.86e-1	5.33e-1
	Land	–	–	–	–	–	–	–	–	–
Tetraethyl orthosilicate	Air	1.25e-2	1.13e-1	2.55e-1	6.30e-1	1.89	3.78	8.23	1.82e+1	3.40e+1
	Land	–	–	–	–	–	–	–	–	–
Tetrahydrofuran	Air	2.90e-2	2.62e-1	5.90e-1	1.46	4.37	8.74	1.90e+1	4.21e+1	7.87e+1
	Land	–	–	–	–	–	–	–	–	–

Table D1 continued . . .

Substance	Test	Release Rate[a] (g/s) for Stack Height (m)								
		0	10	20	30	50	70	100	150	200
Tetramethyl orthosilicate	Air	2.00e-3	8.00e-3	4.44e-2	1.33e-1	4.44e-1	1.09	2.73	8.00	1.85e+1
	Land	-	-	-	-	-	-	-	-	-
Tetramethyl succinonitrile	Air	4.42e-4	4.00e-3	9.00e-3	2.22e-2	6.67e-2	1.33e-1	2.90e-1	6.43e-1	1.20
	Land	-	-	-	-	-	-	-	-	-
Tetrasodium pyrophosphate	Air	7.37e-4	6.67e-3	1.50e-2	3.70e-2	1.11e-1	2.22e-1	4.84e-1	1.07	2.00
	Land	-	-	-	-	-	-	-	-	-
Thallium, soluble compounds (as Tl)	Air	1.47e-5	1.33e-4	3.00e-4	7.41e-4	2.22e-3	4.44e-3	9.68e-3	2.14e-2	4.00e-2
	Land	-	-	-	-	-	-	-	-	-
Thiocyanates	Air	-	-	-	-	-	-	-	-	-
	Land	5.27e-7	2.11e-6	1.17e-5	3.52e-5	1.17e-4	2.88e-4	7.19e-4	2.11e-3	4.87e-3
Thionyl chloride	Air	2.46e-4	2.22e-3	5.00e-3	1.23e-2	3.70e-2	7.41e-2	1.61e-1	3.57e-1	6.67e-1
	Land	-	-	-	-	-	-	-	-	-
Thiram (ISO)	Air	4.91e-4	4.44e-3	1.00e-2	2.47e-2	7.41e-2	1.48e-1	3.23e-1	7.14e-1	1.33
	Land	-	-	-	-	-	-	-	-	-
Tin compounds, inorganic, except SnH₄ (as Sn)	Air	1.97e-4	1.78e-3	4.00e-3	9.88e-3	2.96e-2	5.93e-2	1.29e-1	2.86e-1	5.33e-1
	Land	-	-	-	-	-	-	-	-	-
Tin compounds, organic, except cyhexatin (ISO) (as Sn)	Air	9.83e-6	8.89e-5	2.00e-4	4.94e-4	1.48e-3	2.96e-3	6.45e-3	1.43e-2	2.67e-2
	Land	-	-	-	-	-	-	-	-	-
Titanium dioxide	Air	7.37e-4	6.67e-3	1.50e-2	3.70e-2	1.11e-1	2.22e-1	4.84e-1	1.07	2.00
	Land	-	-	-	-	-	-	-	-	-
Toluene	Air	3.69e-3	3.33e-2	7.50e-2	1.85e-1	5.56e-1	1.11	2.42	5.36	1.00e+1
	Land	3.34e-3	1.34e-2	7.43e-2	2.23e-1	7.43e-1	1.82	4.56	1.34e+1	3.09e+1

Table D1 continued . . .

Substance	Test	Release Rate[a] (g/s) for Stack Height (m)								
		0	10	20	30	50	70	100	150	200
p-Toluenesulphonyl chloride	Air	2.46e-4	2.22e-3	5.00e-3	1.23e-2	3.70e-2	7.41e-2	1.61e-1	3.57e-1	6.67e-1
	Land	–	–	–	–	–	–	–	–	–
Tributyl phosphate, all isomers	Air	2.46e-4	2.22e-3	5.00e-3	1.23e-2	3.70e-2	7.41e-2	1.61e-1	3.57e-1	6.67e-1
	Land	–	–	–	–	–	–	–	–	–
Tricarbonyl(eta-cyclopentadienyl) manganese (as Mn)	Air	1.47e-5	1.33e-4	3.00e-4	7.41e-4	2.22e-3	4.44e-3	9.68e-3	2.14e-2	4.00e-2
	Land	–	–	–	–	–	–	–	–	–
Tricarbonyl(methyl-cyclopentadienyl) manganese (as Mn)	Air	2.95e-5	2.67e-4	6.00e-4	1.48e-3	4.44e-3	8.89e-3	1.94e-2	4.29e-2	8.00e-2
	Land	–	–	–	–	–	–	–	–	–
1,2,4-Trichlorobenzene	Air	1.97e-3	1.78e-2	4.00e-2	9.88e-2	2.96e-1	5.93e-1	1.29	2.86	5.33
	Land	–	–	–	–	–	–	–	–	–
1,1,1-Trichlorobis (chlorophenyl)ethane	Air	1.47e-4	1.33e-3	3.00e-3	7.41e-3	2.22e-2	4.44e-2	9.68e-2	2.14e-1	4.00e-1
	Land	–	–	–	–	–	–	–	–	–
1,1,1-Trichloroethane	Air	2.41e-2	2.18e-1	4.90e-1	1.21	3.63	7.26	1.58e+1	3.50e+1	6.53e+1
	Land	–	–	–	–	–	–	–	–	–
Trichloroethylene	Air	4.91e-4	4.44e-3	1.00e-2	2.47e-2	7.41e-2	1.48e-1	3.23e-1	7.14e-1	1.33
	Land	2.06e-4	8.23e-4	4.57e-3	1.37e-2	4.57e-2	1.12e-1	2.81e-1	8.23e-1	1.90
Trichlorofluoro-methane	Air	3.44e-1	3.11	7.00	1.73e+1	5.19e+1	1.04e+2	2.26e+2	5.00e+2	9.33e+2
	Land	–	–	–	–	–	–	–	–	–
Trichloronitromethane	Air	9.83e-5	8.89e-4	2.00e-3	4.94e-3	1.48e-2	2.96e-2	6.45e-2	1.43e-1	2.67e-1
	Land	–	–	–	–	–	–	–	–	–

Table D1 continued . . . .

Substance	Test	Release Rate[a] (g/s) for Stack Height (m)								
		0	10	20	30	50	70	100	150	200
1,2,3-Trichloropropane	Air	2.21e-2	2.00e-1	4.50e-1	1.11	3.33	6.67	1.45e+1	3.21e+1	6.00e+1
	Land	–	–	–	–	–	–	–	–	–
1,1,2-Trichlorotrifluoroethane	Air	4.67e-1	4.22	9.50	2.35e+1	7.04e+1	1.41e+2	3.06e+2	6.79e+2	1.27e+3
	Land	–	–	–	–	–	–	–	–	–
Triethylamine	Air	2.95e-3	2.67e-2	6.00e-2	1.48e-1	4.44e-1	8.89e-1	1.94	4.29	8.00
	Land	–	–	–	–	–	–	–	–	–
Trimanganese tetraoxide	Air	1.47e-4	1.33e-3	3.00e-3	7.41e-3	2.22e-2	4.44e-2	9.68e-2	2.14e-1	4.00e-1
	Land	–	–	–	–	–	–	–	–	–
Trimethylamine	Air	1.77e-3	1.60e-2	3.60e-2	8.89e-2	2.67e-1	5.33e-1	1.16	2.57	4.80
	Land	–	–	–	–	–	–	–	–	–
Trimethylbenzenes, all isomers or mixtures	Air	1.81e-2	1.64e-1	3.69e-1	9.11e-1	2.73	5.47	1.19e+1	2.64e+1	4.92e+1
	Land	–	–	–	–	–	–	–	–	–
3,5,5-Trimethyl-cyclohex-2-enone	Air	1.23e-3	1.11e-2	2.50e-2	6.17e-2	1.85e-1	3.70e-1	8.06e-1	1.79	3.33
	Land	–	–	–	–	–	–	–	–	–
Trimethyl phosphite	Air	1.47e-3	1.33e-2	3.00e-2	7.41e-2	2.22e-1	4.44e-1	9.68e-1	2.14	4.00
	Land	–	–	–	–	–	–	–	–	–
2,4,6-Trinitrotoluene	Air	7.37e-5	6.67e-4	1.50e-3	3.70e-3	1.11e-2	2.22e-2	4.84e-2	1.07e-1	2.00e-1
	Land	–	–	–	–	–	–	–	–	–
Triphenyl phosphate	Air	2.95e-4	2.67e-3	6.00e-3	1.48e-2	4.44e-2	8.89e-2	1.94e-1	4.29e-1	8.00e-1
	Land	–	–	–	–	–	–	–	–	–
Tri-o-tolyl phosphate	Air	1.47e-5	1.33e-4	3.00e-4	7.41e-4	2.22e-3	4.44e-3	9.68e-3	2.14e-2	4.00e-2
	Land	–	–	–	–	–	–	–	–	–

Table D1 continued . . .

Substance	Test	Release Rate[a] (g/s) for Stack Height (m)								
		0	10	20	30	50	70	100	150	200
Tungsten and compounds (as W)	Air	1.47e-4	1.33e-3	3.00e-3	7.41e-3	2.22e-2	4.44e-2	9.68e-2	2.14e-1	4.00e-1
	Land	–	–	–	–	–	–	–	–	–
Turpentine	Air	4.13e-2	3.73e-1	8.40e-1	2.07	6.22	1.24e+1	2.71e+1	6.00e+1	1.12e+2
	Land	–	–	–	–	–	–	–	–	–
Uranium compounds, natural, soluble (as U)	Air	2.95e-5	2.67e-4	6.00e-4	1.48e-3	4.44e-3	8.89e-3	1.94e-2	4.29e-2	8.00e-2
	Land	–	–	–	–	–	–	–	–	–
Vanadium	Air	4.91e-7	4.44e-6	1.00e-5	2.47e-5	7.41e-5	1.48e-4	3.23e-4	7.14e-4	1.33e-3
	Land	–	–	–	–	–	–	–	–	–
Vinyl acetate	Air	2.95e-3	2.67e-2	6.00e-2	1.48e-1	4.44e-1	8.89e-1	1.94	4.29	8.00
	Land	–	–	–	–	–	–	–	–	–
Vinyl chloride	Air	2.48e-4	2.24e-3	5.04e-3	1.24e-2	3.73e-2	7.47e-2	1.63e-1	3.60e-1	6.72e-1
	Land	–	–	–	–	–	–	–	–	–
Vinylidene chloride	Air	1.18e-3	1.07e-2	2.40e-2	5.93e-2	1.78e-1	3.56e-1	7.74e-1	1.71	3.20
	Land	–	–	–	–	–	–	–	–	–
Warfarin (ISO)	Air	1.47e-5	1.33e-4	3.00e-4	7.41e-4	2.22e-3	4.44e-3	9.68e-3	2.14e-2	4.00e-2
	Land	–	–	–	–	–	–	–	–	–
White spirit	Air	3.54e-2	3.20e-1	7.20e-1	1.78	5.33	1.07e+1	2.32e+1	5.14e+1	9.60e+1
	Land	–	–	–	–	–	–	–	–	–
Xylene, o-, m-, p- or mixed isomers	Air	3.19e-2	2.89e-1	6.50e-1	1.60	4.81	9.63	2.10e+1	4.64e+1	8.67e+1
	Land	4.89e-4	1.95e-3	1.09e-2	3.26e-2	1.09e-1	2.67e-1	6.66e-1	1.95	4.51
Xylidine, all isomers	Air	3.33e-3	1.33e-2	7.41e-2	2.22e-1	7.41e-1	1.82	4.55	1.33e+1	3.08e+1
	Land	–	–	–	–	–	–	–	–	–

Table D1 continued . . .

Substance	Test	Release Rate[a] (g/s) for Stack Height (m)								
		0	10	20	30	50	70	100	150	200
Yttrium	Air	1.47e-4	1.33e-3	3.00e-3	7.41e-3	2.22e-2	4.44e-2	9.68e-2	2.14e-1	4.00e-1
	Land	–	–	–	–	–	–	–	–	–
Zinc	Air	–	–	–	–	–	–	–	–	–
	Land	6.17e-6	2.47e-5	1.37e-4	4.12e-4	1.37e-3	3.37e-3	8.42e-3	2.47e-2	5.70e-2
Zirconium compounds (as Zr)	Air	4.91e-4	4.44e-3	1.00e-2	2.47e-2	7.41e-2	1.48e-1	3.23e-1	7.14e-1	1.33
	Land	–	–	–	–	–	–	–	–	–

(a) Release rates are expressed in "scientific" notation. For example, 0.0018 is expressed as 1.80e-3.

(b) Air significance test data are for any cresol isomer; land significance test data are for total of all cresol isomers

(c) Total anthracene, benzo(a)anthracene, benzo(k)fluoranthene, benzo(a)pyrene, chrysene, phenanthrene, fluoranthene, indeno(1,2,3-cd)pyrene, naphthalene, benzo(ghi)perylene

(d) Total PCBs 28, 52, 101, 118, 138, 153, 180

Table D2:
Significant release rates for pollutants released to inland waters

Substance [1]	Significant release rate (μg/s) at specified river flow rate (m³/s)			Source of EAL [1] [2]
	19.0	2.0	0.4	
Aldrin	0.38	0.04	0.008	SI 2286
Ammonia	152	16	3.2	95%ile as N 78/659/EEC
Ammonia (unionised) (as N)	152	16	3.2	95%ile as N 78/659/EEC
Ammonium (total) (as N)	1182	124	25	95%ile as N 78/659/EEC
Arsenic	1900	200	40	Circular 7/89
Atrazine + simazine	76	8	1.6	Dissolved DoE (1991)
Azinphos methyl	0.38	0.04	0.008	Dissolved DoE (1991)
Biphenyl	950	100	2	Barry *et al* (1994)
BOD$_5$	114000	12000	2400	95%ile 78/659/EEC
Boron	76000	8000	1600	Circular 7/89
Bromoxynil	3800	400	80	Murgatroyd *et al* (1995)
Cadmium & compounds	190	20	4	SI 2286
Carbon tetrachloride	456	48	9.6	SI 2286
Chlorine (HOCl)	190	20	4	78/659/EEC
Chloroform	456	48	9.6	SI 2286
Chloronitro-toluenes	380	40	8	Specific isomers Jerman *et al* (1992)
Chromium	190	20	4	Dissolved Circular 7/89
Copper	38	4	0.8	Dissolved Circular 7/89
Cyfluthrin	0.038	0.004	0.0008	95%ile Circular 7/89
DDT (all isomers)	0.95	0.1	0.02	SI 2286
1,2-Dichloroethane	380	40	8	SI 337
Dichlorvos	0.038	0.004	0.0008	DoE (1991)
Dieldrin	0.38	0.04	0.008	SI 2286
Dimethoate	38	4	0.8	Murgatroyd *et al* (1994)
Endosulfan	0.114	0.012	0.0024	Dissolved DoE (1991)
Endrin	0.19	0.02	0.004	SI 2286
Fenitrothion	0.38	0.04	0.008	DoE (1991)
Flucofuron	38	4	0.8	95%ile Circular 7/89
Formaldehyde	190	20	4	Jerman *et al* (1993)
Hexachloro-benzene	1.14	0.12	0.024	SI 2286
Hexachloro-butadiene	3.8	0.4	0.08	SI 2286

Table D2 continued . . .

Substance [1]	Significant release rate (μg/s) at specified river flow rate (m^3/s)			Source of EAL [1] [2]
	19.0	2.0	0.4	
Hexachloro-cyclohexane (all isomers)	3.8	0.4	0.08	SI 2286
Ioxynil	380	40	8	Murgatroyd et al (1995)
Iron	38000	4000	800	Dissolved Circular 7/89
Isodrin	0.19	0.02	0.004	SI 2286
Lead	152	16	3.2	Circular 7/89
Malachite green	19	2	0.4	Burchmore et al (1993)
Malathion	0.38	0.04	0.008	DoE (1991)
Mercury & compounds	38	4	0.8	SI 2286
Nickel	1900	200	40	Circular 7/89
Nitrite (N)	114	12	2.4	95%ile 78/659/EEC
p-p-DDT	0.38	0.04	0.008	SI 2286
PCSDs	1.9	0.2	0.04	95%ile Circular 7/89
Pentachlorophenol & compounds	76	8	1.6	SI 2286
Perchloroethylene	380	40	8	SI 337
Permethrin	0.38	0.04	0.008	95%ile Circular 7/89
Phosphorus (P)	247	26	5.2	78/659/EEC
Simazine + atrazine	76	8	1.6	Dissolved DoE (1991)
Sulcofuron	950	100	20	95%ile Circular 7/89
Suspended solids	950000	100000	20000	78/659/EEC
Tecnazene	38	4	0.8	Murgatroyd et al (1993)
Tin (inorganic)	950	100	20	Mance et al (1988)
Toluene	1900	200	40	Jones et al (1992)
Tributyl tin	0.76	0.08	0.016	MAC Circular 7/89
Trichlorobenzenes (all isomers)	15.2	1.6	0.32	SI 337
1,1,1-Tri-chloroethane	3800	400	80	Rees et al (1992)
Trichloroethylene	380	40	8	SI 337
Trifluralin	3.8	0.4	0.08	Dissolved DoE (1991)
Triphenyl tin	0.76	0.08	0.016	MAC Circular 7/89
Vanadium	760	80	16	Circular 7/89
Zinc	304	32	6.4	Dissolved Circular 7/89

Notes:
[1] *See Tables B1, B2 for details*
[2] *See Tables B1, B2 for references*

Table D3:
Significant release rates for pollutants released to estuaries

Substance [1]	Significant release rate (μg/sec) at specified dispersion rate (m³/s)				Source of EAL [1] [2]
	15.0	**10.0**	**5.0**	**2.4**	
Aldrin	0.3	0.2	0.1	0.048	SI 2286
Ammonia (unionised)	630	420	210	101	As N Seager et al (1988)
Arsenic	750	500	250	120	Circular 7/89
Atrazine + simazine	60	40	20	9.6	Dissolved DoE (1991)
Azinphos methyl	0.3	0.2	0.1	0.048	Dissolved DoE (1991)
Biphenyl	750	500	250	120	Barry et al (1994)
BOD₅	-	-	-	-	
Boron	210000	140000	70000	33600	Circular 7/89
Bromoxynil	3000	2000	1000	480	Murgatroyd et al (1995)
Cadmium & compounds	150	100	50	24	SI 2286
Carbon tetrachloride	360	240	120	58	SI 2286
Chlorine (HOCl)	-	-	-	-	
Chloroform	360	240	120	58	SI 2286
Chloronitro-toluenes	300	200	100	48	Specific isomers Jerman et al (1992)
Chromium	450	300	150	72	Dissolved Circular 7/89
Copper	150	100	50	24	Dissolved Circular 7/89
Cyfluthrin	0.03	0.02	0.01	0.005	95%ile Circular 7/89
DDT (all isomers)	0.75	0.5	0.25	0.12	SI 2286
1,2-Dichloroethane	300	200	100	48	SI 337
Dichlorvos	1.2	0.8	0.4	0.19	DoE (1991)
Dieldrin	0.3	0.2	0.1	0.048	SI 2286
Dimethoate	30	20	10	4.8	Murgatroyd et al (1994)
Endosulfan	0.09	0.06	0.03	0.014	Dissolved DoE (1991)
Endrin	0.15	0.1	0.05	0.024	SI 2286
Fenitrothion	0.3	0.2	0.1	0.048	DoE (1991)
Flucofuron	30	20	10	4.8	95%ile Circular 7/89
Formaldehyde	-	-	-	-	
Hexachloro-benzene	0.9	0.6	0.3	0.14	SI 2286
Hexachloro-butadiene	3	2	1	0.48	SI 2286
Hexachloro-cyclohexane (all isomers)	0.6	0.4	0.2	0.1	SI 2286
Ioxynil	300	200	100	48	Murgatroyd et al (1995)

Table D3 continued . . .

Substance [1]	Significant release rate (μg/sec) at specified dispersion rate (m³/s)				Source of EAL [1] [2]
	15.0	10.0	5.0	2.4	
Iron	30000	20000	10000	4800	Dissolved Circular 7/89
Isodrin	0.15	0.1	0.05	0.024	SI 2286
Lead	750	500	250	120	Dissolved Circular 7/89
Malachite green	-	-	-	-	
Malathion	0.6	0.4	0.2	0.096	DoE (1991)
Mercury & compounds	15	10	5	2.4	SI 2286
Nickel	900	600	300	144	Dissolved Circular 7/89
Nitrite (N)	-	-	-	-	
p-p-DDT	0.3	0.2	0.1	0.048	SI 2286
PCSDs	1.5	1	0.5	0.24	95%ile Circular 7/89
Pentachlorophenol & compounds	60	40	20	9.6	SI 2286
Perchloroethylene	300	200	100	48	SI 337
Permethrin	0.3	0.2	0.1	0.048	95%ile Circular 7/89
Phosphorus (P)	-	-	-	-	
Simazine + atrazine	60	40	20	9.6	Dissolved DoE (1991)
Sulcofuron	750	500	250	120	95%ile Circular 7/89
Suspended solids	-	-	-	-	
Tecnazene	30	20	10	4.8	Murgatroyd *et al* (1993)
Tin (inorganic)	300	200	100	48	Mance *et al* (1988)
Toluene	1200	800	400	192	Jones *et al* (1992)
Tributyl tin	0.06	0.04	0.02	0.01	MAC Circular 7/89
Trichlorobenzenes (all isomers)	12	8	4	1.9	SI 337
1,1,1-Tri-chloroethane	3000	2000	1000	480	Rees *et al* (1992)
Trichloroethylene	300	200	100	48	SI 337
Trifluralin	3	2	1	0.48	Dissolved DoE (1991)
Triphenyl tin	0.24	0.16	0.08	0.038	MAC Circular 7/89
Vanadium	3000	2000	1000	480	Circular 7/89
Zinc	1200	800	400	192	Dissolved Circular 7/89

Notes:

[1]   See Tables B1, B2 for details

[2]   See Tables B1, B2 for references

Table D4:
Significant release rates for pollutants released to coastal waters

Substance [1]	Significant function of release rate (μg/mg/m/s$^{2/3}$) at specified dilution rate (m^2/s$^{2/3}$)			Source of EAL [1] [2]
	25.0	8.0	2.5	
Aldrin	0.5	0.16	0.05	SI 2286
Ammonia (unionised)	1050	336	105	As N Seager *et al* (1988)
Arsenic	1250	400	125	Circular 7/89
Atrazine + simazine	100	32	10	Dissolved DoE (1991)
Azinphos methyl	0.5	0.16	0.05	Dissolved DoE (1991)
Biphenyl	1250	400	125	Barry *et al* (1994)
BOD$_5$	-	-	-	
Boron	350000	112000	35000	Circular 7/89
Bromoxynil	5000	1600	500	Murgatroyd *et al* (1995)
Cadmium & compounds	125	40	12.5	SI 2286
Carbon tetrachloride	600	192	60	SI 2286
Chlorine (HOCl)	-	-	-	
Chloroform	600	192	60	SI 2286
Chloronitro-toluenes	500	160	50	Specific isomers Jerman *et al* (1992)
Chromium	750	240	75	Dissolved Circular 7/89
Copper	250	80	25	Dissolved Circular 7/89
Cyfluthrin	0.05	0.016	0.005	95%ile Circular 7/89
DDT (all isomers)	1.25	0.4	0.125	SI 2286
1,2-Dichloroethane	500	160	50	SI 337
Dichlorvos	2	0.64	0.2	DoE (1991)
Dieldrin	0.5	0.16	0.05	SI 2286
Dimethoate	50	16	5	Murgatroyd *et al* (1994)
Endosulfan	0.15	0.048	0.015	Dissolved DoE (1991)
Endrin	0.25	0.08	0.025	SI 2286
Fenitrothion	0.5	0.16	0.05	DoE (1991)
Flucofuron	50	16	5	95%ile Circular 7/89
Formaldehyde	-	-	-	
Hexachloro-benzene	1.5	0.48	0.15	SI 2286
Hexachloro-butadiene	5	1.6	0.5	SI 2286
Hexachloro-cyclohexane (all isomers)	1	0.32	0.1	SI 2286
Ioxynil	500	160	50	Murgatroyd *et al* (1995)
Iron	50000	16000	5000	Dissolved Circular 7/89

Table D4 continued . . .

Substance [1]	Significant function of release rate (μg/mg/m/s$^{2/3}$) at specified dilution rate (m^2/s$^{2/3}$)			Source of EAL [1] [2]
	25.0	**8.0**	**2.5**	
Lead	1250	400	125	Dissolved Circular 7/89
Malachite green	-	-	-	
Malathion	1	0.32	0.1	DoE (1991)
Mercury & compounds	15	4.8	1.5	SI 2286
Nickel	1500	480	150	Dissolved Circular 7/89
Nitrite (N)	-	-	-	
p-p-DDT	0.5	0.16	0.05	SI 2286
PCSDs	2.5	0.8	0.25	95%ile Circular 7/89
Pentachlorophenol & compounds	100	32	10	SI 2286
Perchloroethylene	500	160	50	SI 337
Permethrin	0.5	0.16	0.05	95%ile Circular 7/89
Phosphorus (P)	-	-	-	
Simazine + atrazine	100	32	10	Dissolved DoE (1991)
Sulcofuron	1250	400	125	95%ile Circular 7/89
Suspended solids	-	-	-	
Tecnazene	50	16	5	Murgatroyd et al (1993)
Tin (inorganic)	500	160	50	Mance et al (1988)
Toluene	2000	640	200	Jones et al (1992)
Tributyl tin	0.1	0.032	0.01	MAC Circular 7/89
Trichlorobenzenes (all isomers)	20	6.4	2	SI 337
1,1,1-Tri-chloroethane	5000	1600	500	Rees et al (1992)
Trichloroethylene	500	160	50	SI 337
Trifluralin	5	1.6	0.5	Dissolved DoE (1991)
Triphenyl tin	0.4	0.128	0.04	MAC Circular 7/89
Vanadium	5000	1600	500	Circular 7/89
Zinc	2000	640	200	Dissolved Circular 7/89

Notes:

[1]   See Tables B1, B2 for details

[2]   See Tables B1, B2 for references

ANNEX E   Substance unit hazard scores

Table E1:
Exposure, toxicity and unit hazard scores for inorganic substances disposed of as waste from prescribed processes

Chemicals	Aquatic toxicity (AQT)	Total water mammalian toxicity score	Aquatic toxicity score (TW)	S+A+DW+BW water total	Unit hazard score (w)	Total air mammalian toxicity score	V+Da air total	Unit hazard score (a)	Unit hazard score total
Aluminium chloride	6	14	20	18	360	14	5	70	430
Aluminium sulphate	4	14	18	17	306	14	5	70	376
Arsenic trioxide	4	19	23	15	345	19	5	95	440
Cadmium chloride	5	18	23	15	345	21	5	105	450
Calcium chloride	1	6	7	17	119	6	5	30	139
Calcium sulphate	1	6	7	14	98	6	5	30	128
Copper chloride	6	9	15	18	270	9	5	45	315
Copper sulphate	5	10	15	17	255	10	5	50	305
Iron III chloride	3	10	13	19	247	10	5	50	297
Iron III sulphate	2	10	12	16	192	10	5	50	242
Lead acetate	3	19	22	14	308	19	5	95	403
Lead chloride	3	17	20	12	240	17	5	85	325
Lead nitrate	3	17	20	14	280	17	5	85	365
Mercury II chloride	6	21	27	13	351	21	5	105	456
Mercury II nitrate	5	16	21	12	252	16	5	80	332
Nickel II chloride	3	17	20	16	320	20	5	100	420
Nickel II sulphate	3	14	17	15	255	17	5	85	340
Silver nitrate	6	9	15	16	240	9	5	45	285
Sodium acetate	1	6	7	17	119	6	5	30	149

Table E1 continued . . .

Chemicals	Aquatic toxicity (AQT)	Total water mammalian toxicity score	Aquatic toxicity score (TW)	S+A+DW+BW water total	Unit hazard score (w)	Total air mammalian toxicity score	V+Da air total	Unit hazard score (a)	Unit hazard score total
Sodium carbonate	1	6	7	15	105	6	5	30	135
Sodium hydroxide	2	10	12	16	192	10	5	50	242
Tin II chloride	4	10	14	17	238	10	5	50	288
Zinc chloride	5	9	14	16	224	9	5	45	269
Zinc sulphate	3	9	12	16	192	9	5	45	237

Table E2:
Exposure, toxicity and unit hazard scores for organic substances disposed of as waste from prescribed processes

Chemicals	Aquatic toxicity (AQT)	Total water mammalian toxicity score	Aquatic toxicity score (TW)	S+A+DW+BW water total	Unit hazard score (w)	Total air mammalian toxicity score	V+Da air total	Unit hazard score (a)	Unit hazard score total
Acetaldehyde	2	14	16	13	208	14	3	42	250
Acetic acid	2	6	8	9	72	6	3	18	90
Acetone	1	8	9	12	108	8	5	40	148
Acrylonitrile	3	17	20	12	240	17	4	68	308
Aldrin	6	18	24	12	288	18	2	36	324
Benzaldehyde	3	9	12	10	120	9	2	18	138
Carbon tetrachloride	3	21	24	12	288	21	7	147	435
Dichlorobenzene (1,4)	3	12	15	12	180	10	2	20	200
Dichlorethane (1,2)	1	12	13	13	169	10	5	50	219
Dichloromethane	1	11	12	13	156	11	5	55	211
Dieldrin	4	18	22	10	220	18	3	54	274
Endrin	4	13	17	11	187	13	3	39	226
Ethyl acetate	1	8	9	13	117	8	3	24	141
Ethyl acrylate	3	15	18	11	198	13	2	26	224
Ethylene glycol	1	14	15	13	195	14	2	28	223
Formaldehyde	3	17	20	9	180	20	5	100	280
Gamma hexachloro-cyclohexane	5	14	19	11	209	12	2	24	233
Hexachloro-benzene	4	18	22	10	220	16	5	80	300
Hexachlorobuta-1,3 diene	4	17	21	12	252	17	5	85	337
Methanol	1	11	12	13	156	11	4	44	200
Methyl acrylate	3	10	13	12	156	10	3	30	186

Table E2 continued . . .

Chemicals	Aquatic toxicity (AQT)	Total water mammalian toxicity score	Aquatic toxicity score (TW)	S+A+DW+BW water total	Unit hazard score (w)	Total air mammalian toxicity score	V+Da air total	Unit hazard score (a)	Unit hazard score total
Methyl ethyl ketone	1	14	15	12	180	14	4	56	236
Napthalene	3	13	16	9	144	13	2	26	170
Penta-chlorophenol	5	11	16	13	208	11	3	33	241
Styrene	3	15	18	12	216	15	2	30	246
Tetrachloro-ethylene	3	10	13	13	169	10	4	40	209
Tetrahydrofuran	1	9	10	15	150	9	4	36	186
Toluene	5	14	19	9	171	14	3	42	213
Trichloro-ethylene	3	9	12	14	168	9	3	27	195
Trichlorobenzene (1,2,4-)	3	10	13	12	156	10	3	30	186
Trichloroethane (1,1,1-)	2	9	11	13	143	9	5	45	188
Trimethyl benzene	2	9	11	9	99	9	2	18	117
Urea	1	12	13	15	195	12	2	24	219
Vinyl chloride	1	13	14	12	168	13	5	65	233
Xylene (ortho-)	3	15	18	10	180	15	2	30	210

References

Ashmore MR and Wilson RB (1992) *Critical Levels of Air Pollutants for Europe*
Background papers prepared for the United Nations Economic Commission for Europe Workshop on Critical Levels. Egham UK, 23-26th March 1992. Air Quality Division, Department of the Environment, London.

BRE (1991) *An Environmental Priority Setting Scheme for existing chemicals*
Draft for Comment. Directorate for Air, Climate and Toxic Substances, Department of the Environment, July 1991.

Barry M et al (1994) *Proposed environmental quality standards for biphenyl in water*
WRc report to the Department of the Environment, DoE 3151/1.

Burchmore S et al (1993) *Proposed environmental quality standards for malachite green in water*
WRc report to the Department of the Environment, DoE 3167/2.

Clarke RH (1979) *A model for short and medium range dispersion of radionuclides released to the atmosphere* NRPB-R91. National Radiological Protection Board. Chilton, Oxon.

Cleveland Fuels (1992) *Environmental Statement for a proposed waste recovery, treatment and transfer centre, Regent Rd, Liverpool*
Cleveland Fuels Ltd, Liverpool.

Coca Cola and Schweppes Beverages (1991) *Environmental Statement, development at Brackmills, Northampton. Technical Paper 3*
Coca Cola and Schweppes Beverages Ltd.

Cory Environmental (1991) *Environmental Statement, Belvedere refuse to energy project, Volume II*
Cory Environmental.

CRC (1992) *Handbook of Chemistry and Physics (73rd ed.)* 1992-1993
Lide D R (ed), CRC Press Boca Raton, US. 16-22 - 16-24.

Culbard EB, Thornton I, Watt J, Wheatley M, Moorcroft S and Thompson M (1988) *Metal contamination in British Urban Dusts and Soils*
Journal Environmental Quality 17(2), 226-234.

Davis RD (1980) *Control of contamination problems in the treatment and disposal of sewage sludge. Technical Report number TR 156*
Water Research Centre, Medmenham.

Davies BE (1985) *Baseline Survey of Metals in Welsh Soils*
Proc. First International Symposium on Geochemistry and Health.

Derwent RG (1993) *Hydrocarbons in the Atmosphere: Their Sources, Distributions and Fates*
Proceedings of IAI Conference, October 1993, London.

Derwent RG and Jenkin ME (1991) *Hydrocarbons and the long-range transport of ozone and PAN across Europe*
Atmospheric Environment 25A (8) 1661-1678

Derwent RG, Jenkin ME and Saunders SM (1996) *Photochemical ozone creation potentials for a large number of reactive hydrocarbons under European conditions*
Atmospheric Environment 30 (2) 181-199.

DoE (1981) *Chimney heights*
Third Edition of the 1956 Clean Air Act Memorandum. HMSO, London
ISBN 0-11-751556-6.

DoE (1991) *National Environmental Quality Standards for Dangerous Substances in Water: Joint Consultation Paper*
Issued by the Department of Environment jointly with the Welsh Office, Scottish Environment Department and the Department of the Environment (Northern Ireland). November 1991.

DoE (1992a) *Appeals by Ocean Environmental Management Limited and International Technology Europe Limited - Report of the Inspectors 7 volumes*
Department of the Environment, Northern Regional Office, Newcastle upon Tyne, UK.

DoE (1992b) *Decision of the Secretary of State in relation to the local enquiry held to hear the appeal by Cory Environmental Management (formerly Ocean Environmental Management) for land at Seal Sands, Billingham (application no. CS/2262/88)*
Department of the Environment, Northern Regional Office, Newcastle upon Tyne, UK.

DoE (1993) *Reducing Emissions of volatile organic compounds (VOCs) and levels of ground level ozone: A UK Strategy*
Department of the Environment.

EACDP (1996) *Released Substances and their Dispersion in the Environment: Guidance for Applicants for Process Authorisation under Integrated Pollution Control*
Environmental Analysis Cooperative Development Project HMSO

EPAQS (1994a) *Ozone*
Department of the Environment, Expert Panel on Air Quality Standards HMSO, London

EPAQS (1994b) *1,3-Butadiene*
Department of the Environment, Expert Panel on
Air Quality Standards HMSO, London

EPAQS (1994c) *Benzene*
Department of the Environment, Expert Panel on
Air Quality Standards HMSO, London.

EPAQS (1994d) *Carbon Monoxide*
Department of the Environment, Expert Panel on
Air Quality Standards HMSO, London.

EPAQS (1995a) *Sulphur Dioxide*
Department of the Environment, Expert Panel on
Air Quality Standards HMSO, London.

EPAQS (1995b) *Particles*
Department of the Environment, Expert Panel on
Air Quality Standards HMSO, London.

Hall DJ and Kukadia V (1993) *Approaches to the
calculation of discharge stack heights for odour control*
Warren Spring Laboratory Report No. LR 994 ISBN
0-85624-854-1

HMIP (1989) *Determination of Polychlorinated Biphenyls,
Polychlorinated Dibenzo-p-dioxins and Polychlorinated Dibenzo-
p-furans in UK soils*
Her Majesty's Inspectorate of Pollution, Technical
Report HMSO, London

HMIP (1995a) *Determination of Polychlorinated Biphenyls,
Polychlorinated Dibenzo-p-dioxins and Polychlorinated Dibenzo-
p-furans in UK soils*
Her Majesty's Inspectorate of Pollution, 2nd
Technical Report HMSO, London

HMIP (1995b) *Protocol for the Environmental Evaluation of
Achievable Releases in Chief Inspector's Guidance Notes*
WS Akins Environment Report No E5251-R1/Draft

HMSO (1993) *Guidelines on discharge stack heights for
polluting emissions*
Technical Guidance Note (Dispersion) D1 HMSO,
London

HMSO (1995) *Digest of Environmental Statistics No 17
1995*
HMSO, London

HSE (1995) EH40/95 *Occupational exposure limits 1995*
HMSO, London

IPCC (1994) *Radiative forcing of climate change*
The 1994 Report of the Scientific Assessment
Working Group of IPCC. Summary for Policy
Makers. Intergovernmental Panel on Climate
Change, WMO/UNEP

IPCC (1996) Climate change 1995. The Science of
Climate Change

Ireland FE (1970) *The determination of chimney heights in
Britain*
One Hundred and Sixth Report on Alkali etc. Works
1969 HMSO, London

Jerman E et al (1992) *Proposed environmental quality
standards for chloronitrotoluenes in water 4,2-CNT, 4,3-CNT,
2,4-CNT, 2,5-CNT, 2,6-CNT*
WRc report to the Department of the Environment,
DoE 3007/1

Jerman E et al (1993) *Proposed environmental quality
standards for formaldehyde in water*
WRc report to the Department of the Environment,
DoE 3206/1

Jones A et al (1992) *Proposed environmental quality
standards for toluene in water*
WRc report to the Department of the Environment,
DoE 2998/1

Jones JA (1983) *Models to allow for the effects of coastal
sites, plume rise and buildings on dispersion of radionuclides and
guidance on the value of deposition velocity and washout
coefficients*
NRPB-R157 National Radiological Protection Board,
Chilton, Oxon

Leigh Environmental (1990) *Environmental Statement,
Waste Incinerator, Nash Rd, Trafford Park, Manchester*
Volume 3 Environmental Assessment Chemical
Waste Incinerator, Volume 4 Environmental
Assessment Clinical Waste Incinerator. Leigh
Environmental

Mahler EAJ (1967) *Standards of emission under the Alkali
Act*
One Hundred and Third Annual Report on Alkali
etc. Works by the Chief Inspectors 1966 HMSO,
London

Mance G et al (1988) *Proposed environmental quality
standards for List II substances in water - inorganic tin*
Technical Report TR254 WRc, Medmenham

McGrath SP and Loveland PJ (1992) *The Soil
Geochemical Atlas of England and Wales*
Blackie Academic and Professional, London.

Murgatroyd C et al (1993) *Proposed environmental quality
standards for tecnazene in water*
WRc report to the Department of the Environment,
DoE 3206/1

Murgatroyd C et al (1994) *Proposed environmental quality
standards for dimethoate and omethoate in water*

WRc report to the Department of the Environment, DoE 3300

Murgatroyd C et al (1995) *Proposed environmental quality standards for bromoxynil and ioxynil in water*
WRc report to the Department of the Environment, DoE 3627/1

PORG (1993) *Ozone in the United Kingdom*
Third Report of the United Kingdom Photochemical Oxidants Review Group. Department of the Environment, London

Rees Y et al (1992) *Proposed environmental quality standards for trichloroethanes in water*
WRc report to the Department of the Environment, DoE 2942/1

Seager J et al (1988) *Proposed environmental quality standards for List II substances in water - ammonia*
Technical Report TR 260, WRc, Medmenham

Shillaker R O (1992) Priority and Risk Assessment of Chemicals-Human Health Effects
In, Richardson M L (ed), Risk Management of Chemicals. The Royal Society of Chemistry

SRC (1992a) *Soil/Sediment Adsorption Constant Program*
Lewis Publishers, Boca Raton

SRC (1992b) *Biodegredation Probability Program*
Lewis Publishers, Boca Raton

SRC (1992c) *Henry's Law Constant Program*
Lewis Publishers, Boca Raton

SRC (1994a) WS-KOW, *Water Solubility from Log Kow program for Microsoft Windows 3.1*
Syracuse Research Corporation, New York

SRC (1994b) KOWWIN, *Octanol-Water Partition Coefficient program for Microsoft Windows 3.1*
Syracuse Research Corporation, New York

Thames Water Utilities Limited (1991a) *Environmental Statement - Crossness Sewage Sludge Incinerator*
Prepared by Ove Arup Thames Water, Reading, UK

Thames Water Utilities Limited (1991a) *Environmental Statement - Beckton Sewage Sludge Incinerator*
Prepared by Ove Arup Thames Water, Reading, UK

Turner DB (1994) *Workbook of Atmospheric Dispersion Estimates 2nd ed.*
CRC Press Ltd (Lewis Pub.), Boca Raton

UNECE (1991) *Protocol to the 1979 Convention on Long-range Transboundary Air Pollution concerning the Control of Emissions of Volatile Organic Compounds or their Transboundary Fluxes*

Geneva 18th November 1991 United Nations Economic Commission for Europe, Geneva

UNECE (1993) *Manual on Methodologies and Criteria for Mapping Critical Levels/Loads and Geographical Areas where they are exceeded*
Convention on Long-Range Transboundary Air Pollution, Task Force on Mapping, Geneva. Publication of the Federal Environmental Agency, Berlin, Germany Text 25/93

Valentin FHH and North AA (eds) (1980). *Odour Control - a concise guide*
Warren Spring Laboratory Report, prepared on behalf of the Department of the Environment ISBN 0 85624 2144

WHO (1987) *Air Quality Guidelines for Europe*
World Health Organisation Regional Publications, European Series No. 23 Geneva

WHO (1994) *Assessing human health risks of chemicals: Derivation of guidance values for health based exposure limits*
Environmental Health Criteria 170, World Health Organisation, Geneva

WHO (1995) *WHO Air Quality Guidelines for Europe - Update and Revision*
World Health Organisation paper EUR/IGP/EHAZ94.05/PB01 Geneva

Willis PG (1994) *The UK National Air Monitoring Networks, 1994*
Report Number LR 1004 (AP) National Environmental Technology Centre, AEA Technology, Oxon

Woodfield M and Hall D (eds) (1994). *Odour measurement and control - An update*
AEA Technology National Environmental Technology Centre, Culham, Abingdon, UK ISBN 0 85624 8258

Glossary of terms

Term	Definition
Ambient concentration	The existing concentration of a substance in air, water or soil at a given location. In the case of existing processes, this should include the current process contribution which will need to be corrected in calculating the PEC. Sources of data on ambient concentrations are available in *Released Substances and their Dispersion in the Environment*[3] (EACDP 1996).
Best Practicable Environmental Option (BPEO)	For the purposes of IPC the BPEO is strictly the option with the BATNEEC having regard to BPEO. It can be considered (for the purposes of IPC) as the option which in the context of releases from a prescribed process, provides the most benefit or least damage to the environment as a whole, at a **cost that is not excessive**, in the long term as well as the short term.
Corrected ambient concentration	For existing processes this is defined as the Ambient concentration minus the current contribution of the process: For new processes the corrected ambient concentration equals the ambient concentration.
Cost effectiveness analysis	The determination of the least-cost method or means of achieving a particular objective. Cost-effectiveness may also be expressed as the lowest cost per unit of objective achieved.
Environmental Assessment Level (EAL)	The concentration of a substance which, in a particular environmental medium, the EA regards as a comparator value to enable a comparison to be made between the environmental effects of different substances in that medium and between environmental effects in different media, and to enable the summation of those effects. Where there is an EQS then the EAL will be the EQS.
Environmental Quality Standard (EQS)	Concentration of a substance in the receiving environment which must not be exceeded if the environment is to be suitable for a particular purpose or use or to achieve a certain level of protection for a particular receptor(s). In the context of this report the term EQS has been applied only to statutory limits prescribed by the Secretary of State.
Environmental Quotient$_{(Medium)}$ ($EQ_{(Medium)}$)	The sum of $EQ_{(Substance)}$ for each substance released to a particular medium.
Environmental Quotient$_{(Substance)}$ ($EQ_{(Substance)}$)	A dimensionless number derived by dividing the process contribution (PC) of a substance by the appropriate EAL.
Harm	Harm to the health of living organisms or other interference with the ecological systems of which they form a part and, in the case of man, includes offence caused to any of his senses or harm to his property. This definition is taken from section 1 of the Act.
Insignificant release	The release of a substance where the predicted environmental concentration is less than 0.2% of the EAL (see Volume I, Figs 1 and 2).
Integrated Environmental Index (IEI)	The sum of $EQ_{(medium)}$ for releases to air, water and via air to land.

Term	Definition
Option	A particular configuration of process and pollution control techniques to be considered as a package.
Pollution receptor	A part of the environment exposed to a pollutant. Pollution receptors include man, other species, ecosystems, buildings and materials.
Predicted Environmental Concentration (PEC)	The total predicted environmental concentration of a substance at the location where the PC is calculated (i.e. the sum of process contribution and corrected ambient concentration).
Priority for Control	A release is a priority for control where: $PEC \geqslant 0.8$ EAL or $PC \geqslant 0.02$ EAL for one or more substances.
Process contribution (PC)	The concentration of a substance, at the location in the environment where that concentration will be at its greatest, which can be attributed to releases from the process being considered. For example, for releases to air it would be at the location of maximum ground level concentration, and for releases to water it would be after the mixing zone.
Process or abatement option	A collection of process and pollution control techniques to be considered as a package
Technique	Techniques embrace the design, construction and layout of the technology and operation (including staffing) of the process.
Test of insignificance	A test to screen out those substances released in insignificant amounts.
Tolerable releases	Tolerable releases are divided into those which are "priority for control" and those which are "insignificant". Further reduction of releases which are "priority for control" is encouraged and options should be generated with a view to reducing such releases.
Total annualized cost	The measure of the cost of pollution control. Computed first by multiplying capital costs by an appropriate annualization factor based on the interest rate and the lifetime of the relevant pollution control technique. This figure is then added to the typical operating and maintenance cost.

List of acronyms

BAT	Best Available Techniques
BATNEEC	Best Available Techniques Not Entailing Excessive Cost
BPEO	Best Practicable Environmental Option
CFC	Chlorofluorocarbon
DC	Direct Costs
DCF	Discounted Cash Flow
DOE	Department of the Environment
EAL	Environmental Assessment Level
EC	European Commission
EPAQS	Expert Panel on Air Quality Standards
EQ	Environmental Quotient
EQS	Environmental Quality Standard
GWP	Global Warming Potential
HMIP	Her Majesty's Inspectorate of Pollution
HSE	Health and Safety Executive
IC	Indirect (fixed) Costs
IEI	Integrated Environmental Index
IPC	Integrated Pollution Control
IPCGN	IPC Guidance Note
IRIS	Integrated Risk Information System
MDR	Maximum Deposition Rate
MEL	Maximum Exposure Limit
NGO	Non Governmental Organisation
NPV	Net Present Value
OECD	The Organisation for Economic Co-operation and Development
ODT	Odour Detection Threshold
OES	Occupational Exposure Limit
ORT	Odour Recognition Threshold
PEC	Predicted Environmental Concentration
PC	Process Contribution
POCP	Photochemical Ozone Creation Potential
PORG	Photochemical Oxidants Review Group
RC	Recovery Credits
RCEP	The Royal Commission on Environmental Pollution
SI 472	The Environmental Protection (Prescribed Processes and Substances) Regulations 1991, Statutory Instrument SI 472
SSSI	Site of Special Scientific Interest
STEL	Short Term Exposure Limit
UNECE	United Nations Economic Commission for Europe
VOC	Volatile Organic Compound
WHO	World Health Organisation
WRC	Water Research Centre

Associated publications

The following are available from HMSO bookshops (see back cover), their accredited agents, and some larger bookshops.

Series 2

Chief Inspector's Guidance Notes (prepared by Her Majesty's Inspectorate of Pollution)

Fuel Production Processes, Combustion Processes (including Power Generation)

S2 1.01 Combustion processes: large boilers and furnaces 50MW(th) and over
November 1995, £9.95 ISBN 0-11-753206-1
Supersedes IPR 1/1

IPR 1/2 Combustion processes: gas turbines
September 1994, £4.00 ISBN 0-11-752954-0

S2 1.03 Combustion processes: compression ignition engines 50MW(th) and over
September 1995, £7.95 ISBN 0-11-753166-9
Supersedes IPR 1/3

S2 1.04 Combustion processes: waste and recovered oil burners 3MW(th) and over
September 1995, £7.95 ISBN 0-11-753167-7
Supersedes IPR 1/4

S2 1.05 Combustion processes: combustion of fuel manufactured from or comprised of solid waste in appliances 3MW(th) and over
September 1995, £9.95 ISBN 0-11-753168-5
Supersedes IPR 1/5-1/8

S2 1.06 Carbonisation processes: coke manufacture
September 1995, £9.95 ISBN 0-11-753176-6
Supersedes IPR 1/9

S2 1.07 Carbonisation and associated processes: smokeless fuel, activated carbon and carbon black manufacture
September 1995, £9.95 ISBN 0-11-753177-4
Supersedes IPR 1/10

S2 1.08 Gasification processes: gasification of solid and liquid feedstocks
November 1995, £9.95 ISBN 0-11-753202-9
Supersedes IPR 1/11

S2 1.09 Gasification processes: refining of natural gas
November 1995, £9.95 ISBN 0-11-753203-7
Supersedes IPR 1/12 and 1/13

S2 1.10 Petroleum processes: oil refining and associated processes
November 1995, £14.00 ISBN 0-11-753204-5
Supersedes IPR 1/14 and 1/15

S2 1.11 Petroleum processes: on-shore oil production
November 1995, £8.25 ISBN 0-11-753205-3
Supersedes IPR 1/16

S2 1.12 Combustion processes: reheat and heat treatment furnaces 50MW(th) and over
September 1995, £8.50 ISBN 0-11-753178-2
Supersedes IPR 1/17

IPC Guidance Notes (prepared by the Environment Agency)

Mineral Industry Sector

S2 3.01 Cement manufacture, lime manufacture and associated processes
September 1996, £21 ISBN 0-11-310120-1
Supersedes IPR 3/1 and IPR 3/2

S2 3.02 Asbestos processes
September 1996, £15 ISBN 0-11-310118-x
Supersedes IPR 3/3

S2 3.03 Manufacture of glass fibres, other non-asbestos mineral fibres, glass frit, enamel frit and associated processes
September 1996, £21 ISBN 0-11-310121-x
Supersedes IPR 3/4 and IPR 3/5

S2 3.04 Ceramic processes
September 1996, £17 ISBN 0-11-310119-8
Supersedes IPR 3/6

Waste Disposal and Recycling Sector

S2 5.01 Waste incineration
November 1996, £30.00 ISBN 0-11-310117-1
Supersedes IPR 5/1, 5/2, 5/3, 5/4, 5/5 and 5/11

S2 5.02 Making solid fuel from waste
July 1996, £15.00 ISBN 0-11-310114-7
Supersedes IPR 5/6

S2 5.03 Cleaning and regeneration of carbon
July 1996, £13.00 ISBN 0-11-310115-5
Supersedes IPR 5/7

S2 5.04 Recovery of organic solvents and oil by distillation
July 1996, £17.00 ISBN 0-11-310116-3
Supersedes IPR 5/8 and IPR 5/10

Series 1

Chief Inspector's Guidance Notes (prepared by Her Majesty's Inspectorate of Pollution)

Metals Production and Processing

IPR2/1 Iron and steel making processes: integrated iron and steel works
October 1994, £13.00 ISBN 0-11-752961-3

IPR2/2 Ferrous foundry processes
October 1994, £10.00 ISBN 0-11-752962-1

IPR2/3 Processes for electric arc steelmaking, secondary steelmaking and special alloy production
October 1994, £10.00 ISBN 0-11-752963-X

IPR2/4 Processes for the production of zinc and zinc alloys
November 1994, £7.50 ISBN 0-11-753024-7

IPR2/5 Processes for the production of lead and lead alloys
November 1994, £7.50 ISBN 0-11-753025-5

IPR2/6 Processes for the production of refractory metals
November 1994, £6.50 ISBN 0-11-753026-3

IPR2/7 Processes for the production, melting and recovery of cadmium, mercury and their alloys
November 1994, £7.00 ISBN 0-11-753027-1

IPR2/8 Processes for the production of aluminium
November 1994, £8.50 ISBN 0-11-753028-X

IPR2/9 Processes for the production of copper and copper alloys
November 1994, £7.00 ISBN 0-11-753029-8

IPR2/10 Processes for the production of precious metals and platinum group metals
November 1994, £8.00 ISBN 0-11-753030-1

IPR2/11 The extraction of nickel by the carbonyl process and the production of cobalt and nickel alloys
November 1994, £7.50 ISBN 0-11-753031-X

IPR2/12 Tin and bismuth processes
November 1994, £7.50 ISBN 0-11-753032-8

Chemical Industry Sector

IPR4/1 Petrochemical processes
January 1993, £8.50 ISBN 0-11-752738-6

IPR4/2 Processes for the production and use of amines, nitriles, isocyanates and pyridines
January 1993, £9.00 ISBN 0-11-752739-4

IPR4/3 Processes for the production or use of acetylene, aldehydes etc.
January 1993, £8.50 ISBN 0-11-752740-8

IPR4/4 Processes for the production or use of organic sulphur compounds, and production, use or recovery of carbon disulphide
January 1993, £8.65 ISBN 0-11-752741-6

IPR4/5 Batch manufacture of organic chemicals in multipurpose plant
January 1993, £8.00 ISBN 0-11-752742-4

IPR4/6 Production and polymerisation of organic monomer
January 1993, £10.00 ISBN 0-11-752743-2

IPR4/7 Processes for the manufacture of organo-metallic compounds
January 1993, £7.70 ISBN 0-11-752744-0

IPR4/8 Pesticide processes
January 1993, £7.50 ISBN 0-11-752745-9

IPR4/9 Pharmaceutical processes
January 1993, £8.50 ISBN 0-11-752746-7

IPR4/10 Processes for the manufacture, use or release of oxides of sulphur and the manufacture, recovery, condensation or distillation of sulphuric acid or oleum
August 1993, £12.50 ISBN 0-11-752833-1

IPR4/11 Processes for the manufacture or recovery of nitric acid and processes involving the manufacture or release of acid-forming oxides of nitrogen
August 1993, £9.90 ISBN 0-11-752834-X

IPR4/12 Processes for the sulphonation or nitration of organic chemicals
August 1993, £10.70 ISBN 0-11-752835-8

IPR4/13 Processes for the manufacture of, or which use or release halogens, mixed halogen compounds or oxo-halocompounds
August 1993, £11.70 ISBN 0-11-752836-6

IPR4/14 Processes for the manufacture of, or which use or release hydrogen halides or any of their acids
August 1993, £11.00 ISBN 0-11-752837-4

IPR4/15 Processes for the halogenation of organic chemicals
August 1993, £10.70 ISBN 0-11-752838-2

IPR4/16 The manufacture of chemical fertilizers or their conversion into granules
August 1993, £9.80 ISBN 0-11-752839-0

IPR4/17 Bulk storage installations
August 1993, £9.80 ISBN 0-11-752840-4

IPR4/18 Processes for the manufacture of ammonia
December 1993, £9.75 ISBN 0-11-752904-4

IPR4/19 Processes involving the use, release or recovery of ammonia
December 1993, £11.00 ISBN 0-11-752905-2

IPR4/20 *The production, and the use of, in any process for the manufacture of a chemical, phosphorus and any oxide, hydride, or halide of phosphorus*
December 1993, £12.00 ISBN 0-11-752906-0

IPR4/21 *Processes involving the manufacture, use or release of hydrogen cyanide or hydrogen sulphide*
December 1993, £7.00 ISBN 0-11-752907-9

IPR4/22 *Processes involving the use or release of antimony, arsenic, beryllium, gallium, indium, lead, palladium, platinum, selenium, tellurium, thallium or their compounds*
December 1993, £12.00 ISBN 0-11-752908-7

IPR4/23 *Processes involving the use or release of cadmium or any compounds of cadmium*
December 1993, £9.50 ISBN 0-11-752909-5

IPR4/24 *Processes involving the use or release of mercury or any compounds of mercury*
December 1993, £10.50 ISBN 0-11-752910-9

IPR4/25 *Processes for the production of compounds of chromium, magnesium, manganese, nickel, and zinc*
December 1993, £11.00 ISBN 0-11-752911-7

Waste Disposal and Recycling Sector

IPR5/9 *Regeneration of ion exchange resins*
May 1992, £4.30 ISBN 0-11-752650-9

Other Industries

IPR6/1 *Application or removal of tributyltin or triphenyltin coatings at shipyards or boatyards*
March 1995, £6.00 ISBN 0-11-753079-4

IPR6/2 *Tar and bitumen processes*
March 1995, £7.00 ISBN 0-11-753080-8

IPR6/3 *Timber preservation processes*
March 1995, £6.00 ISBN 0-11-753081-6

IPR6/4 *Di-isocyanate manufacture*
March 1995, £8.00 ISBN 0-11-753082-4

IPR6/5 *Toluene di-isocyanate use and flame bonding of polyurethanes*
March 1995, £7.00 ISBN 0-11-753083-2

IPR6/6 *Textile treatment processes*
March 1995, £7.00 ISBN 0-11-753084-0

IPR6/7 *Processing of animal hides and skins*
March 1995, £7.00 ISBN 0-11-753085-9

IPR6/8 *The making of paper pulp by chemical methods*
May 1995, £8.50 ISBN 0-11-753105-7

IPR6/9 *Paper making and related processes, including mechanical pulping, recycled fibres and de-inking*
May 1995, £10.00 ISBN 0-11-753106-5

Technical Guidance Notes

Monitoring

M1 *Sampling facility requirements for the monitoring of particulates in gaseous releases to atmosphere*
March 1993, £5.00 ISBN 0-11-752777-7

M2 *Monitoring emissions of pollutants at source*
January 1994, £10.00 ISBN 0-11-752922-2

M3 *Standards for IPC monitoring Part 1: standards, organisations and the measurement infrastructure*
August 1995, £11.00 ISBN 0-11-753133-2

M4 *Standards for IPC monitoring Part 2 : standards in support of IPC monitoring*
August 1995, £11.00 ISBN 0-11-753134-0

M5 *Routine measurement of gamma ray air kerma rate in the environment*
September 1995, £11.00 ISBN 0-11-753132-4

Dispersion

D1 *Guidelines on discharge stack heights for polluting emissions*
July 1993, £8.00 ISBN 0-11-752794-7

Abatement

A1 *Guidance on effective flaring in the gas, petroleum, petrochemical and associated industries*
December 1993, £4.25 ISBN 0-11-752916-8

A2 *Pollution abatement technology for the reduction of solvent vapour emissions*
March 1994, £5.00 ISBN 0-11-752925-7

A3 *Pollution abatement technology for particulate and trace gas removal*
April 1994, £15.00 ISBN 0-11-752983-4

A4 *Effluent Treatment Techniques*
January 1997, £28.00 ISBN 0-11-310127-9

Environmental

E1 *Best practicable environmental option assessments for Integrated Pollution Control*
April 1997, £35.00 ISBN 0-11-310126-0

Relevant DOE publications

A review of "The potential effects of release of krypton-85"
£4.95, DOE Publications Sales Unit, Block 3, Spur 2,
Room 1/2, Government Buildings, Lime Grove,
Eastcote, HA4 8SE

Integrated Pollution Control: a practical guide
January 1997 ISBN 1-85112-021-1

Processes Prescribed for Air Pollution Control by Local Authorities

A list of these notes is available from:

Department of the Environment
Air and Environmental Quality Division
Romney House
43 Marsham Street
London SW1P 3PY

Tel: 0171 276 8322

Printed in the United Kingdom for The Stationery Office
Dd303281 4/97 C10 G559 10170